100
Years
of Texas
Longhorn
Football

100 Years of Texas Longhorn Football

Gene Schoor

Foreword by Darrell Royal

Taylor Publishing Company
Dallas, Texas

Photos courtesy of the University of Texas at Austin, Sports
Information Department.

Published by Taylor Publishing Company
1550 West Mockingbird Lane
Dallas, Texas 75235
Designed by Hespenheide Design

Library of Congress Cataloging-in-Publication Data
Schoor, Gene.
    100 years of Texas Longhorn football / by Gene Schoor ;
  introduction by Coach Darrell Royal.
     p. cm.
  Includes index.
  ISBN 0-87833-832-2
    1. Texas Longhorns (Football team)—History.   2. University of
Texas at Austin—Football—History.   3. University of Texas at
Austin—Football—Records. I. Title.   II. Title: One hundred years
of Texas Longhorn football.
  GV958.T45S36   1993
  796.332'63'0976431—dc20   93-15867
                                        CIP
Printed in the United States of America
10 9 8 7 6 5 4 3 2 1

ACKNOWLEDGMENTS

No history of the 100 years of Texas Longhorn football, which stretches from 1893 to 1992 with a scope as wide as the game of intercollegiate football, is possible without the help and co-operation of hundreds of interested individuals. To all of them I am grateful.

Many of the former great Texas stars, coaches, managers, and sportswriters took the time from their busy schedules to answer questions and supply material pertinent to the most stirring and inspiring Texas football moments.

First and foremost, a grateful thank you to my editor Jim Donovan for his constant words of encouragement and help on an almost daily basis in a most complicated piece of work . . . and for his consistent advice when the going got tough. Thanks Jim.

Thanks to that inspirational sports information director at Texas, Bill Little, for all the wonderful photographs and for help that was instrumental in the entire project. And to Jason Lovelace, sports editor of the *Daily Texan*, who was ready at the drop of a hat to handle every conceivable question and supply any amount of statistical material.

And thanks to Texas' indomitable football coach for twenty seasons, Coach Darrell Royal, who from 1957 to 1976 provided Longhorn fans with the greatest football in Texas history and three national championships and eleven SWC titles.

And a special note of thanks to those Texas Longhorn players and wives who gave their aid: Russell Exerleben, Mrs. Bobby Layne, Rooster Andrews, Bunny Andrews, Johnny Jones, Eric Metcalf.

And thank you to sportswriters Dave Campbell, Bob St. John, Nick Seitz, Rick Gosselin, Joe Pollack, Pat Putnam, Neil Amdur, Bill Morgan, George Breazeale; the *Dallas Morning News*, *Austin American-Statesman*, the *Daily Texan*, *Sporting News*, *New York Times*, *Sport Magazine*, *Sports Illustrated*, *New York News*; *Hook 'Em Horns*, by Denne Freeman (Strode, 1974); *Bleeding Orange*, by John Maher and Kirk Bohls (St. Martin's Press, 1991); *Here Come the Texas Longhorns*, by Lou Maysel (Burnt Orange Publishers, 1978); and *Texas and Arkansas Football Newsletter*, by Dave Campbell.

Thanks to Associated Press, the *New York News*, the *New York Times*, the Wide World Features Syndicate, and many individual Texas football players for the use of photographs.

CONTENTS

FOREWORD

The history of Texas Longhorn football is like a great country and western music concert—there is a story behind every song, and Gene Schoor has done a good job of spinning the yarns.

When I came to The University of Texas that winter of 1956, it wasn't without a great deal of awe for the folks who had been there before.

I grew up knowing about Jack Crain, and the greatness of the Texas teams of the early '40s. I knew Mr. Bible, and all that he stood for. I had seen, and had the opportunity to meet on the playing field, men like Bobby Layne.

Then, as a coach, I had the opportunity to work with rock-solid people . . . assistant coaches, players, and support staff. I guess now, a few more than fifteen years since I set my bucket down, I realize more than ever that it's the people you remember.

I came to know Clyde Littlefield and Bully Gilstrap and what they had meant to Texas in the early days. And I was blessed to coach some of the finest young people this university—or any university—has ever seen. I have watched them grow, seen them mature, and as time has passed, seen them on their way.

There are a lot of positives in the game of football, and I always believed that in some way we could use those to help folks understand the game of life a little better.

Gene Schoor has brought back a lot of memories, just as he has done with his other fine works on the 100-year histories of such great schools as Notre Dame and Alabama.

In the hundred years, my time on that field was actually only a fifth. And even today, when I walk in the stadium and look around, my thoughts are of those who distinguished themselves there on behalf of The University.

They are the people whom this book is about. Read, enjoy, and remember.

Darrell Royal

INTRODUCTION

The football season of 1992 marked the 100th year of Texas football, and it is my great honor to be asked to write an introduction to a book that chronicles that history.

Gene Schoor, a noted sports author, has assembled a collection of pictures and stories that will warm the heart of any Longhorn. For those of us who played at Texas, it is especially significant.

When I came to The University in the 1950s, there was no way I could ever imagine the impact that playing at Texas would have on my life. I guess I knew it then, and I even understand it more now—the principles that make football a great game are the same principles that allow you to succeed in life.

Football under Darrell Royal meant several things, but prime among them was that you were taught to compete as hard as you could, to respect your opponents, to have loyalty to your teammates, and to play by the rules. You were always prepared, and whatever the outcome, you conducted yourself with class.

You also learned that while football was a big part of your life, it was simply part of a college education that was a preparation for life. What you did in the classroom was every bit as important as what you did on the football field. That commitment to academics—and to the future of the "student athlete"—remains an integral part of Texas today.

None of us who played here will ever be able to repay The University for what it has meant. Gene Schoor has given us the opportunity to look back, and reflect, on the college days that often are the happiest of a person's life.

And as Texas football enters its second century, it is important to take that honored past, and proceed with a commitment that it will stand as it has always stood—for excellence, character, and discipline.

James R. Moffett

PROLOGUE:
THE BIGGEST GAME

There's an old saying in football that a coach is only as good as his material. A nationally known coach who was at the end of a poor season talked to me about his team as we watched them run through a complicated drill. "You can see for yourself, that you can't make chicken salad out of chicken _____."

Perhaps that's true. But every once in a while, an ordinary team can be transformed into a great one . . . that is, if the coach has a smoldering fire in his belly and sweet revenge in his heart.

Jack Chevigny was an outstanding halfback with Notre Dame from 1926 through '28. His teammates on those Irish teams included some of Notre Dame's greatest stars: Frank Carideo, Frank Leahy, Burt Metzger, Johnny Law, Joe Savoldi, Moon Mullins, Jack Cannon, Fred Miller, and Tom Conley, among others.

Upon graduation, after a marvelous career, Chevigny was given a job as assistant to the great coach Knute Rockne, coaching the Irish backfield.

Chev was thrilled at this opportunity to work alongside of his idol, for all of his young life, this was what he'd wanted to do—to become a football coach at Notre Dame. Now he was in fat company, working with America's greatest coach, and Chev soaked up every bit of knowledge from Rockne he could. He was learning every bit of technique possible on the way to becoming a great coach. As a couple of years flew by and Chevigny gained in stature, he was called aside one day by Rockne, who said, "Chev, you're doing a fine job with the backfield, great job. And when I leave here one day, you're going to be the head coach."

In 1928, when Jack Chevigny, Notre Dame's star halfback, tore through Army's great line for a touchdown, he sobbed, "That's one for the Gipper, now let's get another one." That became Notre Dame's battle cry and was used by Ronald Reagan as he sought, and later won, the presidency.

1

Notre Dame's great coach, Knute Rockne, in 1928.

Jack Chevigny was in seventh heaven after that talk with the great Rockne and he worked harder than ever at his job. But then something happened that changed his life forever.

Two years later, Knute Rockne was killed in a plane crash. The tough, hard-boiled ex-tackle, Hunk Anderson, was appointed head football coach.

Chevigny was heartsick, and from the very first day Hunk and Chevigny argued about various points of strategy. By late 1930 Chevigny was fired by Anderson. Jack took it hard. He was bitterly heartbroken, and swore that he would someday get his revenge.

He left Notre Dame and took a job coaching Chicago in the NFL. But his heart was not in the pro field. He then received an offer to coach at St. Edward's University, a small Catholic College in Austin, Texas, and in short order began to turn out a winning football team. His outstanding work attracted the attention of the athletic officials at the University of Texas and when coach Clyde Littlefield resigned as head coach, Chevigny was called in for an interview. Chevigny made such an impression on the Texas officials that he was given a three-year contract as the new head football coach at Texas.

Chevigny immediately appointed an old Notre Dame teammate, Tim Moynihan, as his top aide, and retained three of the assistant coaches who had worked with Littlefield: Marty Karow, Bill James, and Shorty Alderson.

Chevigny in 1933 took over a Texas team that had posted the poorest season since 1917—4 wins, 5 losses, and 2 ties—and the attitude and professional manner in which Chev took charge of the squad assured University officials and ex-alumni that in Chevigny they had selected a coach who was the right man to elevate the football program with the best in the nation.

Back at Notre Dame, Hunk Anderson was replaced by Elmer Layden, one of the immortal "Four Horsemen." Meanwhile, young Jack

Chevigny was working his Texas squad harder than they had ever worked before.

Jack changed the Texas offense in favor of the Notre Dame system developed so successfully by Knute Rockne. The new system stressed marvelous timing and split-second precision, with the four backs shifting at a given signal. At the same time the linesmen were bracing on each and every play, knowing exactly how and when to react. That meant work, work, hours of grueling driving, practice, and more practice. Chevigny and his aides thrived on that kind of effort.

All this time Chevigny brooded over the humiliation of being fired at Notre Dame, and in his mind he began to visualize a dream of someday, somehow, getting his revenge.

In 1934 Notre Dame, looking for an easy touch to open the season, scheduled a game against Texas. When Chevigny heard this, he smiled an enigmatic grin. Weeks before the game against Notre Dame, Chev spent long nights planning strategy to defeat the great Irish team . . . the team that fired him.

Chev drove his players harder in practice. He gave them no quarter, and he was demanding and insistent. His practices were so rough that one of his players called him "The Prussian Field Marshall." And he drove himself and his staff even harder. There were many nights after a grueling practice session that Chev and his coaches, dead tired after hours on the field, would simply collapse and fall asleep in the coach's office, too tired to go home.

The daily drill sessions were long and intensive. Many of the players rebelled. Others accused him of being a heartless, cruel taskmaster concerned only with some crazy idea that he could beat the powerful Notre Dame team . . . a team that in the past decade had won in the Rose Bowl, had won two National Championships in a row, and had run up a string of twenty-six straight wins in a row. Beat Notre Dame? Some of the players actually laughed out loud when Chevigny was out of sight.

But Jack Chevigny carried on, day after day. How could he tell his players, even his coaches, what was in his heart? They'd never understand. So

he kept silent and drove them a little harder. He was even brought up before the University officials and told to go easier on his players.

But before the Notre Dame game came a dress rehearsal. Texas began the season in Lubbock and took a hard-earned win over the Texas Tech Red Raiders by a 12–6 margin. Running back Bohn Hilliard, who had been injured most of the previous season, flashed off tackle and cut in and around several opponents and sprinted 94 yards for one of the most spectacular Texas runs in history. Then, a week later, before some 6000 students at a pep rally, Jack Chevigny told the students that his Longhorn team would make history by beating Notre Dame. But he emphasized that the team would need help from the students, and the crowd went wild with joy as the players were introduced.

On October 6, in Knute Rockne Stadium deep down in the locker room coach Chevigny was talking to his team just before they took the field.

Chevigny said, "Sure, I've worked you hard, harder than you've ever worked before, but this is the biggest game in the history of your great school. And you, all of you will be remembered for what happens on that field today, when you beat Notre Dame." Then he talked about his great mentor, Knute Rockne, who was buried nearby, and he talked about his mother and father, who were gravely ill.

As Jack Chevigny spoke, something stirred in the hearts of the players. Maybe they just began to understand a little of what burned inside of their young coach. "We thought at the time that was the greatest, most inspiring speech we ever heard," said Neils Thompson, a reserve end, "and we were a bunch of demons when we hit the field to play Notre Dame." That afternoon, a strange and curious football miracle came to pass before the wildly cheering crowd of 33,000.

Texas kicked off and the star Irish receiver, George Melinkovich, fumbled the ball. Jack Gray of Texas recovered on the 15-yard line. Three plays picked up a first down and then the great Bohn Hilliard engraved his name in Texas football history as he burst through for a touchdown and kicked the extra point to give Texas a 7–0 lead.

Texas Longhorns' new coach in 1934, Jack Chevigny.

In the second period of a knock-down, drag-'em-out football game, a Texas back fumbled the ball on the 10-yard line. Melinkovich smashed through the lighter, smaller Texas line for a touchdown. But All-American Wayne Millner's extra-point try was just wide of the mark and the Longhorns had a slim 7–6 lead.

The teams battled back and forth through the second and third periods and the final quarter. No holds were barred; the fighting Texas squad seemed to understand the importance of this game to their beloved coach. They fought off every Irish drive, and at the final whistle, it was Texas 7, Notre Dame 6.

As the game ended, Elmer Layden, the Irish coach, crossed the field to the Texas bench, where a mob of reporters was trying to interview Chevigny. But a mob of Texas fans and his players had the coach on their shoulders. Layden reached up and grabbed Chevigny's hand. "Glad you did it, Jack, even though it's my team you had to beat. You've got a great squad here."

Jack Chevigny just murmured over and over again. "We did it. We won . . . beat Notre Dame. A dream come true."

Over the next few days every sportswriter, every reporter, every commentator headlined the incredible Texas victory. Rice had upset Purdue the same day, and the two victories marked the emergence of SWC football. Many of the nation's papers put this sports story on the front pages, for it was the biggest upset in football in 1934 and the biggest story in the history of Texas football. The Texas victory over Notre Dame became the talk of the entire world of sports, and the unbelievable story of Jack Chevigny and his Texas football team went into the record books as one of the great sports miracles of the century.

1893–1926:
THE EARLY YEARS

On March 4, 1893, Grover Cleveland, twenty-fourth president of the United States, was inaugurated for a second term. Adlai Stevenson was his vice president. . . . The United States rushed in the Marines after a violent revolution deposed Queen Liliuokalani of Hawaii, and the Marines raised the U.S. flag over the island after they had put down the insurrection. . . . The world's greatest exposition, "The World's Fair," opened in Chicago as the United States spent more than 22 million dollars on the Fair, which was dedicated to the "Fitting Discovery of America." . . . The nation's first film studio was constructed in West Orange, New Jersey, by the Edison Laboratories. . . . Robert Louis Stevenson's *The Strange Case of Dr. Jekyll and Mr. Hyde* was published in America and created a sensation. . . . In sports, Boston won the American League pennant, Princeton defeated Yale in football 6–0, and Navy beat the Army 6–4 in their annual classic. . . . And in Austin, the University of Texas opened its doors for its tenth year and celebrated the event by organizing the school's first football team, which accepted a challenge by the Dallas Foot Ball Club for a "football match."

The first University of Texas football team, 1893. *Front row, left to right:* Dave Furman, Bill McLean, Walt Crawford (manager), Dick Lee, and Ad Day. *Center row, left to right:* Victor Moore, Paul McLane, and John Philp. *Rear row, left to right:* Ray McLane, Co-captain Jim Morrison, Babe Myers, and Robert Roy. Although the official records list Texas as playing 4 games in 1893, that is not accurate. Only two games, with Dallas and San Antonio, were played that year.

The Texas team had been organized by several students led by the McLane brothers, Paul and Ray. The McLanes had put the squad through several practice sessions (one intrasquad game was watched by 700 spectators), and drilled the players on the fundamental rules of the game as it was played at the time. When the Dallas Foot Ball Club issued the challenge, they were ready and anxious to play. On Thanksgiving Day, November 30, 1893, they took the field at Fairgrounds Park in Dallas to face the "Champions of Texas," as the Dallas eleven proudly called themselves. The Dallas team hadn't been beaten or scored upon in several years, and many city teams refused to play the rough-playing club.

But to the surprise of the Texas contingent and more than 2000 spectators, Texas defeated the highly rated Dallas Club by the score of 18–16 in the first-ever football game played in Texas.

Jesse Andrews, a member of that first University of Texas team, described the game during a fascinating interview in 1956 conducted by the editor of *The Cactus:* "There was little interest in athletics back in 1893," said Andrews. "Some baseball was played and there was some competition in track and field on an interclass basis. But then in the fall of 1893, the McLane brothers, both of whom had played football at Cornell University, entered Texas and began to talk up the game of football. Gradually, interest in the game took hold. The challenge from the Dallas Club was all that was needed.

"The McLane brothers acted as our coaches," said Andrews. They played the end positions on the team. "Our Captain, Vic Moore, was the right guard; I played left guard; Baby Myer was at center; Jim Morrison and Rob Roy were the tackles; Bill McLean was the quarterback; Dave Furman and Dick Lee were the halfbacks; and Ad Day was our hard-running fullback and the heaviest man in our backfield at 155 pounds.

"We were not very big; our average weight was about 150 pounds, while the Dallas team averaged over 160 pounds. But our players had spent a good deal of time during our practice sessions running and we were faster and more aggressive than the Dallas Club.

"You had to be a real he-man to play football in those days," he continued. "We had no shoulder pads, hip pads, or any padding at all. We wore heavy jackets, which were laced across the shoulders, heavy black socks, and heavy shoes. Many of the players nailed cleats on their shoes to give a firm footing. Some of the players allowed their hair to grow rather long as they felt it made them look more rugged and gave them some protection. But in a close scrimmage they complained about having their hair pulled." The team sported old gold and white colors.

The game was started with both teams lined up facing each other in the center of the field, which was 110 yards long. A referee tossed a coin and Texas, who won the toss, received possession of the ball and put the ball in play by the quarterback.

A Texas player flipped the ball to one of his halfbacks. (A lateral was the only legal pass at that time.) As he made the toss, the rest of his team formed a V-type wedge in front of the ball carrier and then all darted forward, intent on gaining ground. On each play the halfback with the ball stationed himself in the center of the wedge and the entire team smashed forward over center or through the guard or tackle positions. A team had to move the ball forward five yards or more in three carries or lose possession of the ball.

"Jim Morrison, our tackle, had the honor of scoring the first touchdown in the history of Texas football," said Andrews. "As we drove downfield towards the Dallas goal, Ad Day who carried the brunt of our attack fumbled the ball as he was hit by several Dallas players, but Morrison caught the ball before it touched the ground and slashed through the Dallas players for the first touchdown in Texas football history. Day then kicked a goal and Texas had a 6–0 margin."

In 1893 a field goal was worth five points, a touchdown was worth four points, and a goal after a TD was worth two points.

Dallas came back with a furious rush, quickly scored a TD, but missed the try for the field goal. It was 6–4, Texas.

Just as the 45-minute first half ended, Texas quickly dashed downfield and fullback Day sprinted the last 25 yards for the second Texas score. Day missed the try for the goal as the first half ended, with Texas in front by a 12–10 margin.

As the second half began, Texas quickly put together several solid gains and once again Day slashed through the Dallas line for a touchdown and Day kicked the goal to give Texas an 18–10 margin.

As the game drew to a close, Dallas' heavier line began to assert itself and they scored a TD and kicked the goal to come to within two points of tying the game. But time ran out and Texas managed to eke out an 18–16 victory—the first in the history of Texas University football.

On December 16, Texas scheduled a game against a makeshift San Antonio town team. This was the first home game for the varsity. The game was held at the local Dam Baseball Park on a cold, blustery day with more than 600 in attendance. Texas quickly battered the less-experienced San Antonio team into submission, scoring five touchdowns, three goals after TDs, and two safeties for an easy 30–0 win.

On February 3, 1894, Texas traveled to San Antonio for the second game scheduled between the teams. The contest held at the San Antonio Jockey Club resulted in another easy win for the University team. Dickie Lee, lightest man on the field for Texas at 135 pounds, starred for the University boys as he ran for two touchdowns and Texas rang up an easy 34–0 win.

The Dallas Club had been clamoring for a return game with the Texas varsity and the game was set for February 22, 1894, at suburban Hyde Park, an exclusive neighborhood. Despite the bitter weather more than 1500 spectators lined the field for the game after paying a pricey admission fee of fifty cents.

Texas quickly put the game on ice as Morrison broke loose minutes after it began and sprinted 50 yards for Texas' first TD at home. Halfback Davey Furman scored two touchdowns, both on spectacular plays, as the varsity easily defeated Dallas for the second time by a 16–0 margin.

The undefeated Texas varsity of 1893 and '94 had so galvanized the students and Athletic Association with their marvelous play that the AA began to take a more active interest in the football program and scheduled games with such highly

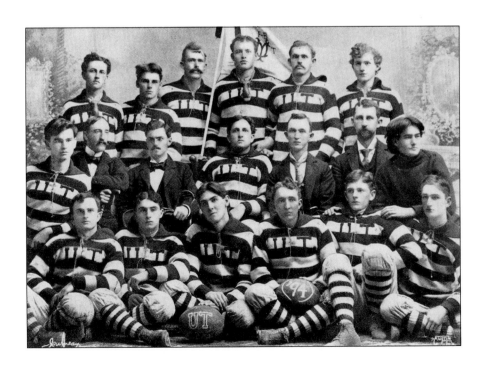

**The 1894 varsity team
won 6 of 7 games played.**

regarded teams as Tulane, Arkansas, Missouri, and Texas A&M. Games had also been set with the Austin YMCA and with San Antonio.

The excitement engendered by the winning team spread to the entire student body and around the entire state, and the spirit was so significant that the AA sought out and hired Texas' first football coach, a man named Reginald D. Wentworth.

Reg Wentworth had played football at Williams College, one of the early pioneers in eastern college football. In the three years Wentworth played at Williams, the team lost only to such top teams as Yale, Harvard, and Princeton. In his senior year, Wentworth captained a solid Williams eleven.

Wentworth took the post at Texas at a salary of $325 per year plus an additional $100 for equipment.

In 1894 there were a number of rule changes. Most important was the abolition of the flying wedge play that had caused so many serious injuries.

By mid-October Coach Wentworth had his Texas team drilled in every phase of the game and they were ready for the first game of the season against Texas A&M. The Farmers, as they were then called, had just begun to play football and had defeated Galveston High School by a 14–6 margin. Texas was their first college opponent. This rivalry was to become one of the greatest, most colorful, and dramatic football series in college football. But in 1894 it was only beginning.

The game was played at the Hyde Park field in Austin. The Farmers proved no match for the well-drilled Texas Varsity, as Texas ran through the A&M defense almost at will, scoring eight touchdowns on the way to a 38–0 victory. Jim Morrison and Ray McLane each scored two touchdowns in this, the very first clash between the two teams, establishing a rivalry that endures to this very day.

Texas A&M was so humiliated by the thrashing that Texas had administered that they promptly dropped football activities for the rest of 1894 and did not play another game for two years.

Tulane University made the long trip to Hyde Park in Austin for the second game of the season and lost a hard-fought battle to Texas. Jim Morrison scored both touchdowns and Ad Day kicked the two goals for a 12–0 victory. Following the A&M game, Texas had engaged in two tuneup games with the Austin YMCA in a two-week period; Coach Wentworth had an opportunity to use every man on his nineteen-man squad as the Y team was beaten 6–0 and 24–0.

The four victories of the season had the Texas Varsity in fine condition for the first Thanksgiving game ever held at Austin, as they played host to the University of Arkansas team. Arkansas was tired from their six-day journey by rail to Austin and were easy victims of the fast-moving Texas Varsity. Cheered on by a hometown crowd of 3000 fans, Texas romped to a 54–0 win. The next week Texas traveled to San Antonio and defeated their rivals by a 57–0 beating.

It was a victorious, cocky bunch of Texans that prepared to receive the ball in the seventh game of the season against a strong Missouri team before a crowd of more than 3000 roaring home fans.

Texas was out to have a good time against Missouri, but the Tigers were not in a playful mood. They had just lost a tough game to Kansas University a week before meeting Texas and their coach, Harry Robinson, had given his squad a tongue-lashing before the kickoff. The Tigers dashed out determined to defeat the strong Texas team. Benefitting from several new plays that their coach had introduced for this big game, the Tigers ran roughshod over Texas by a 28–0 margin that shocked the crowd of more than 3000 eager Texas rooters on hand for the holiday game.

But Texas had much to celebrate. They closed out a season that saw them victorious in six of the seven games played and that set the stage for a more successful 1895.

The defeat by Missouri at the end of the 1894 season did not discourage the Texas players as they opened the 1895 season. They had a new coach from Nebraska, Frank Crawford, and several new players who would distinguish themselves during the next several seasons.

The undefeated 1895 Texas varsity won 5 games and did not allow opponents a single point.

Three-year veteran Ray McLane and tackle Wallace Ralston shared the captaincy during the season. Other members returning from the '94 season included halfbacks Dave Furman, John Maverick, and Jack Michalson, and linemen Victor Moore and Dan Parker. Newcomers included Jim Caperton, Jim "Snaky" Jones, Walt Fisher, Jack O'Keefe, Jim Clarke, Chub Wortham, and Bill Denton.

Texas opened the season at Dallas against their old rivals, the Dallas Foot Ball Club, on November 2 and once more defeated the Dallas eleven by a 10–0 margin. The actual score was disputed, however, with Dallas insisting it was 6–0, Texas. The disputed second TD was scored by Jim Caperton, who had raced to the Dallas 2-yard line and was brought down short of the goal. But when Ed Mosely, the Dallas captain, began to argue with an official, Captain McLane of Texas had his team line up and then scored the second touchdown to give Texas a 10–0 victory.

The following week Texas defeated a hometown rival, the local YMCA eleven; they ran through the locals by scoring at will for a 24–0 win

as Coach Crawford utilized every man on the squad.

One week later, Tulane University, determined to avenge the 1894 defeat by Texas, traveled to Austin. On a field ankle deep in mud, they were again beaten by a superior Texas team. Led by fullback John Maverick, who scored two touchdowns, Texas came to life in the second period after leading 4–0 at the half and easily defeated a rugged Tulane University eleven.

Five days later on Thanksgiving Day, before a hometown crowd of less than 500 fans, Texas rolled to a 38–0 triumph over a lackluster San Antonio squad in a game that was marred by rain, sleet, and snow. The playing field was so muddy, the air so clouded with fog and mist, that it was almost impossible to see any kind of action on the field of play.

The season ended with four victories and without a single point being scored by their opponents. Coach Crawford bid his charges goodbye, suddenly resigned, and left town.

However, late in February, the Galveston team offered Texas a $250 guarantee for a game, and Texas accepted. On February 22, 1896, Texas defeated Galveston on two marvelous touchdown runs by Jim Caperton and Snaky Jones to give Texas an 8–0 triumph.

Harry Robinson, who had coached the Missouri Tigers to a 28–0 win over Texas in 1894, the first loss by Texas in twelve games, was named head coach at Texas in 1896, and Robinson and the Athletic Association came up with some major changes in the Texas schedule. Games were set with such major schools as Tulane, LSU, Missouri, and four regional rivals to make up an interesting seven-game season.

Julius House, a guard, and Snaky Jones, an end, were named co-captains of the '96 team, which ran up three straight wins: over Galveston by a 42–0 margin; San Antonio by a 12–4 margin; and then Tulane 12–4 at New Orleans. Although they won a rough, tough battle against Tulane, Texas paid dearly for the victory. They took a fierce battering from the bigger, heavier Green Wave eleven and were in poor shape when they faced LSU just three days after the Tulane game. As a result, LSU took a 14–0 win over Texas.

Thanksgiving Day at Austin once again brought the Dallas Club to town, and Texas displayed the finest form of the season as they completely outplayed Dallas 22–4. Jim Caperton, Clarence Cole, and Snaky Jones were outstanding for Texas as they registered their fourth win of the season.

In the final game of the season, the Missouri Tigers, charged up as a result of a 28–0 win over Dallas a few days earlier, barged into Austin and handed the varsity a 10–0 defeat after a bruising battle.

As the game began, Texas seemed on the way to an easy score as they reached the Tigers' 2-yard line as Caperton flashed through and around the Missouri defense. Suddenly the Tigers' defense held and they took the ball over. They drove downfield in quick darting smashes at the Texas line to register two rapid-fire TDs and a 10–0 win, despite the fine efforts of Jim Caperton, who appeared to be all over the field, both on offense and defense. He was

so battered, however, that he was escorted off the field a few minutes before the game's end.

The season ended for Texas with four victories, two losses, and a 0–0 tie against Dallas.

Walter Kelly, a fine end on the Dartmouth 1895–96 teams, was selected as the new physical director for men at the University of Texas in 1897. As part and parcel of his new job, he was handed the job as football coach. During the early part of the year, much of Kelly's time was spent completely revamping the schedule for the 1897 season. As a result, only one game was set with a college team; the other seven games in an eight-game schedule were set with local town teams, including two big games with Dallas.

Dan Parker, Jr., an outstanding end for four years, was named captain of the Texas varsity. Other returnees included Walt Schreiner, Lamar Bethea, Chub Wortham, Jim Clarke, and Otto Pfeiffer.

In the opening game of the season at Austin, the varsity defeated San Antonio by a 10–0 margin. Although weakened by an attack of dengue fever, the Texas squad then managed to eke out a 22–4 win over Dallas. The game was marked by the appearance of a player named Ed Scott wearing a Dallas uniform. Coach Kelly and Parker of Texas charged that Scott was actually a professional football player. But after an argument that lasted fully an hour the game was started. Scott was allowed to play, but it made little difference to the outcome.

Just two days after the Dallas encounter, Texas dropped a 6–0 decision to the Fort Worth University Panthers as Charley Leavell, in an attempt to try a field goal, fumbled the ball and Fort Worth recovered across the Texas goal for the only score of the game.

Stopping off at Waco on the way back to Austin, Texas defeated Add Ran (later to become Texas Christian) by an 18–10 margin. This was the third game in what proved to be a much-needed shot in the arm for Texas, for they went on a scoring rampage to defeat their next four opponents: Houston by a 42–6 margin; San Antonio, 12–0;

Fort Worth, 38–0; and in the final game of the season, at Austin on December 11, they defeated Dallas in the most exciting game of the year by a 20–16 margin.

In that game Bob Stanage, Dallas' fine halfback, returned a Texas punt 60 yards for a TD; then, on a play at his own goal line, he plucked the ball out of midair after Dan Parker fumbled the ball and raced the entire length of the field, some 104 yards, for Dallas' second TD. It was 12–0, but Texas suddenly woke up. Freshman halfback Cade Bethea quickly scored two touchdowns and Texas was back in the game. With five minutes to play, fullback Otto Pfeiffer drove over for another Texas score. Bethea then scored a TD, and Texas was out in front by a 20–16 margin as time ran out. As the game ended the 1500 Texas fans stomped out onto the field in a frenzy of excitement, hoisted the victorious Texas players onto their shoulders, and marched off the field with their heroes. It was a thrilling moment in Texas' early football history.

Dave Edwards, a great Princeton tackle who played on the Tigers' undefeated 1896 team, was selected as the new Texas head football coach for the 1898 season and initiated a number of new training methods in his approach to the game. He drove the players through a rigorous series of physical conditioning exercises that had the squad panting before practice actually began. Then, at the end of a tough hour-long practice session, every player on the squad had to jog one mile to the gym, where they could wash and change clothes. Some of the veteran players actually questioned his no-nonsense approach to the game, but when the season opened, the players were in the best physical condition they had ever enjoyed. Edwards also had ordered new uniforms with padded orange and maroon shirts, heavy canvas pants with added hip and thigh protection, and long, striped orange and maroon stockings.

Edwards also scheduled several challenging games with colleges and universities in addition to town teams. Games were set with Add Ran (TCU), Texas A&M, Galveston, Sewanee University, and Dallas.

R. W. "Chubb" Wortham, a four-year veteran lineman, was elected the team's captain, and other returnees included Lamar Bethea, Jim Hart, and Walt Schreiner.

Texas opened the season with Add Ran in a game at Waco. The Add Ran team, coached by for-

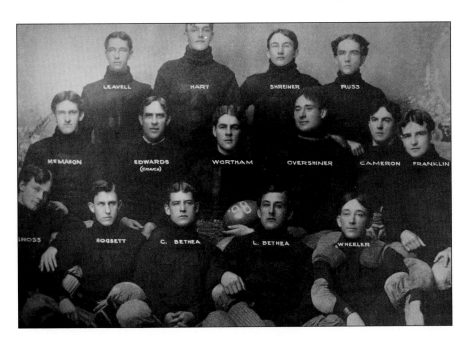

Captain Chub Wortham (with ball) led the 1898 varsity to a 5–1 record, including a 48–0 win over the Texas Aggies.

mer Texas star Jim Morrison, was an easy victim, losing to Texas 16–0. Following the Add Ran game was a match with Texas A&M one week later. It was the first game since the 38–0 drubbing in 1894. This time the finely tuned Texas team drubbed A&M by a 48–0 score. The game featured several outstanding plays by quarterback Sam Hogsett and halfback Cade Bethea. Hogsett picked up an A&M fumble and flashed downfield 60 yards for a touchdown, while Bethea scored on a flashy 25-yard dash for another score. Galveston was beaten 17–0 in a game at Austin; a week later, in a return game with Add Ran, Texas had a 29–0 lead when a tussle broke out among several players. After both players who had started the fracas were banished from the game, coach Jim Morrison, still not happy with the official's decision, decided to pull his team off the field. The game was declared over with Texas the winner, 29–0.

Sewanee, a tiny Tennessee school with an enrollment of less than a hundred, was on the way to developing one of the strongest teams in the nation. They visited the Texas campus and came away with a 4–0 victory in one of the most bitterly fought battles ever seen in Austin. Late in the game Sewanee blocked a Texas punt, recovered the ball, and scored a touchdown as the Sewanee quarterback quickly lateralled the ball to his end, John Hurt. Hurt scampered 60 yards for the only score of the game.

The big Thanksgiving Day game with the Dallas Tigers provided the holiday excitement for some 2500 Texas fans in a game at Austin. Texas responded by giving their rooters a 26–0 win. The season ended on a victorious note for the varsity, who won 5 and lost 1.

Many years later, while serving as an alumnus member of the athletic council, Jim Hart, who had been a star tackle for three years, wrote: "The year 1898 marked the beginning and a realization of just how important football could be to the development of the growth of the University."

In 1899 Texas had its seventh football coach in seven years in the person of Maurice Clark, a football and basketball star at the University of Chicago. Clark was outstanding during his playing days; the Maroons defeated Michigan, Notre Dame, Illinois, and many other top teams in compiling a record of 23 wins in twenty-nine games during a three-year period from 1896 to 1898. Clark introduced a number of new formations and plays that he brought over from his mentor, Amos Alonzo Stagg, Chicago's great coach.

Among the new rules prevalent in football during the 1899 season was the change in scoring. A touchdown was now five points instead of four. A goal after a touchdown was now one point instead of two. A field goal was five points and a safety counted two points.

Jim Hart, a three-year veteran and one of the most versatile players on the team, was named captain for the 1899 season. Hart's regular position was at end, but he also played at tackle, and was a quarterback when the occasion warranted. Hart remained quite active in University affairs long after his graduation, and his son, Jim Hart, Jr., served as the school's first chancellor.

The first game of the season was against their annual rival, the Dallas Tigers. A mob scene erupted as Texas fans charged that quarterback Semp Russ, after being tackled near the sidelines, was jumped on by Dallas' captain, Ed Mosely, and that Mosely then whacked Russ with a big stick. Finally, after much argument and delay, with Texas leading 11–6 and with 11 minutes left to play, the game was called "because of darkness."

The following week saw Texas pound out a 28–0 win over San Antonio, and then travel to the Alamo City to take a hard-fought battle over Texas A&M 6–0. The A&M squad walked off the field in protest after Texas was awarded the ball on a blocked kick on the A&M 2-yard line. The game was held up for 20 minutes as the teams argued the point. Then the A&M captain pulled his team off the field with some 28 minutes left to play.

A week later, on November 9, Texas faced Sewanee University (now the University of the South) at Austin, where a crowd of more than 2000 fans attended the game. Sewanee, the winner of four straight games in 1899 over such teams as Georgia, Georgia Tech, and Tennessee, was unscored on and had one of the great teams in the nation. But they were hard-pressed to score a 12–0 victory over Texas in a game that provided thrills to all present. Sewanee quarterback Harry Siebels scored both touchdowns for the victors.

After defeating Texas, Sewanee traveled to Houston the next day and defeated A&M 10–0; then to New Orleans, defeating Tulane 23–0; then to LSU, where they beat the Tigers 34–0; and then to Mississippi, beating Ole Miss 12–0 on November 14. Five shutout victories in six days—the most remarkable achievement in college football. In a nine-day trip Sewanee, traveling in special sleeping cars and carrying their own food and water, traveled 3000 miles and ended the season with 12 wins and no losses. In the 12-game schedule, Auburn was the only school to score against the purple and white, though they went down to defeat in a bitter 11–10 battle. Sewanee scored 322 points and permitted only those 10 points for one of the most remarkable records in the history of college football.

After the Sewanee game, Texas traveled to Nashville to play Vanderbilt. In the first game between the two schools Texas lost 6–0. Semp Russ, Texas' 140-pound quarterback, was injured in the game, and when Texas played Tulane two days later at New Orleans, tackle Jim Hart shifted to quarterback and kicked a late 23-yard field goal; that, added to an earlier TD, gave Texas a hard-fought 11–0 win. It was the first field goal in Texas history.

Five days later in Austin, Texas and Tulane once again faced each other, and this time Texas easily defeated the Green Wave 32–0.

The annual Thanksgiving game at Austin saw Texas, despite injuries to key players, notch an impressive 29–0 victory over LSU. Fullback Charley Cole scored twice on two smashes through the LSU line in a leisurely holiday battle. The win over LSU closed out the nineteenth century with a 6–2 record for the Texas football team. It entered the twentieth century with some twenty returning varsity lettermen, a new coach, a new school song, and a new and more aggressive brand of football,

and faced a succession of strong opponents—all of whom would go down to defeat in the most impressive year in Texas football history.

In 1890 the classic Army-Navy rivalry had begun, and within a five-year period, the game developed into the most popular sports event in the nation. In Chicago, Amos Alonzo Stagg started his long regime in 1892. In 1895 California and Stanford began one of the classic rivalries on the West Coast. Glenn Pop Warner began his marvelous career at Georgia that year, earning the munificent sum of thirty-five dollars per week. 1895 also saw the birth of the Western Intercollegiate League, forerunner of the Big Ten Conference, and by 1898 two great and heroic figures arose at Harvard, Percy Haughton and Charles Daly. Out in Wisconsin, Pat O'Dea was winning immortality with his incredible kicking feats and in the South, Sewanee was churning up the land.

By 1900, college football was well on its way to becoming a major sport, trailing only baseball in popularity. The game, however, was still a rough, tough, crude one, devoid of craft and strategy. There were quick savage bursts through the line and endless battles at the line of scrimmage. Force was the only important offensive weapon—players piling on the ball-carrier, roughing the kicker, wedge plays that led to serious injuries.

In 1900, after several very successful seasons of play, Texas hired still another new coach, Sam Thompson. He had been a star player with Princeton's undefeated eleven in 1896 and 1897, losing only to Yale in the final game of the '97 season. He was bright, understood the game, and realized the importance of a well-conditioned squad.

When he studied the facilities at Texas he was dissatisfied, and decided to do something to improve the situation at once.

Depressed and disappointed by the state of the facilities and outmoded equipment, Tommy aided the AA in the establishment of Clark Field as the new home field for the team. He also got the AA to erect a fence around the field, making it easier at game time to collect admission charges. The fence

The 1900 eleven won all 6 games of the season. (Captain Walt Schreiner with ball.)

also gave the players a sense of privacy and some secrecy. Thompson designed new uniforms for the team that consisted of solid white canvas jackets that fit over maroon-and-white striped shirts. The vests and shirts contained some padding at the shoulders. The pants were made of heavy moleskin with added layers of cloth over the hips and knees and provided additional protection for the players.

A veteran squad of more than twenty lettermen was on hand to greet the new coach for the first practice session. They soon learned that their new coach was a no-nonsense martinet who was determined to give Texas an outstanding team in his first year.

Back for his fifth year and elected captain was Walt Schreiner, the fleet 145-pound end. Back also were Marshall McMahon, tackle; Leopold Sam; Walt Monteith; and fullback Jim Hart. Jim McCall, a husky 190-pound center and Sam Fenner Leslie, a strapping halfback, were among the brightest freshman prospects.

In the first game of the season at Austin, a young inexperienced Oklahoma squad was easily defeated by a 28–2 margin as coach Thompson utilized every member of the team. Then, Vanderbilt

was beaten 22–0 as four Texas halfbacks, Hart, Leslie, Russ, and Johnny DeLesdernier, scored touchdowns. The following week Texas A&M was beaten in a game at San Antonio 5–0 in a bruising battle. DeLesdernier burst over left tackle the game's only TD after Texas recovered a blocked A&M punt at the A&M 8-yard line.

Next up was Missouri. The Tigers had outplayed and outscored Texas in the two previous games the teams played in 1894 and in '96, but in 1900, Texas was determined to avenge both those defeats.

Coach Thompson worked his charges for three weeks prior to the game, running them hard each day until they were ready to drop from exhaustion. He also added a few new plays, and then tacked on a long one-mile jog on the way back to the gym.

When Missouri arrived in Austin for the game, Texas was ready and out for blood.

Sam Leslie, the huge 200-pound fullback who had played very well in the first three games, was deliberately kept on the bench as punishment for allowing his weight to zoom to 225 pounds. With Leslie on the sidelines, Missouri ran up a 5–0 lead in the first half, but when the second half began, Coach Thompson inserted Big Sam into the lineup and Sam played like a wild man. He singlehandedly tore the Tigers' line apart for gains of ten, fifteen, and twenty yards each time he carried the ball, and in short order Texas had a 17–5 lead.

With only a few minutes left in the game, Leslie was given a rest, and Missouri managed to score a touchdown and kick the goal. But Texas had too much of an edge and took the victory 17–11. As the game ended the delirious Texas players dashed over to their coach, hoisted Thompson onto their shoulders, and paraded about the field to celebrate the biggest victory of the season.

The following week in a game at Austin, Texas romped to an easy win over the Kansas City Medics, 30–0. A few days later on Thanksgiving, Texas defeated their rivals from Texas A&M by an 11–0 score.

The victory over the Aggies brought the season to a close. Texas celebrated their finest year with six consecutive victories that gave them undisputed claim to the unofficial Championship of the Southwest.

In 1901, the second season of the twentieth century, the University of Texas rehired their undefeated coach, "Tommy" Thompson, for another year. The most ambitious football schedule yet was organized by the Athletic Association, a lengthy 11-game schedule that called for games with the leading college teams in the Southwest. The Texas officials must have thought that the Texas team consisted of iron men, for the schedule called for the final five games of the season to be played within a span of thirteen days. To make matters worse, four of the five games—Missouri, Kirksville, Kansas, and Oklahoma—were on the road.

As difficult as the new 11-game schedule was, Coach Thompson was faced with an even more frustrating problem. Virtually none of the regular lettermen had returned. Captain Marshall McMahon, an outstanding tackle, was back. So was halfback Sam Leslie, end Vance Duncan, Bill McMahon (Marshall's kid brother), tackle Tom

James, Walt Hyde, a fullback from A&M, and quarterback Rem Watson.

In the opening game of the season against the Houston town team Texas romped to an easy 32–0 victory. Against Nashville University a week later, Little McMahon tore around his own left end and dashed 65 yards for a spectacular touchdown as the game opened. But from that point on, it was Nashville's game. They scored on a 50-yard sprint by their fullback, and it was a 5–5 tie the rest of the way as both teams drove up and down the gridiron but failed to score.

The Oklahoma Sooners traveled to Austin for the third game of the season. After the two teams struggled for three periods the score was 6–6. There were just two minutes left to play in the game when Little McMahon faked a line buck, then skirted his own right end, stiff-armed a couple of tacklers, and sped 55 yards for a touchdown that gave the Horns an exciting, last-minute 12–6 victory.

A week later in San Antonio, Texas had little trouble defeating the Aggies 17–0 in a game that was played at midday. Three days later, at Waco, Texas inaugurated their long rivalry against Baylor and defeated the Bears 23–0. Four days later, back home in Austin, Texas defeated the Dallas Athletic Club 12–0.

A few days later Texas began the arduous 1500-mile road trip with an impressive 11–0 win over Missouri. Rem Watson, the shifty Texas quarterback, took the kickoff on the first play of the second half, tore through his right side, and raced downfield for 95 yards and a touchdown. It was the fifteenth win in the last 16 games for Texas over a two-year period.

In the second game of the road trip, Texas locked horns with the Kirksville (Missouri) Osteopaths. The strong Osteopaths had easily beaten Missouri in an earlier game. According to Coach Thompson, the Osteopaths were composed of outstanding players, who were "pickups," and not regular members of the institution, and they were practically invincible at home.

The Osteopaths' offense mystified Texas with tricky plays and within three minutes of the kickoff,

Vance Duncan captained this rugged 1902 squad through a difficult 10-game schedule.

Kirksville had scored twice. At halftime it was 36–0. Finally, after the Osteopaths had run the Texas defense dizzy, scoring a total of 48 points, both coaches called the game with some 15 minutes remaining to play.

After the game the Texas players claimed that the Osteopath players had used their own coach as the referee and, as one Texas player put it, "they held us and fouled us at every opportunity."

Three days later, badly bruised and with morale at a low ebb, Texas rolled into Lawrence to face a strong Kansas eleven. They dropped a 12–0 game to the Jayhawks. A few days later Kansas defeated Kirksville 17–5—the same Kirksville team that beat Texas 48–0.

Just one day after the tough Kansas game, Texas battled Oklahoma and took a 5–0 lead early in the game. In the second half, quarterback Rem Watson returned a punt 55 yards for another Texas score. The game ended with Texas in front by an 11–0 margin.

Battered and bruised after 1500 miles and five road games, an exhausted Texas team returned to Austin to meet A&M in the big Thanksgiving game, just three days after the Oklahoma victory. With a number of substitutes in the lineup, Texas battered A&M with a withering attack, scoring 5 touchdowns in a 32–0 rout.

The resounding victory over the Aggies after the 10-day, 1500-mile road trip resulted in a most successful 8-2-1 season for Texas. They had concluded the season with convincing victories against the strongest college rivals in the Southwest.

Once more Texas had a new football coach as Tommy Thompson left after two outstanding seasons. New coach John Hart had been a fine halfback for the undefeated 1901 Yale University team. But when the 135-pound, five-foot-five Hart called his first practice session most of the Texas players doubted that Hart had ever played the game. However, once practice was called, Hart quickly demonstrated why he was selected as Texas' coach. He ran through Texas tacklers in a scrimmage again and again and demonstrated how and why he had led Yale University to 11 consecutive wins the previous season.

Only three regular members of the 1901 team reported back for the 1902 season, including Vance Duncan, a fine end, Dave Prendergrast, a solid tackle, and Rem Watson, quarterback of the '01 team.

In the first game of the season at home, against Oklahoma, Rem Watson dashed 55 yards for a quick score as the game began. The Oklahoma team, playing without a coach, quickly lost interest in the game and was beaten 22–6. One week later at the Dallas State Fair Grounds, Texas fullback Johnnie Jackson scored two quick touchdowns in the first half as Texas defeated a strong Sewanee eleven 11–0. A crowd estimated at more than 5000 enjoyed the fine play of the Texas squad.

The game with Sewanee, a tough bruising battle, evidently took a great deal out of the players; they seemed to have lost a good part of the pep and spark of their offense as the team then lost in San Antonio to the LSU Tigers, 5–0, then was held to a sluggish 5–5 tie by A&M. But a quick turnaround led by a spirited Dave Prendergrast gave Texas a 27–0 victory over San Antonio's Trinity University in a game at Austin.

The all-Indian Haskell Institute of Kansas (not to be confused with the Haskell Institute of Carlisle, Pennsylvania, where Jim Thorpe got his start) visited Austin for a game against Texas and came away with a 12–0 win. Two touchdown sprints by the tricky, clever ball-handling backs, George Baine and Chauncey Archiquette, resulted in TD runs of 75 and 60 yards for the Indians.

Following the Haskell game, Texas embarked on a three-game road trip. The first game, against Nashville in Dallas, resulted in an 11–5 win for Texas; next was a 10–0 win over Alabama, then a 6–0 victory over Tulane that halfback Ed Crane called "the roughest game I've ever played in."

To close out the season at Austin, the Aggies made up for seven straight losses at the hands of Texas by drubbing the varsity 12–0 to give the Aggies a claim to the Southwest Championship.

Though his team had lost 3 games and tied 1, Coach Jim Hart was satisfied with his six wins over some of the Southwest's leading colleges.

Ralph Hutchinson had been the star quarterback on the 1898 and '99 Princeton teams. They were two of the greatest Tiger teams ever; the 1898 team won 11 of 12 games, while the 1899 eleven won 12 and lost 1. In 1903 Hutchinson was selected to coach the Texas team. "Hutch" had previous coaching experience at Dickinson and at Princeton.

Hutch quickly realized that his material at Texas was thin; only two veteran players had returned for the 1903 season, including one of the bright stars, quarterback Rem Watson, and tackle Nick Marshall. Newcomers to the team included Lucian Parrish, a lineman; Don Robinson, all-around star who reportedly had played the game at several colleges; and Bill Scarborough, a huge tackle.

Now known as the Longhorns, Texas took the field against the School For Deaf & Dumb in the first game of the season and defeated them 17–0. The Haskell Indians again visited Texas and in a game played at the Dallas Baseball Park defeated Texas 6–0 in a defensive battle that was marked by close line play and fine punts by both teams. Indian halfback Herb Falls picked up a blocked punt and raced 20 yards for the only score of the game.

In the first of two games this season, Oklahoma tied the score against Texas near the end of the game. Texas fumbled an Oklahoma punt, and the Sooners recovered the ball and scored from the 8-yard line. The kick was good and the final result was a hard-fought 6–6 tie.

In the fourth game of the season Texas, now hitting on all cylinders, rolled over Baylor 48–0, then shut out a strong Arkansas team 15–0 in the first game in nine years against the Razorbacks. Then, a 5–5 tie against Vanderbilt that was called "one of the great games" by one scribe ended with Texas storming toward the Vanderbilt goal line only to have darkness put a halt to all activities.

Texas won the return game against Oklahoma on the road by an 11–5 score in a closely fought battle in which the key play involved a horse. The score was tied at 6–6 when Don Robinson recovered an Oklahoma fumble that bounced under a horse. Robinson dove underneath the animal, recovered the fumble, which was over the goal line, and scored the winning TD. This was undoubtedly the most unique fumble recovery in the history of college football. Final score: Texas 11, Oklahoma 7.

THE TEXAS FOOTBALL TEAM WHICH WILL PLAY CHICAGO THIS AFTERNOON.
[DRAWN FROM TELEGRAPHIC DESCRIPTION.]

RALPH WILDER

This cartoon appeared in the *Chicago Herald* prior to the Texas-University of Chicago game in 1904.

In the traditional Thanksgiving battle at Austin, the Aggies opened the game with a rush, scoring a quick touchdown to give them a 6–0 lead. But an aroused Texas squad bounced back and ripped A&M for four touchdowns and a 29–6 victory in a game that brought the season to a successful close. The 1903 record included 5 victories, a 6–0 loss to Haskell, and ties with Oklahoma and Vanderbilt.

Coach Hutchinson, after surveying his 1904 University of Texas football squad, predicted that the Longhorns would have an outstanding season. "With such veterans as Rem Watson, quarterback, Neill Masterson, Dave Prendergrast, Grover Jones, Don Robinson, Lucian Parrish and Bill Scarborough, we have the nucleus of a team that could defeat any team in the Southwest," he said.

And as the season progressed, Hutchinson's prognostication was quite accurate, for the only two teams to defeat Texas were the Haskell Indians and the University of Chicago.

In the season's opener against TCU at Austin, team captain Rem Watson took the opening kick-off, dodged two tacklers, and then outran the rest of TCU's defenders for a 60-yard touchdown that stunned TCU and delighted the hometown crowd. Before the game was over Texas had driven through and around TCU for a 40–0 win in the first game between the two teams in six years.

The following week Trinity was beaten 24–0. Then, in the third game of the season at Austin, the Haskell Indians picked up their third straight win over Texas by virtue of a 40-yard field goal by Haskell's great kicker, Pete Hauser. The game ended 4–0.

In their first invasion of the middle west, Texas was invited to play the Washington University team of St. Louis at the Louisiana Purchase Exposition World's Fair. The Longhorns' smoothly working offense easily defeated Washington 23–0 as Don Robinson scored two touchdowns.

But in the Longhorns' first bid for national recognition, against the University of Chicago's great team directed by one of football's coaching immortals, Amos Alonzo Stagg, Texas was routed in a flurry of touchdowns. Captained by all-American quarterback Walter Eckersall, Chicago had too much speed and experience for the Texas team. In one of the first offensive drives of the game, Texas drove to the Maroons' 2-yard line. There were high hopes that Texas would score. But Scarborough had the ball knocked from his hands in a drive into the line. Walt Eckersall scooped up the ball on the 10-yard line and with Grover Jones in pursuit raced the entire length of the field for Chicago's first score.

Stunned by the suddenness of that score, Texas never recovered and played the rest of the game as if they were in a fog. As a result, Chicago romped to a 68–0 victory—the worst defeat in Texas history. Chicago piled up 11 TDs, nine extra points, and a field goal by Eckersall.

In the locker room after the game, Coach Hutchinson tried to soften the defeat. He pointed to the fact that Chicago had beaten such teams as Indiana, Purdue, Iowa, and Northwestern, the strongest teams in the Big Ten Conference, and was considered one of the great teams in the nation.

Back home once again after the Chicago disaster, Texas defeated Oklahoma 40–10. Leading at halftime 17–10 and strongly pressed by a gutsy Sooner team, Texas rallied in the second half and scored four touchdowns. A week later in Austin, Texas trampled over Baylor 58–0 as every member of the Texas team saw action. Bill Blocker broke away for several big gains, including an 80-yard touchdown run near the close of the game.

The annual Thanksgiving game at Austin featured Texas vs. Texas A&M and once again Texas defeated their bitter rivals, this time by a 34–6 score. It was the seventh victory for Texas over the Aggies in the eight games the two rivals had played since the series began in 1898.

The victories over TCU, Trinity, Oklahoma, Baylor, and Texas A&M gave Texas 6 victories over Southwest teams in 6 games and a strong claim for the Championship of the Southwest.

With six of the seven varsity linemen of the 1904 team not in school for the 1905 season and a rugged nine-game schedule booked, Coach Ralph Hutchinson realized that he would be fortunate to have a break-even season. To replace such regulars as Grover Jones, Marrs McLean, Bill Scarborough, Dave Prendergrast, Ben Glascock, and Norm Marshall, all thoroughly schooled linemen, Hutch was fortunate in having Bob Ramsdell, a 175-pound tackle and the first of three Texas-football-playing Ramsdells; Henry Fink; Harry Weinert, a 200-pound guard; Magnus Mainland, another 190-pound guard; Brodie Hamilton at center; and end Bowie Duncan as the players he could count on to bolster his line. In the backfield Hutch could count on quarterback Bill Blocker; the heady, swift Don Robinson and Ed Crane at the halfback posts; and Red Hastings and Fred Householder, two rugged fullbacks, to start the season.

In the opening game of the season Texas was able to punch across two touchdowns against TCU for an 11–0 victory in a game held at Austin. Then the Haskell Indians visited the Austin campus for the fourth game of the Series and against defeated

Texas, this time by a 17–0 score. The game was shortened to 45 minutes in an agreement by the two coaches prior to the start of the contest.

A visit by Baylor got Texas back on the winning track. Bobby Ramsdell rammed in 3 touchdowns in a 39–0 rout of the Bears.

The 3-game road trip that followed was beset by financial problems. Texas first traveled to Nashville to do battle with an undefeated Vanderbilt University team. Coached by Dan McGugin, who had been the head coach at Michigan, Dan had developed one of the strongest teams in Vanderbilt history. Prior to playing Texas, Vandy had routed Maryville College, 97–0, defeated a strong Alabama team 34–0, lost to Michigan, and trounced Tennessee 45–0. In a game that starred Vandy's great halfback, Honus Craig, who scored TDs on runs of 70, 87, and 35 yards, a superior Vanderbilt team defeated Texas 33–0.

Texas then defeated Arkansas at Fayetteville by a 4–0 margin in a close, rough battle. A field goal by Winston McMahon was the only score. A few days later at Oklahoma City Texas was beaten 2–0 when Sooner tackle Bob Severin tackled Don Robinson behind his own goal line for the safety that was the margin of victory.

Coach Hutchinson protested the Oklahoma game, pointing to the "horrible officiating." Said Hutch, "Even the safety call was wrong. Robinson hardly made an effort to run the ball because Severin was clearly offside on the play." There was a minute of play left in the game, but Sooner fans stormed the field and Hutch pulled his team from the field of play.

One week later, little Transylvania University from Lexington, Kentucky, defeated Texas in Austin 6–0.

Next was former powerhouse Sewanee. With 3 wins and a tie with Georgia Tech, they took a 10–6 lead with only 12 minutes left to play, but flashy fullback Red Hastings quickly scored two more TDs to give Texas a 17–10 win.

Then, in the season's finale at Austin on Thanksgiving Day, Texas completely outplayed the Aggies as Red Hastings again dashed for two touchdowns. Texas ran up a 27–0 victory to close out a lackluster 5–4 season. It was a season that saw Texas outplayed by Haskell and Vanderbilt, lose close games to Oklahoma and Transylvania, and then come back strong against two rivals, Sewanee and the Texas Aggies.

At the end of his third and final season at Texas, Coach Hutchinson pointed out that at least three of the games were lost because of poor and unprofessional officiating. "Had we won two of those games," said Hutch, "we would have a seven and two season and that would have been wonderful with the inexperienced team we had."

The 1905 football season ended in an uproar of national protest against the brutality of college football. The *Chicago Tribune* in a front-page story compiled a list of serious injuries and deaths due to football; it showed that in 1905 there were eighteen deaths and more than 159 serious injuries. Then, in midseason, President Theodore Roosevelt called representatives of Yale, Harvard, and Princeton to the White House and told them it was up to them to save the sport . . . by removing every objectionable feature. "Brutality and foul play, inefficient officials should receive the same punishment given to a man who cheats at cards. And," said the President, "if you people, leaders of the sport, don't clean up this sport, I will banish the game."

The presidents of Stanford, New York University, and the University of California all suspended the sport for one year.

At a meeting on December 28, 1905, sixty-two schools participated in a meeting to change and reform football under the aegis of the Intercollegiate Athletic Association, and they adopted a program to save the game.

At other meetings, culminating in a January 12, 1906, meeting in New York, a number of rule changes were adopted:

1. Reduce the length of the game from seventy to sixty minutes.
2. Establish a neutral zone separating the teams by the length of the ball.
3. Increase the distance to be gained in three downs from 5 to 10 yards.
4. Guards, centers, and tackles not permitted to drop behind the line of scrimmage on offense . . . unless they fall back at least 5 yards.
5. All punts striking the ground makes all members of the kicking team on-side, except the punter.
6. The field must be marked by lengthwise stripes 5 yards apart.
7. The forward pass is now legal.

The new rules toned down the savage and brutal play in football, cut down the piling on, kicking, and gouging, and abolished the wedge-type play. The legalization of the forward pass was the most revolutionary change in the game, for it made for a wide-open style of play that brought big plays and excitement to the fans.

And in 1906 the University of Texas once more selected a new football coach, a coach who was to make history in a most unique manner.

The new coach, Henry Schenker, was highly recommended by the great Walter Camp and Yale's great coach and former all-American, Tommy Shevlin. Schenker supposedly played for a couple of years with the Yale team, but the official records show he never graced a varsity lineup.

When Coach Schenker called his first practice session it was obvious he was in way over his head and did not at all understand the intricacies of the game. He ineffectively attempted to show how a lineman had to use a hip or shoulder to block out an opposing player. Further, he had no idea of how the quarterback should function in handing the ball off to another back. He was clumsy and his efforts were met with ridicule.

Fortunately, the Longhorn captain was Lucian Parrish, a four-year all-star player who was bright and sharp (he later would be elected to Congress). He spoke to the Athletic Association about Schenker's complete lack of football knowledge and the AA agreed to help.

Parrish called the squad to a special meeting soon after and discussed the new coach. "Men," he said, "we have an unfortunate problem with the new coach. Now, whatever he tells you try to follow

Lucian Parrish, an outstanding guard, was elected captain of the 1906 team. An honors student, Parrish was elected to congress later in his career.

through . . . But it will probably be the wrong thing to do. But keep your mouth shut, then at the end of practice, come to me and I will see that all the mistakes are rectified."

In a rather odd setup, two professors were called in as sort of assistant coaches. W. E. Metzenthin, a young German instructor and a former player in college, and Dr. Caswell Ellis, professor of pedagogy, were on hand for every practice and every game.

What kept the 1906 season from being a complete washout was the fact that several of Texas' veteran players returned. No less than eleven varsity players with at least two or three years of experience gave the Longhorns a cadre of veterans with the background to play the game with a minimal amount of coaching.

It was fortunate, too, that the 1906 schedule called for a number of games with schools and organizations that would not provide much opposition—like the Texas 26th Infantry team.

In the opening game of the season, Texas defeated the military team from Fort Worth by a

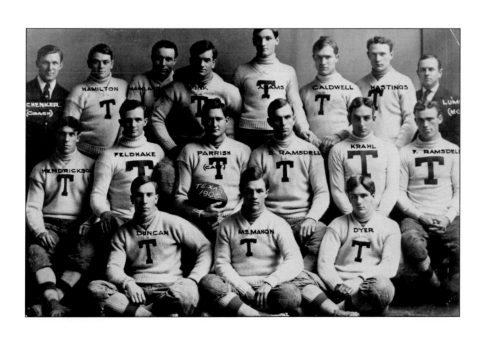

The 1906 Texas football team was coached by two of the university's professors. One of the professors, Henry Schenker, played football with Yale. The team won 9 and lost 1.

The Texas Varsity attempts a wedge-style play against Daniel Baker in a 1906 game.

21–0 score, then handily rolled over TCU 22–0 and West Texas Military Academy 28–0. Then, in the fourth week of the season, just as the team was adjusting to their unique coaching setup, they traveled to Nashville and were soundly beaten 45–0 by an overpowering Vandy eleven coached by Dan McGugin. The previous week Vandy had overpowered Alabama 78–0 and would win 8 of 9 games that year.

Following the Vanderbilt loss, Texas pulled itself together and managed to defeat Arkansas in Fayetteville 11–0 in a game that saw halfback Fred Ramsdell pick off an Arkansas forward pass at the Texas goal line and race 100 yards for a touchdown.

The following week at Oklahoma City, Texas decided to try an on-side kick against the Sooners late in the game. Behind 9–4 with just three minutes left to play, halfback Bellard Caldwell, substituting for Ramsdell, who was out with an injury, faked a run around his right end. Then he suddenly stopped and kicked the ball across the field to left end Henry Fink. Fink scooped up the ball just as it hit the turf, and dashed over the goal line to tie the score.

Winston McMahon kicked the extra point, and Texas managed to pull out a thrilling, come-from-behind 10–9 win . . . just as the gun sounded to end the contest.

Back home again after ten days on the road, Texas defeated its Indian rivals from Haskell by a 28–0 margin. It was Texas' first win over Haskell

after suffering shutout defeats in four consecutive games against the Indians.

Texas displayed a fine forward pass attack in Austin the next week against Daniel Baker College. The McMahon-to-end-Bowie Duncan combination set up a number of successful plays, including one 40-yard pass play for a touchdown, as Texas routed Daniel Baker 40–0. Halfback Verne Hendrickson was outstanding in Texas' eighth game of the season against Washington University as they defeated the St. Louis eleven 17–6 in a fiercely fought battle that went right down to the final gun.

The final game of the season was the Thanksgiving game against Texas A&M. The Longhorns, utilizing the forward pass with increasing success, easily defeated A&M 24–0 to close out one of the most successful seasons in their 14-year football history. Their 9–1 record once again gained them recognition as the Southwest Champions. This, despite one of the most extraordinary coaching situations in the history of college football.

Bill Metzenthin, the young German professor who had volunteered his services in 1906, agreed to coach the Longhorn squad in 1907. Metzenthin had played football at Franklin & Marshall College and then at Columbia University in 1903 and '04. It was a period in which the Blue & White ranked among the finest teams in the nation. In 1903 Metz played with a Columbia squad that won 9 of 10 games, including victories over Penn, Cornell,

Bill Metzenthin, A UT German professor, volunteered to serve as the football coach in 1906. He was appointed head coach for 1907 and 1908.

Williams, Swarthmore, and Amherst. Coached by all-American Bill Morley, Columbia lost only to Yale, Pennsylvania, and Amherst in three seasons.

Fifteen lettermen reported to Coach Metzenthin, guaranteeing him a veteran at every position for the 1907 season. There was initially some unhappiness when sophomore Bowie Duncan, a fine end, was elected team captain over some of the older, more experienced team members. But that was forgotten as the season began.

In the opening game at the Dallas State Fair Grounds, Texas battled to a 0–0 tie with their rivals, Texas A&M, in a game that saw both teams play below par.

In the second game, played at Austin, LSU was beaten 12–5 in a game that saw 175-pound fullback Bill Krahl blast through the Tigers for two last-minute touchdowns. Texas eked out a 12–5 victory.

In the third game of the year, the Haskell Indians were roundly defeated after a bitterly fought

first half that ended with Texas out in front by a 12–10 score. In the second half, however, Coach Metzenthin lashed out against his veterans, saying they were playing like a bunch of prima donnas. Texas came roaring back in the second half with six touchdowns in a 45–10 rout of the Indians. Halfback Fred Ramsdell inspired his teammates as he ripped off a 70-yard sprint for a TD at the beginning of the second half and quarterback Ben Dyer took a Haskell punt and raced 60 yards for another score. It was Texas' biggest margin over the Indians in the six games the teams had played.

Texas began its annual road trip against Arkansas in Fayetteville and defeated them 26–6. Three days later the listless Longhorns lost a bitter 5–4 battle to Missouri. Arnie Kirkpatrick missed three field goals from within the 25-yard line after successfully kicking a 30-yarder.

Back home in Austin, Texas engaged the Baylor Bears on a rainy, muddy afternoon, but the fine play of halfback Ed Slaughter gave the Longhorns a 27–11 win.

A week later, in a game played at Austin, halfback Fred Ramsdell took the opening kickoff against Oklahoma and raced 55 yards for a brilliant touchdown. The play provided the impetus for Texas, and Bill Krahl tossed passes to Bowie Duncan and Ed Slaughter for two additional touchdowns. The Longhorns stormed to a 29–10 win over Oklahoma for their fifth win of the year.

A crowd of more than 6000 spectators turned out for the annual Thanksgiving battle in Austin against the Texas Aggies. Once again the Longhorns, playing inspired football, outplayed A&M in a stubborn defensive battle between two fine football teams. Texas was so determined to win this game they played the entire game without making a single substitution.

Fred Ramsdell's punting was the big difference. His kicks drove the enemy far into their own territory time after time. Two of his kicks were recovered by Texas and both recoveries gave Texas the ball deep in Aggie territory. Finally, after recovering one of A&M's kicks, Bill Krahl drove across the Aggies' goal line for a touchdown. At the end of the half, it was Texas 5, Texas A&M 6.

Late in the second half A&M, eager for another score, tried a complicated forward pass play that backfired. Ramsdell, always on the alert, leaped high into the air, took the ball right out of the hands of an A&M player, then shot off for the goal line and scored what proved to be the winning TD in a bruising but thrilling game.

The victory over A&M ended the season for Texas with a very successful 6–1 record, and Texas was again proclaimed the Southwest Champion.

When Coach Bill Metzenthin looked over the squad of some twenty-three players reporting for practice for the 1908 season, he noted that there were some thirteen lettermen who had played through the grueling 1907 season, one of the most successful seasons in the school's 15-year football history. Therefore, he rationalized, with such solid veterans returning and half a dozen solid-looking freshmen, 1908 could be another banner year.

But what Metzenthin didn't take into consideration was the fact that the Athletic Association had scheduled games with nine of the leading teams in the Southwest. Perhaps the one team that was not supposed to give the Longhorns any trouble was a small college in nearby Georgetown, Southwestern, that had played but two games in its history. But Southwestern proved to be a tartar. . . .

The opening game of the season found Texas facing the Texas Christian team at Austin. Fuzzy Feldhale, a fine tackle, was shifted to halfback, and he smashed into the TCU line for two touchdowns that brought victory to the Longhorns by an 11–6 margin.

In the second game, also at Austin, the Longhorns met and easily defeated the Baylor Bears. Feldhale, recently elected team captain, starred in every aspect of the game and scored touchdowns as Texas took a 27–5 win over Baylor. But against the University of Colorado in the first game ever played between the two schools, Colorado romped to a 15–0 victory as the Longhorns fumbled several punts that were recovered by Colorado for touchdowns.

The Southwestern game scheduled just four days prior to the annual Texas Aggie game was sup-posed to be a breather. But the schedulemakers had no idea that the tiny Southwestern college would spring one of the biggest upsets in Texas history.

Utilizing a short, accurate passing game, Southwestern ran up two quick touchdowns and held on for dear life as the Longhorns snapped out of their lethargy and began to push the Southwestern defense all over the field. But Texas had awakened too late, and before anyone realized it, Southwestern had a big victory by an 11–9 margin.

Just four days later in Houston, determined to shrug off the loss to Southwestern, Texas applied tremendous pressure against A&M as the game began and scored quickly on Ed Slaughter's pass interception for a TD. Then Bowie Duncan kicked two beautiful field goals, one for 25 yards and another for 35 yards, to wrap up a 24–8 win over the Aggies. It was the sixth straight win for the Longhorns over A&M.

Once again the schedulemakers at Texas, intent on making it tough for their football team, had slated three games within an eight-day period. Now, just four days after the Aggies game and seven days after the Southwestern loss, Texas traveled to Norman, Oklahoma, for a game with the Sooners. Oklahoma had won seven of eight games to that point and had one of the strongest teams in the Big Six Conference.

The Longhorns arrived in Norman amidst a fierce winter storm on a day that Oklahoma folks said was the coldest day in ten years. The Texas players' hands were so cold they could not handle the ball. Players stuffed cardboard and paper into their shirts and pants to keep warm. Substitutes carried coats and hats while they sat on the sidelines and froze.

Tired out, worn to a frazzle, and freezing cold, Texas was no match for the Sooners, who punched out a 17–0 halftime lead and increased the margin of victory with 33 additional points to completely rout Texas 50–0. It was the worst beating since the 68–0 defeat inflicted by Chicago in 1904.

Still tired and with morale at a low ebb, the Longhorns went down to another defeat one week later in a game against Tulane at New Orleans. The

Green Wave had not beaten Texas in six previous engagements, but an effective, accurate passing attack gave them a 28–15 win.

Faced with their first losing season in fifteen years, the players looked forward to their annual Thanksgiving game at Austin against the rival Texas Aggies. But the Aggies, pumped to new heights by a 32–0 win over Southwestern the week before, jumped out to a 12–0 lead at the half as their great kicking ace, Lou Hamilton, made good on kicks of 33, 20, and 47 yards.

In the locker room between halves end Bowie Duncan, a four-year star and former captain, began to talk to the squad about coming from behind and winning. Midway through his speech he began to cry and could not finish. The emotion stirred the entire team and they dashed out onto the field for the second half and ran up two quick touchdowns to trail A&M by an 11–12 score as the crowd of 5000 fans roared their approval of the Texas drive.

Then quarterback Ben Dyer took an A&M punt, broke to the sidelines, reversed his field, and was off on an amazing 50-yard dash through the entire A&M team to give Texas a 16–12 lead. Texas continued to pound away and scored 12 more points to win one of the most thrilling games ever played in Austin. Final score: Texas 28, A&M 12.

The win over the Aggies gave Texas a winning 5–4 season, but Coach Metzenthin, severely criticized by all the sideline experts and the alumni, tendered his resignation at the end of the season.

By 1908 most of the major colleges had incorporated the forward pass into their offensive bag of tricks. Amos Alonzo Stagg of Chicago even added a double pass: a pass to an end, followed by a forward pass. In 1909 Bob Zuppke of Illinois originated the screen pass and used it to the dismay of his opponents. But there were a number of coaches who were not in favor of the pass or had no player who could effectively throw the ball. Simply put, the forward pass play, to be effective, meant that a coach had to devote a great deal of time, effort, and energy teaching it to his team. They often felt they lacked the talent to effectively introduce this new threat.

Texas' new coach, Dexter Draper, had been a three-year star tackle with the University of Pennsylvania team, an all-American tackle in 1907, and a member of Penn's great teams in 1905, '06, and '07 that lost but three games in three years. He was a burly, tough lineman who disdained the lighter, swifter type of player. He liked his football players with plenty of heft and strength. He immediately quarreled with the team's captain, 150-pound end Ben Dyer, about the kind of offense he wanted for the 1909 season.

Draper shifted the speedy Dyer to the quarterback spot, and with such veterans as Fuzzy Feldhale and Emil Stieler; two 190-pound guards, Cullen Bailey and Jack Persons at the tackles; Arnie Kirkpatrick, Marshall Ramsdell, Bart Moore, and Les Spoonts in the backfield; plus the addition of several newcomers, Texas faced Southwestern in the opening game of the season.

Texas scored quickly in the first five minutes of play. At the half it was 12–0, Texas, and they coasted the rest of the way in an easy win over Southwestern. In the second game against Haskell, played in Dallas, Texas had an 11–6 lead over the Indians when Ben Dyer, eager to score again, fumbled an Indian punt. The speedy Indians recovered the ball and raced over for a quick touchdown and an extra point as they snatched a 12–11 win from Texas.

Coach Draper shook up his backfield for the next game, against Trinity. Dyer was moved from quarterback to halfback, and Arnie Kirkpatrick was moved from his fullback spot to quarterback. Both players responded with outstanding games as they defeated Trinity 18–0. The following week both Dyer and Kirkpatrick again performed like stars as Texas defeated TCU 24–0. Kirkpatrick sped 50 yards for a TD, then Dyer raced to a 40-yard touchdown as the Longhorns picked up their third win in four games.

Preparing for their old rivals, the Texas Aggies, the Longhorns heard rumors that the Aggies had loaded their team with a group of all-stars, including a couple of players who had played with the Haskell Indians and the Nesser Brothers team (later the Massilon Tigers, a professional team). True or not, the new players were good enough to defeat Texas by a 23–0 score. Lou Hamilton, a three-year star for the Aggies, broke loose for a 90-yard touchdown sprint, and that single play broke the spirit of the Longhorns and they went down to an easy defeat.

Texas then traveled to New Orleans for a game against Tulane; the Green Wave managed a 10–10 tie with Texas.

Next up was the big game against Oklahoma. In a discussion with Coach Draper before the game, Captain Ben Dyer insisted the team was losing games because Draper was not utilizing the veterans properly and was playing men out of their regular positions. Draper responded by moving Dyer to an end spot and starting Bart Moore and Marshall Ramsdell, the third member of the Ramsdell family to play for Texas, in the backfield. Both players responded magnificently in the game against Oklahoma. Ramsdell scored two touchdowns and Moore drove 45 yards and then 50 yards on kickoffs to give Texas two additional opportunities to score. Texas played as if the championship depended on this game and easily defeated OU 30–0. The result was in sharp contrast to 1908, when Oklahoma romped to a 50–0 finish over Texas.

In the final game of the season, Texas displayed its best form of the year, but it was not good enough; the Aggies and their "supposedly ringer players" defeated the Longhorns by a 5–0 score. After the game there were charges and counter-charges that Charley Moran, the Aggies' football coach, had used at least half a dozen illegal players, including Ted Nesser, a professional with Massilon. At the end of the season, not one of the A&M players involved in the rumors returned to school.

Texas finished the season with a 4-3-1 year. It was the poorest year since Texas began its football program in 1893.

Bill Wasmund, a fiery member of the 1905 Lafayette College team that won 8 of 10 games in the strong Eastern College Football League and a 6–6 tie with Pennsylvania, was selected to replace Dexter Draper for the 1910 season. Wasmund was the fourteenth head coach at Texas in eighteen seasons.

At the first practice session, Wasmund noted with satisfaction that he had nineteen lettermen back from the 1908 squad, including one of Texas' great triple threat stars, captain and quarterback Arnie Kirkpatrick, and Bart Moore, Hap Massingill, Joe Russell, Hans Helland, Lee Spoonts, Offie Leonard and Little Brown, all backfield members. Linemen included Joe Estill, Ed Harold, Frost Woodhull, Marshall Ramsdell, Johnny James, Sam Wolfe, and Les Stallings. All in all, Wasmund and his aides were delighted with the spirit and abilities of the players he had inherited and felt that 1910 would see a vastly improved Longhorn squad on the field.

Texas opened up the season at home against tiny Southwestern and rang up an easy 11–6 victory that saw Coach Wasmund utilize every man on the squad.

In the second game, against Haskell, also at Austin, Wasmund used sweeping end runs and a number of forward passes to turn the game into a rout of the Indians by a blistering 68–3 score. Then followed another romp, this time over Transylvania. Texas scored a point a minute in winning by a 48–0 margin.

In the first real test of the season against a strong Auburn team, the first game ever played between the two schools, Texas jumped to a 3–0 lead early in the game, when Arnie Kirkpatrick booted a 30-yard field goal. Then Auburn mounted a strong offense and moved to the Longhorns' 10-yard line before they were stopped. Then Texas took over the ball and Kirkpatrick boomed a punt to the Auburn 40-yard stripe, a 50-yard kick. The ever-alert Joe Estill scooped up the loose ball and raced 40 yards for another Texas score and a 9–0 victory. (In those days a punt became a free ball.)

The hard-fought Auburn victory was not without its price, however, for a number of the Longhorn stars came away from the fray with injuries—injuries that hampered Texas the remainder of the season.

The record indicates that Texas scored an unusual 1–0 victory over the Baylor Bears in a game played at Waco. Baylor, however, claimed the game should have been a 6–6 tie. During the game there were many timeouts due to arguments between the two coaches, Wasmund of Texas and Ralph Glaze of Baylor. There were a number of penalties against both teams and then the play that brought the game to a dramatic end; Baylor punted the ball from their 2-yard line and Texas took over. Kirkpatrick, in attempting to pass, dropped the ball and Baylor end Riley Hefly scooped it up and started for the far goal line. But the play was ruled dead because the ball had hit the referee. Two of the three officials ruled in favor of Baylor, but the other official insisted the play was dead. Baylor's coach ordered his team off the field and the game went to Texas by forfeit.

Despite the constant rumors regarding the number of new players in the Texas Aggies line-up—players who were thought to be "ringers"—A&M was still regarded as the underdog in the annual game at Houston. But this time the Aggies played their very best game of the season and defeated the Longhorns 14–8. The Aggies' victory was their eighth in a row and they went on to a marvelous 9–1 record.

Back once more in the kindly confines of their home grounds Texas defeated LSU by a 12–0 score and then dropped the big Thanksgiving Day game at Austin to the Oklahoma Sooners by a 3–0 margin. This was a game that saw both teams drive to their opponent's goal line only to lose the ball without a score. Time after time both teams threatened to break the game wide open. Three times the Longhorns were inside their opponent's 5-yard line but simply could not drive across for a score. Finally, with the game coming to a dramatic close, Trim Cupshaw booted a 25-yard field goal to give the Sooners the margin of victory. The game closed out the season for both teams.

Despite the losses to Texas A&M and Oklahoma, Texas ended the season with a 6–2 record for the best season in four years and the Athletic Association agreed to renew Coach Billy Wasmund's contract for an additional year.

Before issuing calls for his first practice for the 1911 season coach Bill Wasmund organized a pre-season training and conditioning camp at Marble Falls for a two-week period. Most of the camp consisted of short, fast sprint drills and calisthenics, and

when the squad reported to Austin in preparation for the regular season they were in the best shape a Texas team had ever been in.

On October 1, just six days prior to the opening game of the season with Southwestern, Coach Wasmund was found unconscious on the ground outside his apartment on campus.

At first there were rumors of foul play, but Wasmund, a known somnambulist and subject to falls and nightmares, apparently had fallen from his second-floor apartment, and was severely injured. He was rushed to Seton Hospital, where his condition worsened. Four days later he was dead.

The gloom and doom about the campus was widespread, for Coach Wasmund had become one of the most popular coaches and teachers despite a gruff, brusque manner. Before his death, Wasmund suggested that the Athletic Association contact Fielding Yost, the illustrious Michigan coach, for advice on a successor. Yost, quite familiar with the progress made at Texas, suggested Dave Allerdice, a former teammate of his, for the position.

Allerdice had starred for the Wolverines on Michigan's fine 1907–09 football teams that had won 16 of 19 games played. In 1909 Allerdice had captained a Michigan team that lost only to the fighting Irish of Notre Dame while defeating Syracuse, Ohio State, Minnesota, Marquette, and Pennsylvania. He was an outstanding athlete, a fine student of the game, and had all the qualifications for the job. He seemed to be just the right man for Texas football at this crucial period.

Clyde Littlefield, who was to develop into an outstanding fullback under Allerdice, recalled the day he first met the new coach. "I was immediately taken with his manner and approach to the game. He had the finest disposition, a marvelous sense of humor and knew how to handle his players. He was the right man at the right time for Texas football, and I was most fortunate to play for a fine coach like Dave Allerdice."

During Wasmund's hospitalization two assistant coaches—Burt Rix, who also coached track and baseball, and Bill Disch—drove the football squad through their paces and prepped the team for the opening game of the season, which had been postponed given the circumstances to allow the coaches more time to get their squad ready for the difficult eight-game schedule.

Coach Allerdice had only five days to prepare for the opening game of the season against Southwestern and the Longhorns were just plain lucky to beat Southwestern 11–2 on a rain-soaked muddy field that slowed both teams to a walk. The Bears of Baylor were next on the schedule. Again playing on a rain-swept, sloshy field in Austin, the Bears were beaten in the first five minutes of play as Texas quickly smashed across two touchdowns, then held the Bears scoreless in an 11–0 victory.

Marsh Ramsdell, shifted from a tackle position to the backfield by Allerdice, was in marvelous form as he raced for two touchdowns against a strong, determined Arkansas team for Texas' third win of the season, 12–0.

Sewanee, on a two-year streak with 12 wins in 14 games, arrived at Austin a week later thirsting to avenge two previous beatings at the hands of Texas. But it seemed as if they were in for another defeat as Johnny James scooped up a Sewanee fumble early in the game and dashed 35 yards for a TD, giving Texas a 5–0 lead. Texas held onto that lead until the final three minutes. Then, just as the Texas rooters were beginning their victory parade, a mixup in the Texas backfield resulted in a poor center snap as the ball shot over quarterback Puett's head. The ball was finally recovered by Texas on their 5-yard line. On first down Kirkpatrick attempted to punt, but the kick was blocked and Sewanee recovered for a TD that tied the score. Then as the crowd of 2500 fans held its breath, Sewanee kicked the extra point as the gun went off for a thrilling 6–5 victory over the stunned Longhorns.

The following week was the annual grudge match against the Texas Aggies—a game that was always accompanied by arguments, clashes, and even riots by the students of both teams.

Disturbed by the manner in which previous Longhorn-Aggie games had ended with brawls and fights between the rooters of both teams, Texas officials were insistent that the game officials control the behavior of the teams on the field and that the Aggie officials control their excited fans. When those assurances were forthcoming, preparations proceeded for the kickoff at Houston.

Charley Moran, the Aggies' coach, had taken over in 1909 and in that first year the Aggies drubbed Texas 23–0. In 1910 the Aggies had won again by a 14–8 margin as the arguments raged back and forth about the Aggies using "ringers." There was bad blood between the two schools and more than 1200 Longhorn fans traveled to Houston to cheer their team on to victory.

The game began. As the excitement in the stands rose to a feverish pitch, a smash into the line by the Aggies resulted in an injury to Texas' crack guard, Marion Harold. Doctors rushed onto the field and it was disclosed that Harold had suffered a broken leg.

In the second period Kirkpatrick punted to the Aggie 15-yard line. On the following play, a smash into the Texas line failed to gain much, but on the play Frost Woodhull dove into the ball-carrier, Art Bateman, who fumbled the ball. Then Arnie Kirkpatrick scooped up the ball and dove the last couple of yards over the goal line for a Texas touchdown. That single play gave the game to Texas by a 6–0 score after a wild, wooly, and exciting battle.

While Texas fans paraded at Austin the day following the victory over the Aggies, W. T. Mather, chairman of the Texas Athletic Association, sent this message to the Aggie officials:

"I beg to inform you that the AA of Texas has decided not to re-new any athletic relations with Texas A&M for the year 1912."

There were many reasons given for the cancellation of athletic activities between the schools. The action was taken because of the explosive behavior of students before and after the game, and the alleged use of professional players by A&M.

Five days after the hard-earned win over A&M, and beset by injuries to Woodhull, Puett, Kirkpatrick, and Harold, Texas barely managed to defeat Auburn 18–5. Arnie Kirkpatrick played the game of his young life, even though he had suffered injuries in the A&M battle. Kirk scored all of the Longhorns' points in a spectacular one-man show.

On Thanksgiving Day in Austin, still crippled by the same injuries, Texas nevertheless put up a

Arnie Kirkpatrick, Texas' quarterback from 1909 to 1911, was their first triple-threat star. In the 1911 game with Auburn, Arnie scored all 18 points to single-handedly defeat Auburn.

game battle against Oklahoma before going down to defeat 6–3.

Despite the shock of losing their beloved coach, and several injuries to key players throughout the season, the Longhorns finished the season with 5 wins while losing 2. And the Athletic Association was so delighted with the way that Dave Allerdice handled the team that he was given a contract for 1912.

In 1912, as he began his second season at Texas, Coach Allerdice worked feverishly to prepare his team for the opening game of the season against a TCU eleven that had lost every game played between the two schools since the series began in 1904 with a 40–0 Texas victory. But this time TCU, with its finest team ever, had been prepping for Texas since the first day of spring practice and were confident of victory. A crowd of more than 2500 rabid and cheering fans were on hand as Texas and TCU faced each other for the kickoff to open the season.

Texas displayed a quintet of outstanding backfield men including Nels Puett at quarterback, Len Barrell, Little Brown, and Coke Wimmer as alternating halfbacks. Their amazing fullback was Clyde Littlefield, who had a brilliant career at Texas in football, basketball, and track. Littlefield would go on to earn twelve varsity letters, four in each of the three sports, before he graduated in 1916.

As the game began, Texas used a smashing running attack; then, when TCU massed to stop the line rushes, Littlefield opened up with brilliant passing, and the Horns rolled to an impressive 30–10 win over the unbeaten TCU eleven.

A week later, tiny Austin College nearly broke the hearts of the Texas rooters, as they battled the Horns right down to the final minute before surrendering a 3–0 spine-tingling decision to Texas.

The following week, the high-flying Oklahoma Sooners, who had racked up 127 points in the two games they had played, had their scoring machine tuned up for a victory over Texas and they were right on target. Texas, minus the use of Littlefield and several other regular players who had left school, did not play up to their potential; as a result, the Sooners pounded out a 21–6 win over the Longhorns.

In the fourth game of the season against their old rivals, the always colorful Haskell Indians, Clyde Littlefield returned to the lineup to lead the Longhorns to a hard-fought 14–7 win over the Haskell eleven. Three days later at Waco, Texas defeated Baylor 14–7 in a battle marked by a misunderstanding in the matter of downs for Baylor. The mixup gave Texas the ball in Baylor territory and they scored to break open a close game. Final score: Texas 19, Baylor 7.

In the annual Thanksgiving game, Mississippi held Texas to a 7–0 halftime lead. But in the third period Texas ran up three touchdowns, and then added three more in the fourth period to rout Mississippi 53–14. The following week, Little Brown scored two touchdowns early in the game as Texas easily defeated Southwestern, 28–3.

In the final game of the year, quarterback Nelson Puett, all 140 pounds of him, raced for three touchdowns as Texas closed out the season in a blaze of glory. They ran up a 48–0 win over

Arkansas in a game that was officiated by famed coach Amos Alonzo Stagg.

The 7–1 season gave Texas its most successful year since 1907, but there was something missing. That something was the annual battle against the Aggies, and it didn't seem right that the traditional rivalry was not to be played that year.

Coach Dave Allerdice in his third season had to be delighted with the seventeen veterans returning from his victorious 7–1 season of 1912. Returning stars included Little Brown, the acrobatic Paul Simmons, quarterback Len Barrell, and the marvelous passing star, Clyde Littlefield. Linemen included Pete Edmond, Charlie Turner, and Bob Simmons at the end position; Gene Berry, Fats Carlton, Grady Niblo, and Gaddis Bass, all outstanding tackles; Louis Jordan and Hebe Goodman, a pair of tough guards; and Pig Dittmar and Bill Murray at center. There was also a plentiful supply of high school graduates out for the team for the first time.

In the opening game of the season against Fort Worth Polytechnic College, the Longhorns were held to a 7–7 tie with three minutes left to play. But Bill Murray blocked a Poly punt and Gene Berry recovered the ball, and then Little Brown dashed in for a touchdown to give Texas a hard-fought 14–7 edge. A week later, Paul Simmons sparked a four-touchdown spurt as Texas defeated Austin College 27–6. Simmons broke away for two brilliant touchdown runs as the Longhorns showed a vast improvement over their previous effort.

The Longhorns played like champions as they ran roughshod over Baylor University in the third game of the season at Austin. Coach Allerdice played every one of his twenty-six men as the Longhorns scored 12 touchdowns in a 77–0 rout of the Bears.

Sewanee was next on the schedule, in a game played in Dallas. The Longhorns triumphed in a thrilling battle that was not decided until the final whistle. The game was just three minutes old when Len Barrell sprinted 40 yards to the 3-yard line, where fullback Milt Daniel crashed over for the Texas score. The point was missed, and Texas led 6–0. Sewanee then scored a touchdown, kicked the extra point, and led 7–6 until the final minute of the third period. Then Milt Daniel jumped high in the air to intercept a Sewanee pass and sprinted through the entire Sewanee team, some 69 yards, for the winning touchdown. Final score: Texas 13, Sewanee 7.

One week later Southwestern, always a problem for Texas, was defeated under an avalanche of touchdowns in a 52–0 rout. In the following game, Texas defeated Oklahoma in a rugged defensive tussle by a 14–6 margin. Four days later in the frenetic schedule, Texas ran roughshod over Kansas A&M for its twelfth straight win without a defeat. Little Brown, Paul Simmons, and Milt Daniel led the Horns in a spectacular offensive display that ended in a 46–0 Texas win.

At 205 pounds, Alva "Fats" Carlton was one of the top Texas tackles from 1913 to 1916.

Fresh from an incredible upset over a great Army team, Notre Dame's Fighting Irish invaded Austin and took on Texas, defeating UT 30–7. The Irish were led by Captain Knute Rockne (center with ball) and quarterback Gus Dorais (on Rockne's left). In the top row, far right, is Coach Jesse Harper.

Then, for the final game, the Fighting Irish blew into Austin. The entire state was agog with excitement over the impending struggle on Thanksgiving Day. It was the biggest day in Texas football to that point.

The Irish were led by Captain Knute Rockne and Fred Gushorst at the ends; Freeman Fitzgerald and Emmett Keefe at guards; and Deak Jones and Ralph Lathrop were the tackles. Fast, brainy Gus Dorais was the quarterback who could toss swift, accurate 40- to 50-yard passes; Joe Pliska and Sam Finegan were the two shifty halfbacks; and six-foot-four Ray Eichenlaub was a punishing fullback.

The Irish were fresh from an incredible upset over a great Army team, 35–13, and a crowd of more than 10,000 Texan fans were on hand for the titanic struggle.

Texas opened the game by kicking off to Notre Dame. Big Ray Eichenlaub caught the ball and flipped a lateral to Knute Rockne, who drove to midfield before he was brought down. Then Gus Dorais took over and steadily marched his Irish team toward the Texas goal line. Drives into the line alternated with short passes to Rockne; then, when the Horns expected another line smash, Dorais tossed to Rockne for a touchdown and it was Notre Dame by a 7–0 margin.

CAPT. DORAIS

The outstanding Notre Dame quarterback Gus Dorais.

A sample of the action in the Notre Dame game as Texas halfback Paul Simmons is hit so hard by two Irish players that he does a somersault.

Captain Knute Rockne in 1913.

In the second period, the Longhorns opened up with an offense that caught the Irish by surprise. With Simmons carrying the ball, the Horns advanced to midfield. Then, after a fake into the line, Simmons lateraled to Milt Daniel. Daniel then quickly tossed a pass to Len Barrell, who eluded three Irish tacklers and sped 30 yards for a Texas TD that tied the score. The Longhorn fans went wild with joy.

Then the Irish went to work with a will. In smashing drives, mixed with two passes from Dorais to Rockne, the Irish marched straight downfield, but were stopped at the Texas 20-yard line. Not to be denied, the Irish kicked a field goal. It was 10–7 Notre Dame at the half.

At the start of the second half, Notre Dame quickly took command and once again began to pound the Texas line with Eichenlaub driving over the tackles, then up the middle for huge gains— right over the Texas line, which stubbornly gave ground on each play. Then, just as they stopped the Irish ground game, Dorais would flip a pass to Rockne or to halfback Joe Pliska for a score. The game ended with Notre Dame on top by a score of 30–7.

Gus Dorais had completed 10 of 21 forward passes for 200 yards. But it was the great line smashes by Eichenlaub that hurt Texas the most; the Irish had gained 339 yards with their vicious running attack.

Coach Allerdice, in summing up the game, said, "We were beaten by a far stronger, tougher team with more experience. But we gave it our best and I'm delighted that not a man in our lineup gave up. We lost to a better team . . . this time. And Gus Dorais and Knute Rockne taught us a lot about the forward pass and how they mixed up their passing game and then came in with a solid ground game. And that big Eichenlaub, he was a tough man to stop with his plunges into the line."

The loss to Notre Dame ended the unbeaten streak season for the Longhorns. But the 1913 season was one of the most successful and satisfying in Texas football history, for it brought the Texas Longhorns national prominence, and even the staid *New York Times* reported the Texas-Notre Dame game in feature articles on the sports pages.

Texas officials were so delighted with Coach Dave Allerdice's work during the past three years that they signed Allerdice to an unprecedented two-year contract that called for an increase in salary and additional funds to hire two assistants for the 1914–15 seasons.

Meanwhile, Athletic Director Theo Bellmont continued to upgrade the football program and facilities. He also drew up a tough schedule for 1914, with games against Trinity College, Baylor, Rice, Oklahoma, Southwestern, Haskell Institute, Mississippi, and Wabash College. It was a tough lineup of college teams, and it posed a major hurdle for Coach Allerdice, for he had lost a number of outstanding players from the 1913 squad. Some were players who could not be replaced, among them two top halfbacks, Paul Simmons (who had starred in every game he played), and Milt Daniel, tackle Gene Berry, and several other stalwarts.

In the opening game of the 1914 season at Austin, Texas battered Trinity College 30–0 in an awesome display of offensive strength. But the big surprise of Texas' offense that afternoon was the

Len Barrell was an outstanding Texas fullback who scored 14 touchdowns in 1914. With his field goals and points after touchdowns, Barrell racked up 121 points that year, making him UT's all-time scoring leader.

amazing forward passing by halfback Clyde Littlefield, who tossed the fat football around as if it was the size of a baseball. Littlefield's spectacular toss to Charlie Turner, a 60-yard play, brought the big hometown crowd up on its feet roaring. But the Texas defense was just as spectacular, for the defense allowed the Trinity backs just one first down in the entire game.

The Baylor Bears came into Austin the following week. The Longhorns were invincible as they ran through and around and over Baylor, mix-

Pete Edmond was quarterback Clyde Littlefield's favorite receiver from 1913–1915.

ing the running game with great passes by Clyde Littlefield to trounce Baylor by a 57–0 score in a game that was shortened to 40 minutes. Len Barrell rushed for 165 yards, fullback Bert Walker rushed for 135, and Doc Neilson and Walker each scored two touchdowns. Next on the Longhorns' schedule was another home game at Austin against Rice. Showing consistent improvement, Texas completely outplayed the Rice team by battering them 41–0. End Pete Edmond caught a 42-yard pass thrown by Littlefield in a spectacular play for a touchdown.

One week later, at Dallas, the Texas Longhorns faced an Oklahoma team that had run up a record 230 points in trouncing three rivals in the three games they had played. The Oklahoma team won with an attack that deployed speed and deception, and they were out to avenge the 1913 defeat handed them by Texas.

On the opening kickoff Hap Johnson of Oklahoma took the ball and raced through the entire Longhorn team for 85 yards and a touchdown. Stunned by this lightning strike, Texas fought back. Then Clyde Littlefield went to work. With a right arm that was bandaged and ached with

every movement, Clyde shot a quick, accurate spiral to Charlie Turner for a TD that tied the score. On the next series of downs, Littlefield tossed two short passes to Turner and the flashy end scored another TD to give Texas a lead they would never relinquish. Then it was Littlefield again with a spectacular 50-yard pass to Edmond, who sped 18 yards to complete a 69-yard play for another TD. Then Littlefield again passed to Turner for huge gains and Turner carried into the line for another TD. Final score: Texas 32, Oklahoma 7.

A week later Southwestern was battered in a 10-touchdown blitz, 70–0, in a game that was followed by a 23–7 beating of the Haskell Indians. The following week Mississippi traveled to Austin to do battle with Texas. They proved an easy touch for the Longhorns as Texas ran away with the game by a 66–7 margin. Len Barrell scored three touchdowns (and 24 points, still a school record) and Clyde Littlefield was spectacular with sensational passes that had Mississippi defenders chasing the ball all over the field in a vain effort to stop the aerial bombardment. One of Clyde's tosses was a 55-yard shot for a touchdown.

In the final game of the season on Thanksgiving Day at Austin, Indiana's Wabash College proved to be an easy Thanksgiving Day opponent for the Longhorns. A great Texas defense led by Pete Edmond, Charlie Turner, Louie Jordan, Hebe Goodman, and Pig Dittmar held the Wabash backs to just five first downs, and they absorbed a 39–0 beating at the hands of the Texas offense. Len Barrell scored three touchdowns and kicked three extra points to raise his season total to a record 121 points for the season.

The victory over Wabash gave Texas 20 wins in its last 21 games, and for Coach Allerdice the 1914 season would be one he would remember for a long, long time. His Texas Longhorns went through the eight games undefeated, scoring a record total of 358 points while holding the opposition to 21 points.

At the end of the season, Coach Allerdice named an All-State football squad. It was composed of twelve players . . . all of them from the University of Texas.

Three of Texas football's most outstanding captains: Captain Louis Jordan, 1914; Captain "Pig" Dittmar, 1916; and Captain Billy Trabue, 1917.

Early in 1914, Texas Athletic Director Theo Bellmont, who had drastically improved the football program since his appointment in 1913, contacted all the large colleges in the Southwest to ask if they would be interested in setting up a conference that would provide strict eligibility rules for not only the football program, but for all collegiate athletics. Most of the major colleges agreed, and at a meeting on December 8, 1914, the Southwest

Conference was formally organized. Charter members were Texas, Texas A&M, Baylor, Southwestern, Arkansas, Oklahoma, and Oklahoma A&M.

Among the rules that were adopted was a strict one limiting varsity athletes to three varsity seasons, and a strict adherence to amateur codes, including no off-campus football practice.

Once the agreement had been approved, officials of the University of Texas and Texas A&M immediately agreed to resume football, and a home and home schedule was agreed on. The first game between the two rivals would be played at College Station, home of the Aggies.

When Coach Allerdice called the first practice of the year he looked over his veterans, including a group of the stars who had produced an unde-

Halfback Clyde Littlefield was called "One of the greatest forward passing stars of the day" by sportswriter Grantland Rice in 1914. In the opening game of the 1915 season against TCU, Littlefield was responsible for 7 touchdowns, 4 from passes he threw, as Texas routed TCU 72–0. In 1927, Littlefield was appointed head coach, replacing Doc Stewart.

feated season in 1914. He agreed with his new assistant coach, Eddie Tremkmann, that he was blessed with some of the finest young college players he had seen in years. Returning was his great passing star, Clyde Littlefield; the marvelous running back, Paul Simmons; a fine quarterback in Billy Trabue; a pile-driving fullback, Bert Walker; two top-notch ends in Pete Edmonds and Charlie Turner; a trio of fine tackles in Fats Carlton, K. L. Berry, Baker Duncan; an All-Southwest center in Pig Dittmar; and enough sophomore prospects to ensure him another outstanding season. It would be too much to hope for another unbeaten year, but it could very well happen, he thought.

In the first game of the 1915 season at Austin, the Longhorns simply rolled over and through Texas Christian University for eleven touchdowns in a one-sided 72–0 plastering. The game was a complete rout from the opening kickoff. TCU simply was never in the game. Texas' next victim, Daniel Baker College, was buried under a 92–0 riot of touchdowns. Halfback Paul Simmons and Clyde Littlefield starred in the game with both men responsible for four touchdowns each. Simmons had TD sprints of 55, 60, and 20 yards and a 4-yard smash into the line, while Littlefield tossed TD passes of 2, 37, 42, 33, and 47 yards. Littlefield was responsible for seven touchdowns in this scoring spree that saw Coach Allerdice play every man on the squad.

Texas' first SWC conference game with Rice on October 16 enabled the Longhorns to extend their winning streak to 11 straight games and 23 out of the last 24 games, as they scored on the first series of downs and battered the inept Rice squad by a 59–0 margin.

Oklahoma rolled onto the State Fair Grounds for their game against the Longhorns with an undefeated record of nine in a row over the past two years and fresh from a 24–0 win over a strong Missouri eleven. This was going to be a battle of giants, and the entire state of Texas was aroused and excited as the two great unbeaten teams faced each other. The game attracted more than 11,000 fans—the largest crowd ever to watch a football game in Texas.

Tommy Newman stops A&M halfback Icky Elam. Second from far left is Texas' great tackle, Bibb Falk.

The big crowd roared on the opening kickoff as Texas kicked to Oklahoma halfback Jackie Geyer. Just as he started upfield, Geyer was hit hard by two Texas tacklers. He fumbled the ball, Texas recovered, and three big plays later fullback Bert Walker slashed off-tackle for a touchdown. Edmonds kicked the extra point and it was 7–0 Texas. But Oklahoma came right back, driving off-tackle and piling up some big gains. Then halfback Frank McCain tossed a 22-yard pass to halfback Johnson, who went 10 more yards for the Oklahoma score. Geyer kicked the extra point and it was a 7–7 tie.

In the second half the game seesawed back and forth with neither team having the edge. Then, late in the third period, Texas connected on several short passes by Littlefield, and two big off-tackle plays brought the ball to the Oklahoma 5-yard line. On the first play quarterback Bob Simmons faked a handoff to Littlefield and smacked through the Oklahoma center for the touchdown that gave Texas a 13–7 lead. The extra point was missed.

In the final period, the rugged Oklahoma backs pounded the Texas line for several gains. Then Jack Geyer pitched a 20-yard pass to Hap Johnson, and the score was tied when Johnson scored. With time running out Geyer booted home the extra point, and Oklahoma had its biggest win of the year by one point, 14–13.

The following week, back home in Austin, Texas drubbed Southwestern 45–0 as Charlie Turner scored three touchdowns on passes from

Littlefield. Turner repeated his three-touchdown spree one week later as Texas defeated a strong Sewanee eleven 27–6 in a game at Houston.

A tough, strong Alabama squad invaded Austin for the game against Texas. This was an Alabama team that had won 5 out of the last 6 games and was determined to make Texas its next victim. But the muddy, rainy weather hampered both teams, slowing the game down. Texas managed to score three touchdowns to give the Longhorns a hard-earned 20–0 win, their sixth of the season.

Meeting for the first time in five years, Texas traveled to College Station for a game that had in previous years produced much controversy, argument, and even riotous behavior on the part of both student bodies. Texas A&M shocked the Longhorns by handing them a 13–0 defeat in the biggest upset of the season for Texas. Twelve Longhorn fumbles contributed greatly to the Texas defeat as John Gerrity, feisty captain of the Aggies, Fanny Coleman, and Rip Collins starred for the Aggies in a game that cemented the once-solid relations between the two Texas rivals.

In the final game of the season, Notre Dame's Fighting Irish visited Austin once again for the second meeting between the two schools. Led by Dutch Bergman, Charley Bachman, and Stan Lofall, the Irish were too fast, too strong, and too shifty, and simply overpowered Texas with a grueling, grinding ground attack that provided five touchdowns and a 36–7 win for the Irish. Texas'

Texas guard, Louie Jordan (sans helmet) is on the turf after halting a Notre Dame drive near the Texas goal line in 1915.

Notre Dame halfback Stan Cofall attempts to score a TD and is stopped by Texas end Pete Edmonds on the Texas 8-yard line. Paul Simmons, a Texas back (*left*) also closes in on the play in the 1915 game.

only score came in the third period when end Charlie Turner blocked an Irish kick. Texas recovered the ball. As Bob Simmons drove over the Irish goal line, he fumbled the ball, but Texas halfback Windy Kelso fell on it for the Texas touchdown.

The loss to Notre Dame in the final game of the season gave Texas a 6–3 record, a successful season at any other school. However, Texas alumni were unlike any other group and they demanded more from a football coach. They were not happy at the three defeats and voiced their opinions in words and stories in the local papers.

Allerdice had noted the continuous opposition to his coaching by alumni and early on in the season

had confided to a few close friends that he would resign at the end of the season . . . and he did.

In his five years, Allerdice teams compiled a 33–7 record. It was the finest five-year period in Texas football history, and his players and many fans regretted the resignation of a fine coach and an outstanding leader.

Gene Van Gent, an all-around star at the University of Wisconsin and captain of the undefeated 1912 Badger football team, was appointed to replace Dave Allerdice for the 1916 season. Van Gent had spent two seasons as an assistant football

Notre Dame's quarter-back, Gus Dorais watches the flight of a ball he has just kicked for a field goal against Texas in a 1915 game. Captain Knute Rockne (*far right*), also watching the kick, is playing left end for the Irish.

Coach Dave Allerdice compiled a remarkable 33–7 record in his five years as Texas head coach.

coach at Missouri and had the background and experience to handle the burgeoning football program at Texas. He brought Jim Clay, an assistant coach at Missouri, along with him, while H. J. Ettlinger continued on as the freshman coach.

Van Gent was heartened by the return of some twenty-two members of the 1915 squad along with a number of sparkling new prospects. Returning veterans included Maxey Hart, Harry Dolan, Bob Blaine, and Joe Secor; tackles Fats Carlton and Ned Boynton; guards Gill Johnson,

Henry Casey, and Tom Austin; team captain Pig Dittmar, the All-Conference center; quarterback Bill Trabue; halfbacks Rip Lang, Lee Sens, and Fred Moore; and Homer Watts and Bert Hedick at the fullback posts.

In the opening game of the season, against Southern Methodist University, the Texas players wore numbers on the backs of their jerseys for the first time and the fans were quick to show their appreciation by cheering loudly for their favorite players. The Longhorns presented a smooth, well-

Texas' coaching staff, headed by Gene Van Gent and Bill Juneau. Van Gent handled the line and Juneau coached the backfield with Barry Whitaker and H.J. Ettinger as assistants. *Left to right:* **Whitaker, Ettinger, Van Gent, and Juneau. In 1920, Whitaker took over as head football coach.**

oiled football machine and ground out 11 touchdowns in a 74–0 rout of SMU. The crowd was brought to their feet time after time with Bill Trabue's sharp passes and quick slants into the SMU line for score after score. The game featured a spectacular 85-yard sprint by halfback Shorty Beall, who weaved in and out through every member of SMU's team for the score. The game was an impressive display of offensive might.

In the second game of the season, at Austin, Rice was defeated by a 16–2 score in a costly game for Texas as several key players were injured. Then, against Oklahoma State in San Antonio, end Maxey Hart, the 150-pound dynamo, caught 6 passes (two of them for touchdowns) thrown by Homer Watts. The passes—one for 40 yards, another for 24 yards—were so accurate that the crowd rose to their feet and roared a tribute to both players in the 14–7 victory. One week later, Maxey Hart again was the clutch performer in the game against Oklahoma (in Dallas) as he recovered a blocked punt and ran it across for a touchdown that gave Texas a hard-fought 21–7 victory.

After four straight wins, Texas was upset 7–3 by an aggressive Baylor squad. Texas was unable to penetrate the Bears' defense and Baylor had their first win in eleven years over a Texas team.

The next contest was on the road against Missouri. Years later, Captain Pig Dittmar remembered the game as if it happened yesterday. "A substitute, a guy named Peoples, tried a field goal from the 28-yard line, near the end of the game with the score 0–0. He kicked this old fat ball, and it hit the upright," said Dittmar, "then bounced onto the crossbar and went over for the 3–0 win for Missouri."

On a cold, wintery day in Austin, Texas scored an impressive 52–0 win over Arkansas as 143-pound Billy Trabue took an Arkansas punt and returned it 75 yards to bring the biggest crowd to ever attend a game in Austin to their feet. More than 10,000 fans attended the game. Several days later, Texas scored its sixth victory by defeating a tough Southwestern team 17–3.

Thanksgiving Day saw the Texas Aggies in their first visit to Austin since 1909. Clark Field in

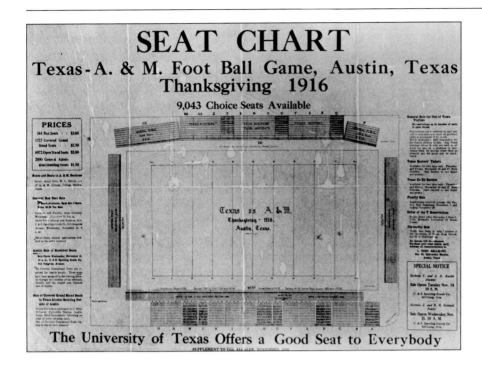

Rip Lang was Texas' star in a 1916 game against A&M. Lang teamed up with quarterback Bill Trabue to execute a perfect Statue-of-Liberty play and defeat A&M.

Austin was jammed with more than 15,000 fans eager to see the two squads battle.

The Longhorns played their best game of the year. In the second period, with the score 7–7, halfback Rip Lang took the ball from quarterback Bill Trabue on a double reverse and then dashed 40 yards through the entire Aggie defense for the touchdown that gave the Longhorns the lead. In the fourth period Bill Trabue returned an Aggies punt and raced 65 yards for the third touchdown and a 21–7 win.

The victory over their bitter rivals, the Aggies, before the largest crowd ever to watch a football game in Texas gave the Longhorns a successful 7–2 season.

Captain Pig Dittmar was later named to the second Walter Camp All-American Team. Fats Carlton, Maxey Hart, and Rip Lang were selected to the All-SWC Team.

On April 6, 1917, President Woodrow Wilson signed a joint resolution of Congress proclaiming a state of war with Germany, and more than 1000 students at Texas along with the football coach,

Gene Van Gent, left to enter military service. To replace Van Gent, William Juneau, a former captain of the University of Wisconsin team in 1902 and a former coach at Marquette University, took over as coach.

After more than half of the varsity volunteered for military service, Juneau found that he had several veterans left from the 1916 squad. Quarterback Bill Trabue, fullback Homer Waits, and Fred Moore, Grip Penn, and Gordon Conley were the only members of the squad with any varsity experience.

Texas opened its twenty-fifth year of varsity football with a 27–0 victory over Trinity College and then a week later ran up a 35–0 win over Southwestern.

A veteran Oklahoma team had run up a record score of 179–0 against Kingfisher College just a week before the Texas game, and they were out to avenge their 1916 loss to Texas. In the game played in Dallas, Sooner star Wally Abbott tossed a touchdown pass to end Spot Durant and then scored a second TD on a beautiful 65-yard dash after intercepting a pass thrown by quarterback Trabue. The final score was Oklahoma 14, Texas 0. The following week at Austin, Rice utilized a tricky spread offense and scored two touchdowns for a 13–0 win. Next the Baylor Bears jolted Texas with a 3–0 loss, the only score a 35-yard field goal by tackle Jack Roach as the game ended. This was the first time in twenty-five seasons of football that the Longhorns had dropped three games in succession.

Oklahoma State battled Texas throughout their game the next week in a furious attempt to avenge their defeat by Texas in 1916. But quarterback Billy Trabue, out with injuries most of the year, managed to limp into his post and guide the Longhorns to a TD and a 7–3 win over State.

The Longhorns visited College Station for their seventh game of the season. The Aggies, under new head coach Dana X. Bible, had the biggest, toughest-looking team in years. They were undefeated in six straight games, but were held scoreless in a tight 0–0 game until the final moments of the game, when A&M battered the Longhorn line on three successive drives. Then,

just before the gun ended the game, Jim McMurray, a big, tough 200-pound tackle, switched to fullback for one play. He rammed over from the 5-yard line for an A&M touchdown and the Aggies had a 7–0 victory.

In the final game of the season, Arkansas traveled to Austin for the big Thanksgiving Day game and was soundly defeated by the Longhorns 20–0. The game was a tight, tense one for nearly three quarters, but Texas then broke loose for all 20 points while holding Arkansas scoreless.

The twenty-fifth season was not a successful one for Texas as they wound up with a 4–4 record. But there were to be better years in the immediate future as the war would wind down and former Texas stars would be returning.

Most of the male students enrolled at Texas in the fall of 1918 were enrolled in the SATC, the Students Army Training Corps. They wore army uniforms, lived on the campus in army shacks, and followed army rules and regulations. This also applied to the football squad that reported to coach Bill Juneau. Reveille awakened them at 5:30 A.M., and classes and military duties occupied them until 5:30 P.M. Then it was dinner, and finally football practice under special lights erected on Clark Field. Practice ended at 8:30 and taps were sounded at 9:00. But just as the squad had settled into this strict routine and had beaten Texas Christian University in the opening game by a 19–0 score, a Spanish flu epidemic swept through the campus and the University closed down and did not resume classes until late in October. Consequently, several scheduled games were cancelled.

The team, however, continued to practice in the hopes that the flu epidemic would end, and games were played against such makeshift teams as the Penn Radio School and Ream Flying Field. The games were played as exhibitions and Texas easily won two games from Penn and one from Ream.

Then, as the flu epidemic ended and the Armistice was at hand, Texas defeated Oklahoma State 27–5. Several days later Texas won another exhibition game against the Camp Mabry Auto Mechanics School by a 22–0 score. Three days later

Texas defeated Rice 14–0. SMU was the next victim on Texas' list and the Southern Methodist team was easily beaten 32–0.

In the final game of the year at Austin, Texas faced off against the Texas Aggies, who were also undefeated. The Aggies had compiled a remarkable record under their new coach Dana Bible. In 1917 A&M had won all of the eight games scheduled and did not allow their opponents a single point. In 1918 A&M ran their string of consecutive wins to 13 straight before the battle against the Longhorns, and the entire state of Texas was excited about the battle expected when these two titans of the gridiron met head on. Despite the war, more than 10,000 fans jammed every inch of Clark Field to cheer for their respective teams.

In the opening moments of the game, the Longhorns took the kickoff and proceeded to grind out yardage on each and every play. Drives by Lou Smyth, Fran Domingues, and Joe Ellis, brought Texas to the 12-yard line. Ellis drove in from there for the lone touchdown of the game. It was 7–0, Texas, and that's how it ended.

The win over A&M closed out the schedule for Texas with a 9–0 season, although several wins were games against inferior service teams.

A scheduled game with Oklahoma for December 7 to decide the SWC championship was cancelled when the flu epidemic reared its ugly head again. The SWC office decided not to name a champion.

On September 26, 1918, one of the great battles in the history of modern warfare began on the French-German frontier. The battle, which lasted for a period of three weeks, involved more than 1,200,000 U.S. troops. The objective was to cut off the Imperial German Army's supply line, the Sedan-Mezieres railroad; the battle successfully forced a general German withdrawal from the entire area. As the American forces furiously engaged and destroyed the spirit of the German ability to fight on after suffering untold losses, a general armistice on November 11 brought the American advance to a halt as the Americans seized the railroad and brought peace. Three weeks later, on October 5, the German Chancellor asked for peace terms and the war was at an end.

Back in the United States college football, which had almost been abandoned by dozens of colleges during the 1917–18 period, began to enjoy its greatest boom. Never before had there gathered together on the American campus the wealth of experienced football material that assembled in 1919. From cantonments, army camps, and navy stations in this country, and from American Expeditionary Forces in Europe, there streamed back thousands of fine young athletes, hardened and matured by their training and experiences and returning as men in the full vigor of manhood. After what they had been through, football with its body contact appealed more than ever to them. It offered rugged physical exercise in a game they loved and comparative relaxation from the grim, deadly business in which they had been engaged. Coaches found them more difficult to handle because the "Rah, Rah" idealism had been knocked out of most of them. But the coach who knew his business and could command men had a veritable gold mine to work with.

At the University of Texas, the Longhorns found themselves with not one but two head coaches for the 1919 season. Gene Van Gent, who had been head football coach in 1916, had obtained a leave of absence when he went into the military and he came back to take over his old post in 1919. But Bill Juneau had taken over the team in 1917 and in 1918 had come through with an undefeated season. University officials decided they would have both men coach the 1919 squad, with Juneau as the head coach. Van Gent would handle the line.

Eighteen varsity lettermen reported for the first practice, including a number of returning servicemen who were to give the Longhorns the nucleus for some of the strongest teams in the SWC in the next few years.

Returning from the 1918 eleven were Captain and end Doc Graves; tackle Bibb Falk; Tom Dennis, fullback; Louie Smyth; Bud McCallum and Joe Ellis, two fine halfbacks; Tilly Ferguson at the quarterback post; and end Maxey Hart. Other

Tilly Ferguson (extreme left with ball) advances the ball into Texas A&M territory in the last game of the 1918 season. Texas defeated A&M 7–0.

bright prospects included Bert Hedick and Bill Brennan, two solid backs, and center Bachman Greer.

In the season's opener at Austin, center Bachman Greer was outstanding against Howard Payne University from Brownsville, Texas. He was all over the field. He blocked a punt in the first period and recovered the ball over the goal line for a touchdown. Then in the second period Greer recovered a second Howard Payne fumble, scooped it up, and dashed 15 yards for his second touchdown. Texas coach Juneau utilized every man on the squad in taking an easy 26–0 win. In the second game of the season, Southwestern came to Austin with a highly touted team, but were routed by a spirited Longhorn squad 39–0.

Phillips University was a small school from Enid, Oklahoma, coached by Michigan star Johnny Maulbetsch, who had played with the great Wolverines in 1914. Phillips had too much sheer power for Texas and a driving, 200-pound fullback in Dutch Strauss, who was unstoppable inside the 20-yard line. As a result Phillips pounded out a 10–0 upset win over Texas.

With its usual power-laden team, Oklahoma had chalked up eight wins in nine games and against Texas rang up win number nine. They

defeated an injury-ridden Texas team playing without their regular quarterback, Rats Watson. As a result, the Sooners won 12–7.

The next week Baylor showed a strong offense and tough defense against Texas during the first half, but then wilted under the savage drives of the Texas backs, who scored four touchdowns in the second half to take a 29–13 win. Texas halfback George McCullough starred against Rice the next game as he scooped up two fumbles for two touchdowns as Texas romped by a 32–7 score. A week later against Arkansas Bobby Cannon, a speedy halfback ran like a jackrabbit around and through the Arkansas line and tossed passes to both his ends, one of them a bullet pass to McCullough good for 45 yards, as Texas spurted to a 35–7 victory. Then, in the eleventh meeting between the Haskell Indians and the Longhorns, Texas scratched out a 13–7 win over the feisty Indians. Finally, in the last game of the year, it was the big Thanksgiving Day match against the Aggies.

Coach Dana X. Bible was back once more at A&M after missing the 1918 season due to his military service. This 1919 squad was one of his greatest teams. The Aggies had won nine games in a row, amassing a total of 268 points along the way, and hadn't allowed an opponent to cross their goal line all season long. The Aggies had shut out such rivals as Southern Methodist, Trinity, Southwestern, Baylor, and Texas Christian, and they were loaded with a marvelous, tricky offense and a no-nonsense defense.

After an even first period, the Aggies recovered a Texas fumble at the Longhorn 20-yard line. They quickly drove to the 5-yard line, where Jack Higginbotham cracked into the Texas goal line for a touchdown.

Texas did manage to reach the Aggies' 5-yard line with Oscar Eckhardt carrying the brunt of the offense, but the Aggies stopped them, took over the ball, and ran the play upfield. The game ended with the Aggies in front 7–0.

And once more the voices of dissent were heard on the campus as Texas finished the season with a 6–3 record and a 3–2 SWC record—and the unhappiness resulted in a new coach for 1920.

Gene Van Gent had coached the line and Bill Juneau the backfield during the 1919 season. There were bound to be difficulties in this situation and both coaches admitted they were hard-pressed to make it work.

The season had been a frustrating one. Texas had lost to Phillips College and Oklahoma, then played raggedly in a loss to bitter rival Texas A&M in the final game of the season. The Athletic Council decided a new coach was needed, and immediately went out to secure one.

They found him right on the Texas staff of assistant football coaches. He was Berry Whitaker, and he had served as assistant to Juneau in 1919.

An all-around football and track star, Whitaker had been a steady halfback for the Indiana University Hoosiers during 1913, '14, and '15, when the Hoosiers played a fairly consistent brand of Big Ten football. After graduation, Whitaker was hired as a physical education teacher in the Austin public schools and as part of that position he had coached the Austin High School football team to an undefeated year. In 1917, Whitaker was appointed director of the intramural program at Texas and it was only a matter of time before Coach Van Gent, knowing Whitaker's foot-

Maxey Hart was a fast, shifty end who played with the Longhorns from 1916 to 1920. In 1920, Hart was elected captain and the Texas Varsity team won 9 and lost 0.

ball background, lured him away from the intramural program and made him an assistant football coach.

In 1920 Whitaker was selected as the new football coach to replace Juneau. He brought in two assistants, Charles Sneddon, a lineman and former Ohio State star, and Clyde Littlefield, one of the great early forward passers for Texas during the 1912, '13, '14, and 1915 seasons.

"I will never forget one game that Littlefield played," said Whitaker. "That was in 1915, against Daniel Baker College. That Littlefield was amazing in that game. He ran for three touchdowns and threw the ball around the field from all angles. He scored on four touchdown passes, passes that went 37 yards, 42, 43, and 47 yards. In all Clyde was responsible for seven touchdowns in that game. So I figure here's a coach who can give me one hell of an offense."

Coach Whitaker greeted a 1920 squad that included some of the most talented members of the 1919 team and previous squad members who had returned from the armed forces. Such veterans as Maxey Hart, the team captain and a great receiver; halfbacks Bud McCallum and Tom Dennis; George Green and George Hill in the line; center Swede Swenson; quarterbacks Rats Watson and Icky Elam; and a number of promising newcomers who had all the coaches smiling and happy to be on hand for this 1920 football season.

In the first game of the season, opening at home, Texas crushed Simmons University under a barrage of 9 touchdowns led by quarterback Icky Elam and halfbacks Joe Ellis and Bill Barry. The Longhorns used every one of the 33-man squad and ran through and around and over Simmons to carve out a 63–0 triumph. Two additional victories, over Southwestern by 27–0 and Howard Payne by 41–7, convinced the student body and alumni that Texas had one of their great teams in the making. However, the coaching staff realized that the schedule prepared by Athletic Director Theo Bellmont was one of the easiest on record, and kept the team on an even keel.

"I didn't want the players to think they were that good," said Coach Whitaker, "I pointed out that the games with Oklahoma, Rice, SMU, and the Texas Aggies were still ahead and I drove them as hard as I could.

"And this all paid off," said Whitaker, "as Oklahoma State gave us hell for three-and-a-half quarters. It was 7–0 in our favor until Icky Elam broke out in the clear on a naked reverse and ran 35 yards for a touchdown. Then when we got the ball on a fumble, Elam slipped away for 20 yards and another score and we had ourselves a hard-earned 21–0 win."

In the fifth game of the season, at Austin, once again Coach Whitaker had the opportunity to utilize every man on the squad as the Longhorns routed Austin College in Sherman, Texas, under a barrage of touchdowns and a 54–0 win. And now the complaint from the alumni was that the 1920 schedule was too easy. "We should be playing the best teams in the country," said a former player, "instead of the prep school teams we've played."

The sixth game of the season was against a Rice team that had as its running star halfback Eddie Dyer, who later on would become one of baseball's most successful managers with the St. Louis Cardinals. Dyer had led the Rice Owls to four straight wins prior to the Texas game, but the Longhorns' defense kept Dyer bottled up throughout the game and wrapped up the big win when Bud McCallum intercepted a pass thrown by Dyer and raced 65 yards in the final quarter for a touchdown. That put the game beyond the reach of Rice. Texas 21, Rice 0.

Phillips was easily beaten by a 27–0 score for Texas' seventh win of the year. The Phillips game was just the preparation needed for the SMU battle at Austin as the Longhorns roughed out a 21–3 win over Southern Methodist for their eighth win of the year, and settled in for the big Thanksgiving Day game vs. the Aggies.

Texas A&M stormed into Clark Field for the game against the Longhorns with the most impressive statistics of any college football team in the nation. The Aggies had won 18 games in a row over a two-year period—and had not allowed a point to be scored on them in all of those eighteen games. It was one of the most amazing runs of all time and spoke highly of the incredible defense of the Aggies.

The Longhorns had an imposing string of their own. They had put together eight straight wins with just ten points scored against them in that span. The big game excited every football fan in the state, and more than 20,000 frenzied fans jammed every inch of old Clark Field for what looked to be the most exciting game in the history of the Southwest Conference.

Instead of a wide-open offensive free-for-all, the game became a strictly defensive battle as both teams relied on their great line strength to bottle up any unusual offense.

Behind their marvelous kicking star, Roswell Higginbotham, who booted the ball for a 49-yard average each time he punted, the Aggies kept the

Longhorns back in their own territory for much of the game. His kicking gave the Aggies the edge in the first half of the game.

The first break came when Rats Watson of Texas fumbled an Aggie punt at the Texas 40-yard stripe and the Aggies recovered the ball. Jack Mahan and then Higginbotham drove through the Texas line and advanced to the 20-yard line, where Moran calmly booted a field goal. The Aggies had a 3–0 lead.

Now it was Texas' turn as Ellis and Bud McCallum took turns crashing through the Aggies' rugged defense. Two Texas drives by Watson, then a high-arching pass from Barry to Dennis. Dennis leaped high into the air, caught the ball by cradling it in one hand, and was downed on the 4-yard line. Then fullback Fran Domingues rammed in for the Texas touchdown. The kick was good and Texas had a 7–3 lead.

Both teams struggled vainly for another score, pounding each other's line, putting the ball into the air, but all to no avail. Both defensive teams were at their best and stopped every advance.

But time was on the Longhorns' side, and they won the game after one of the most hotly contested battles in the rivalry between the Longhorns and the Aggies. When it was over, Texas had won their most coveted victory over A&M, and had ended with a bang the most brilliant year in the 28 years of Texas football.

The season ended with 9 wins, no defeats, no ties, for Texas' first SWC championship.

And Coach Berry Whitaker was honored and feted all year long and well into the next season— and was granted a new two-year contract extension.

Everyone in the state of Texas who had any interest in college football—sportswriters, columnists, alumni, and the ordinary campus followers— just knew that the Longhorns would, in 1921, produce another outstanding team like the one Coach Whitaker had produced in 1920. And why not, with all those fine players?

For when Whitaker and his top aide, Clyde Littlefield, were on hand to greet the varsity stars who earned their letter in 1920, there were nineteen lettermen on hand for the first practice session of 1921.

In the first game of the season, Texas easily routed Austin's St. Edward's University by a 33–0 score. The game was shortened to eight-minute quarters to hold down the rampaging Horns. Sherman's Austin College was the next victim, and every man on the Texas squad saw action in the game as Texas routed Austin 60–0. But in the third game of the season, against little Howard Payne, perhaps the Longhorns were too cocky, for they were only able to muster a 21–0 win.

Texas was rated a four-to-one favorite to defeat Vanderbilt, but they had not counted on the experience and guile of Vandy's fine coach, Dan McGugin, who had just guided his team to a 21–14 upset win over a solid Kentucky team just a week earlier. Now on top of their game, Vanderbilt put up a stubborn defense, stopping the Texas backs time after time. When Texas attempted to go to the air, Vandy intercepted five Longhorn attempts, turned two of those passes into touchdowns, and upset Texas 20–0. In the final period, when there was still time to possibly turn the tide against Vandy, a Texas pass from the Vandy 8-yard line was taken out of the hands of a Texas receiver by Vanderbilt halfback Lynn Bomar, who raced 50 yards for the touchdown that took the game out of the Longhorns' reach.

While the stunning upset defeat started the alumni voices of disapproval, it only slightly annoyed Coach Whitaker. "It comes with this job," said the coach, sadly. "You've got to win every game to stay even."

The Longhorns rallied a week later, pulling themselves together and manhandling the Rice Owls by a lopsided 56–0 score. Southwestern did no better and were also beaten by a raging Texas team, this time by a 44–0 score. Texas held the Southwestern offense to just two first downs.

Then it was Mississippi State's turn. The Horns buried State under an avalanche of 7 touchdowns on the way to 54–7 beating. This was Texas' sixth win in seven games played and they were prepped for the big game on Thanksgiving Day against a formidable Texas Aggie eleven.

A crowd of more than 15,000 excited fans were on hand for this classic. Both coaches predicted victory. But the fans, expecting to see a high-powered offense by both teams, were disappointed as both squads played a cautious defensive battle, much like the year before.

With both teams trying hard, but playing a waiting game, the air was tense with anticipation. Both teams played raggedly. The Aggies fumbled seven times. Each time Texas recovered the ball and drove downfield. They reached the 3-yard line, then another series of plays to the five, then to the 9-yard line, and each time they were stopped by the fierce play of the Aggies' great defense.

Near the end of the battle, Texas missed two field goal attempts: one from the 38-yard line was missed by Punk Stacy, and another by Stacy at the 50-yard line was blocked. The game ended with both teams battling furiously for just one score—that never came. The final was a bitter, bruising 0–0 tie.

If statistics were to decide the game Texas had the edge as they had a 7–3 edge in first downs and gained 146 yards to just 57 yards for A&M. But when it came to deciding the SWC Championship, both A&M and Texas had similar percentages. Texas A&M with 3 wins, no losses, and 2 ties had a percentage of 1.000%. Texas with 1 SWC win, no losses, and 1 tie also had 1.000%.

After a long, hard look, the SWC awarded the title to Texas A&M.

Texas players Hook McCullough, a great pass-catching end; Tom Dennis, a marvelous tackle; and center Swede Swenson were named to the All-SWC Team.

With the exception of the games against Vanderbilt and Texas A&M, Texas had played a smart, fast-paced brand of football all through the season and was one of the highest-scoring Longhorn teams on record. With 6 wins, 1 loss, and 1 tie, the Longhorns rang up a total of 268 points while holding opponents to just 27 points in eight games. And for coaches Whitaker, Sneddon, and Littlefield, the 1921 season was a most successful

one. But for the alumni it was a time to growl and howl and they did . . . all winter long.

Despite a magnificent two-year record of 15 victories, 2 defeats, and 1 tie, Coach Berry Whitaker had to withstand a withering blast of criticism at his coaching methods, techniques, and conduct in the spring of 1922. The unhappiness on the part of the alumni around the state resulted in a special meeting with the Athletic Council. It was claimed that Whitaker taught his players unethical tactics and that he was personally disliked by members of the squad. At the meeting, and after the charges were heard, a resolution was passed by the alumni group that no changes should be made in the coaching position.

Whitaker's position was made more secure when the Athletic Council agreed to hire an additional assistant. The new assistant was Milt Romney, a quarterback from the University of Chicago, who had led his Maroons to victory in six of seven games in 1921 for the best Chicago record since 1905. Romney was assigned to handle the Texas backfield.

The most important rule change since the major overhaul in 1912 eliminated the free kick for the extra point after touchdown. The new rule called for the scoring team to try to score the extra point by the kick, pass, or by a run from scrimmage.

With twenty-two varsity lettermen returning for the 1922 season, Coach Whitaker concentrated on solving his major problems. Who would replace Rats Watson and Icky Elam, his two outstanding quarterbacks who had graduated? After several practice sessions Whitaker handed the position to a youngster who had played for him at Austin High School in 1915, Punk Stacy. A husky 165-pounder, Stacy could run, pass, and kick and was a heady, steady signal caller.

With Stacy set at quarterback, Whitaker's main goal was to get his team into the best physical condition for a schedule that included games with six major college teams: Oklahoma A&M, Vanderbilt, Alabama, Rice, Oklahoma, and the finale against Texas A&M.

Fast action in this photo shows three Texas defenders—Oscar Eckhardt, Joe Ward (*center*), and Swede Swenson (*right*)—converging on an Oklahoma back in their 1922 game. Texas won 19–7.

Austin College was the first opponent on the schedule and the Longhorns did not have an easy time of it. Austin battled to the final gun, and the 19–0 Texas win was an unimpressive opener. The second game was against Phillips and Texas showed great improvement in a 41–10 win over a good Phillips squad. Oklahoma A&M was even better and scored a touchdown the first time they got possession of the ball. But the Longhorns came back in fine style and managed to blast Oklahoma for three touchdowns in a 19–7 win.

Now Texas was set for the game against Vanderbilt, who came into the game fresh from a 0–0 moral victory over a strong Michigan team. A crowd of more than 11,000 jammed the Dallas field and thousands more listened to a broadcast over Dallas radio station WFAA. It was the first such broadcast of a football game in Texas.

Taking the opening kickoff the Longhorns drove steadily up the field in short drives into the Vandy line. Stacy, Oscar Eckhardt, and Jim Marley took turns pounding the Vandy line until Stacy was downed on the Vandy 15-yard line. Two tries to advance the ball failed, and Stacy dropkicked a field goal from the 22-yard line to give Texas a 3–0 lead.

Vanderbilt came back with a vengeance when they recovered a Texas fumble. Then Gil Reese, Vandy's fleet halfback, raced 52 yards for a touchdown. The kick was good and Vandy had a 7–3 lead. Vandy recovered another Texas fumble and Reese scored again to give Vanderbilt a 13–3 lead at halftime.

In the third period, a fighting mad bunch of Longhorns stormed back, forced a Vandy fumble, and Texas recovered the ball. Texas fullback Jim Marley smashed 20 yards to the Vandy 5-yard line. Yancy Culp cut off-tackle and cracked through the Vandy line for a touchdown that narrowed the score to 13–10 in favor of Vanderbilt.

With time running out in the fourth period Jim Neely, Vandy's halfback, tossed a beautiful 48-yard pass to his end, Lynn Bomar, who was stopped at the 2-yard line. On the first play, Reese smashed through the line for the Vanderbilt touchdown to make it 20–10 Vanderbilt. With less than a minute to play the Longhorns mounted a furious drive. But it stalled at the Vanderbilt 2-yard line as the game ended.

Back in Austin after the tough loss to Vanderbilt, Texas ripped into a strong Alabama defense and cracked it wide open. The Horns forced seven fumbles to score 19 points, defeating the Tide 19–0. George Gardere and Buddy Tynes, two rugged Longhorn stars, were out of the Southwestern game, but Texas easily disposed of Southwestern 26–0. Next, Rice was defeated 29–0. The Longhorns were now in their best form of the year, and ripped apart a strong Oklahoma team 32–7. Halfback Bobby Richardson had his finest hour, tossing two touchdown passes and kicking his ninth field goal of the year, a record not broken until 1963.

In the final game of the season, on Thanksgiving Day, Texas played host to the Texas Aggies in the 23rd renewal of their classic rivalry. The largest crowd to ever attend a game at Clark Field, 20,000 fans jammed every inch of the old field and shouted for their favorite team.

With a schedule that included such teams as Howard Payne, Tulsa, Southwestern, and Ouachita College, the Aggies had dropped games to Payne, Tulsa, Baylor, and Southern Methodist, but that old trickster, Dana Bible, had prepared his team for the ultimate battle of their lives. His five-to-one under-dogs utilized two tricky pass plays to score two touchdowns and defeat Texas in a battle that had the crowd roaring and standing on their seats from the opening kickoff to the last minute.

King Gill, the Aggies' fleet speedster, took a pass from quarterback T. L. Miller and raced 25 yards for a touchdown to give the Aggies a 7–0 lead. Late in the second period fullback Jim Marley smashed into the Aggies line from the 3-yard stripe to make it 7–7 at the half.

In the third period the Aggies completely dominated the game; then, in the fourth period, with five minutes to play, they broke the game open. Once again it was King Gill who took the ball on a reverse and reached the Texas 4-yard line. Three tries later fullback McMillan dove in for the winning score. The game ended with Texas driving hard down the field. The Aggies had one of the big upsets of the year, 14–7.

Several days after the Aggies game, Texas coach Berry Whitaker resigned his post.

When the Athletic Council at the University of Texas went out to hire a football coach for the

1923 season to replace Berry Whitaker, they came up with one of the most unusual personalities in the history of Texas football. His name was Edward "Doc" Stewart and he had an unusual background for a job with a major football team. Stewart had been a member of the chorus of a Methodist church, where his father was the minister. He then attended Mt. Union College, where he played football and basketball. Transferring to Western Reserve University, Doc became the school's best pitcher. When his father was transferred to a church in Massilon, Ohio, Stewart left school and became city editor of the Massilon newspaper.

In 1904, when the baseball activity slowed down, Stewart organized and coached the Massilon Tigers, one of the very first professional football teams. And when the team needed a substitute quarterback, the 145-pound Stewart pitched right in and played with the team.

For some unknown reason, Doc Stewart then turned to college coaching at Mount Union, Purdue, Oregon, Nebraska, and then Clemson, where he worked with both football and basketball teams. In between seasons, Stewart sold automobiles until the agency went bankrupt and finally, in 1923, Doc Stewart wound up as football coach at the University of Texas. Incidentally, Stewart got his nickname simply because in his travels he turned up one year at the medical school of Western Reserve University.

To his credit, Doc Stewart knew his football, probably better than most of the previous Texas coaches. In short order the sixteen varsity letter-men and a squad that numbered more than thirty-four players, many of them freshmen and transfer players, realized that Doc Stewart was intent on developing a winning team at Texas. He was a stern taskmaster and worked his players like a drill sergeant. And Stewart was an excellent teacher. He would gather his squad about him, explain a certain play, and detail the movement of each player. He would then select eleven men and have them walk through the play so that every man on the squad knew their assignments. If a player was uncertain about a movement Stewart would slow the action and repeat the details over and over.

Quarterback Bobby Robertson said, "I never had the fundamentals explained to me like Coach Stewart. It's so simple the way he tells it, why, anybody can play for him."

When the season opened against Austin College, the Longhorns were in the best physical and mental condition possible and Stewart had the team raring to play. As the game opened, Bobby Robertson took the kickoff and sped 35 yards to midfield. The spirited run by Robertson opened the floodgates. Oscar Eckhardt on two tries banged through for 38 yards and a touchdown. Several plays later, Eckhardt darted 25 yards for another Texas score, and the Longhorns went on to a 31-0 win. Phillips University was buried in the next game under a barrage of 7 touchdowns, four of them by fullback Jim Marley, who was a raging tiger in this game. Halfback Eckhardt once again starred as he ran for two touchdowns against Tulane as Texas flattened the Green Wave in Beaumont 33-0.

Vanderbilt, confident of continuing their 18-game winning streak over a two-year period, and victorious over Texas the past two seasons, was soundly defeated in Dallas by the Longhorns. They were pounded into submission by a 16-0 margin. The crowd of more than 18,000 roared as Eckhardt tossed a 35-yard pass to halfback Buddy Tynes and Tynes raced to the Vandy 9-yard line. Then Eckhardt blasted over for the first score. Late in the game, with the score 10-0, Texas worked the ball to the Vanderbilt 20-yard line. Again Eckhardt bulled his way across the goal line. The final was 16-0, Texas.

The next two victims were Southwestern and Rice, who lost 44-0 and 27-0, respectively. The Baylor Bears, out to avenge their 1919 loss to Texas, were lying in wait in Waco.

With five straight victories and a 0-0 tie with the Texas Aggies, the Bears were confident they had Texas' number this year. And the game began with the Bears attempting an on-side kick. The play caught Texas by surprise and Baylor recovered the ball on the Texas 37. But their attack stalled and the Horns took over. They failed to move the ball, and late in the second period Baylor recovered a Texas punt that carried just ten yards. The Bears then smashed in for a touchdown and it was 7-0, Baylor.

The game seesawed back and forth with the Bears missing five field goals that would have put the game out of reach. In the final period, Eckhardt and fullback Joe Ward worked the ball to the Bears' 2-yard line. Then, on a reverse, Ward scored for Texas. It was a 7-7 game as the gun sounded to end the struggle. "This was the toughest game we had to play all season long," said Coach Stewart. "I'm glad it's behind us."

Oscar Eckhardt had a great day for himself a week later. He was all over the field as he led the Longhorns to their eighth victory of the season against the Oklahoma Sooners by a 26-14 margin. The victory set the stage for the big Thanksgiving Day tussle between Texas and Texas A&M in College Station.

The Aggies put up a tremendous defensive battle from the opening kickoff, but their offense could only get two first downs in the entire game. A wet, muddy field hampered both teams.

On the twelfth play of the game, Eckhardt sent a high, booming punt into Aggie territory. It seemed as if the ball would never come down, but when it did, halfback Clem Pinson of A&M fumbled the ball and Buddy Tynes recovered for Texas on the 5-yard line. His momentum carried him across the goal line for the only score of the game. It was the Longhorns' first win over A&M at College Station and gave Coach Doc Stewart a remarkable season record. Texas wound up with an 8-0-1 record, scoring 241 points and allowing their rivals just 21 points. Oscar Eckhardt, Ed Bluestein, F. M. Bralley, and Jim Marley had been selected All-SWC.

But Texas fans were disappointed when the faculty representatives of the SWC voted the league championship to Southern Methodist, who had a 5-0 league record. Texas was not considered for the title as they'd only played four teams in the SWC Conference.

In a national magazine story, *New York Times* sportswriter Allison Danzig called Texas "the uncrowned" national champions along with Dartmouth and Yale. It was consolation of a sort.

K. L. Berry was an outstanding guard among the 1924 eleven.

In 1924, Doc Stewart had a major rebuilding job on his hands. He had lost his great halfback, Oscar Eckhardt; his quarterback, Bob Robertson; one of the top ends in Texas football, Bully Gilstrap; tackle Ed Bluestein; rugged center F. M. Bralley; and a host of other backs and linemen. Matter of fact, the only veterans Stewart had left were Captain Jim Marley, fullback; and three linemen, Bud Sprague, Matt Newell, and Cotton Dayvault.

At the same time that Stewart was rebuilding his football team, the hardworking Athletic Director, Theo Bellmont, had drawn up a plan to replace the wooden stands at Clark Field with a concrete stadium that would seat some 27,000 spectators. The Board of Regents approved the plan, and the re-financing was settled. The new stadium, covering some thirteen acres, would be ready for the big Thanksgiving Day game with the Texas Aggies.

The lineup set by Coach Stewart for the opening game against Southwestern included Stookie Allen and Matt Newell as ends; Bud Sprague and Heinie Pfannkuche were the tackles; Swampy Thompson at center; K. L. Berry and Cotton Dayvault the guards; Bertie Foster, quarterback; Stud Wright and Clint Slover at the halfback spots; and Jim Marley, fullback.

Southwestern was easily defeated 27–0 and a week later Phillips went down by the same score. Next, Howard Payne did everything but win the game in a bitter struggle, but Texas managed to eke out a 6–0 win in a surprisingly rough battle.

Southern Methodist roared into the State Fair Grounds at Dallas on the wings of a sensational 13-game winning streak over the past two seasons. They expected a hotly contested battle. The big game attracted a capacity crowd of 16,000 fans, all wild with excitement and hoping their team would win.

But instead of exciting plays and daring strategy, both teams were extremely cautious, and played a waiting, defensive battle. Late in the first period, an SMU field goal forced Texas to open up their game plan. On a fake run and pass play, Texas halfback Reed Thompson tossed a beautiful aerial to Bert Foster, who was slammed down on the 5-yard line. On the next play, fullback Jim Marley banged across the SMU goal line for a touchdown, and Texas had a 6–3 lead.

But SMU came back like a whirling dervish. Under the direction of Logan Stollenwerck they scored a touchdown that gave the Mustangs a 10–6 win. It was a game that saw players on both teams so battered they would have to miss several games in the weeks ahead.

Back home at Austin, Texas prepared to do battle against the Florida Gators. With five varsity men out of action the Horns were sorely pressed to gain a 7–7 tie with the hard-fighting Gators.

Then Rice University, under their new coach John Heisman, who would become a legend in a few years, tore into Austin. The Owls filled the air with forward passes, laterals, and reverses, and scored three touchdowns to topple Texas in a 19–6 upset.

The new football stadium was completely ready for play on November 8 and a crowd of more than 13,500 poured into the new stands to watch a championship Baylor team defeat Texas 28–10. The score was only 7–2 in favor of Baylor at the end of the half, but in the second half, Baylor's fine backfield stars tore off runs of 38 and 22 yards for two quick scores, and the Bears left Austin with a 28–10 win.

On a quick trip to Fort Worth, the Longhorns walked away with a 13–0 win over TCU, newest member of the Southwest Conference.

In the Thanksgiving Day battle with Texas A&M, Governor Pat Neff dedicated the new Memorial Stadium to the many thousands of Texans who served in World War I, stating that the Stadium would also honor the more than 5000 Texans who had died in the service of their country.

The game turned out to be a hard-fought defensive battle with little offense on the part of either team. Texas tried and missed on two field goal opportunities of 29 and 38 yards by quarterback Stud Wright.

Late in the game, with the score still 0–0, substitute halfback Rosy Stallter scampered back on a fake reverse play, then turned and tossed a short pass to halfback Potsy Allen. Two Aggie players, Bob Berry and Milt Dansby, deflected the ball but did not catch it, and it bounced high into the air and into the waiting arms of Allen. Allen was off and running from the 35-yard line into the end zone. 33,000 frenzied Longhorn fans went mad with joy as their team the Longhorns pulled out a last-minute 7–0 win over the Aggies.

Years later when this play was discussed, Allen said, "I was not surprised when the ball flipped into my arms. I was waiting for the pass and looking for the ball all the way."

The Longhorns' 5-3-1 record landed them in sixth place in the SWC, far behind the champion Baylor Bears. It was their worst conference finish ever.

With twenty veterans returning for the 1925 season, Coach Doc Stewart was delighted with his team's prospects—until he and his coaches studied the 1925 schedule. In previous seasons there had always been two or three soft touches, smaller

schools that provided just enough of a contest to test the Longhorns and get the team in the proper condition and frame of mind to face the big challenges to come. But in 1925, the schedule-makers had come up with the most difficult eight-game slate in the 33-year history of Texas football. Following the opening game with Southwestern were such major opponents as Mississippi, Vanderbilt, Auburn, Rice, Southern Methodist, Baylor, Arizona, and the Texas Aggies. Not a soft spot in the list. And every one of those teams would be pointing toward the Texas game.

Watching practice one day, early in the season, Stewart took particular notice of a youngster who had transferred from Austin College and played football there. He was fast, shifty, could cut on a dime, and run faster than any man on the squad. His name was Mack Saxon, and although he only weighed 165 pounds, Saxon soon developed into the best runner and passer on the team—and he could kick hell out of the ball. In quick order, Saxon was the number one back.

In the season's opening game against Southwestern, Stud Wright handled the team beautifully from his quarterback spot. In the second period he took a punt from Southwestern and dashed 60 yards for a touchdown that sparked a parade of four additional scores, and Texas had a 33–0 win to start the season. Against Mississippi, after a scoreless first half, Mack Saxon spun off-tackle in the third period, eluded four defensive tacklers, and sped 55 yards for a touchdown. Following Saxon's marvelous run, the floodgates opened. Three more TDs and Texas had a 25–0 win over Mississippi.

Vanderbilt entered the fray against Texas fresh from a stunning 35–7 victory over a strong Tennessee team. They simply had too much drive for Texas as they went on to a 14–6 win. The game was tied at 6–6, though, at the end of the first half. In the last minute of the third period, quarterback Wright was injured and taken out of the game, and Fred Thompson took over the kicking chores. Vanderbilt blocked the first kick by Thompson and recovered the ball in the end zone for a safety. Near the end of the game, Vandy scored a TD on a 35-

yard pass from Bill Spears to halfback Gil Reese and the Commodores had a 14–6 victory.

For some time Coach Stewart had been worried about his quarterback, and the Vandy game confirmed his suspicions. Stud Wright had won that position on opening day and had performed fairly well. But with Auburn, Rice, SMU, Baylor, and the big game against the Aggies coming up in rapid order, Stewart realized he had to get more of an all-around game from his quarterback.

In the first practice after the Vanderbilt battle, Doc took Mack Saxon aside and told him he wanted him to work especially hard. "I'm going to give you a shot at quarterback, Mack. I think you can be the player to move and inspire the team. What do you think about that?"

"Coach, I'll do anything I can to win and I'll try my best to give you everything I've got," said Saxon.

Throughout a long week, Stewart personally devoted much of his time to his new quarterback. He had Saxon practicing hours on end to properly receive the pass from center, then shift his feet to fake or hand the ball off to other backs. The coach had Saxon work on the reverse, where the quarterback hands off to an end or back coming from the opposite side. He drilled Saxon on his passing, working over and over on short quick passes to his ends or to another back.

When the week was over Mack Saxon was the new Texas quarterback, and Stud Wright was shifted to halfback for the Auburn game.

The result? Saxon was sensational. In the second period against Auburn, he intercepted a pass and flashed downfield on a spectacular 70-yard sprint for a touchdown. Then, a few plays later, Wright tossed a 37-yard pass to Saxon and he picked up another TD. In the final period, Saxon tossed an aerial bomb to his end, Matt Newell, a 40-yard play for another touchdown, and Texas romped 33–0 over Auburn.

In a game in Austin against Rice, the Longhorns, although playing with a patched-up lineup due to injuries, ripped the Owls for a 27–6 win. Then, against SMU in the sixth game of the season and with both teams playing a defensive game throughout the afternoon, Texas was held to a 0–0 tie. On the final play of the game, Texas had the ball at the SMU 17-yard line, but a pass by Rosy Stalter was intercepted and Texas' last chance to score failed.

On November 7, Texas did battle with a tough Baylor team in a game that was notable for two reasons: the Texas victory by a 13–3 margin, and the broadcast of the game for the first time by KUT, the University's new radio station. In the game Mack Saxon recovered a fumble and dashed ten yards for a touchdown. Then Matt Newell scooped up a fumble by a teammate and ran the ball over for another score.

In the last home game of the season, Texas easily defeated Arizona 20–0 for a 6-1-1 record and just one tie in SWC play. But Texas A&M, defeated but once by TCU, was also in the race for the SWC championship. Interest in this final game between Texas and the Texas Aggies was at such a high level that even the governor attended the game. More than 26,000 excited fans jammed College Station on Thanksgiving Day for the championship game.

Texas fans anticipated a big win over A&M, but they were sadly deflated by the Aggies' clever ballhandling and opportunistic ways. The Aggies took advantage of every Texas misplay—there were several—and scored a touchdown each time to upset the confident Longhorns in a 28–0 rout, despite the spectacular play of Mack Saxon, whose splendid defensive tackles stopped at least two more scores.

With the defeat by the Aggies, the Longhorns ended the season with a respectable 6-2-1 record and tied with TCU for second place in the Southwest Conference. But second place in any situation was never good enough for the Texas fans and alumni, and the voices of discontent bubbled and boiled and then suddenly broke out into open dissension within the athletic department.

When peace was finally restored in the athletic department in 1926, Doc Stewart felt confident that he could remain as Texas' head coach as long as he continued his winning ways. He was especially confident about his job since his record showed 19 victories with just five losses and three ties. Most impressive was his two out of three wins over Texas' bitterest rivals, the Texas Aggies. And in 1926 Stewart was certain that his Longhorns could again beat the Aggies in their big Thanksgiving Day game, for he had a backfield that looked to be one of the most potent offensive units he had ever worked with. Captain Mack Saxon was back at quarterback, and the rest of the men were among the most versatile he had ever worked with: Rosy Stallter, Bill Ford, John Estes, Potsy Allen, and Rufe King.

In Saxon, his six-foot, 165-pound speedster, Stewart had a quarterback who was both brainy and tough. He could run like the wind, he could pass that round football like a pitcher throwing strikes, and he could kick the ball fifty or more yards on every attempt. Saxon was a threat to break a game open every time he got his hands on the ball and he was a proven player, having demonstrated his all-around abilities in 1925.

The line, however, was a problem, for Stewart had just half a dozen experienced players back, including two top ends in Clem Higgins and Clint Slover, a great center in Pottie McCullough, and four or five promising freshmen and transfer players.

The opening game with Southwestern Oklahoma Teachers College provided a good test for his makeshift line and his backfield unit. They came through in a workmanlike manner, holding Southwestern to just 7 points as they racked up a 31–7 victory. Perhaps Texas became too cocky this early in the season as they ran into a surprise in the second game, against Kansas State. The short, accurate, tricky pass offense utilized by Kansas State shocked the Texas defense and before they could settle down, Kansas State had two touchdowns and a 13–3 upset win.

Back home again, still stunned by the Kansas State defeat, the Longhorns responded by breaking off a spectacular play against Phillips University just as the game got underway. On the opening set of downs, Phillips attempted a tricky lateral-then-forward pass play, but halfback Bill Ford read the entire play, dashed for the ball, intercepted the pass, and sped 70 yards for a touchdown. From then on it was an easy 27–0 triumph.

A veteran Vanderbilt eleven, winners of two of three games against the leading teams in the South, pounded out a close 7–0 victory over the Longhorns in a game in Dallas that saw both teams exhausted from the beating they inflicted on each other. The score was 0–0 in the final minutes of the third period when Bill Hendrix, on a well-executed double reverse, surprised the Texas defense and drove around his own end for 25 yards before he was stopped at the Texas 3-yard stripe. On the next play he smashed off-tackle for the score that won the game for Vandy by a 7–0 margin.

A week later in Houston fullback Rufe King intercepted a pass late in the final period against Rice for a touchdown. King's score opened the gates for two more touchdowns in a 20–0 win for Texas.

In the sixth game of the season, at home after two games in a row on the road, the Longhorns were throttled by a great Southern Methodist team that would go through the conference undefeated. Ray Morrison's unit, with their all-American quarterback Gerald Mann, rallied furiously with a barrage of passes and scored two touchdowns late in the game. Though Texas played tough, the two scores gave SMU the edge in a 21–17 win.

With 5 victories in 7 games, including a stunning 20–7 win over the Texas Aggies, the Baylor Bears were not to be denied in their game against Texas. The Bears kicked a field goal early in the game, then scored a touchdown in the third period to take a 10–0 lead. Late in the fourth period, Texas rallied and scored on a long pass from King to Mack Saxon, but that was the Longhorns' only score, and Baylor took a 10–7 victory in Waco.

The eighth game of the season against Southwestern on Armistice Day provided the Longhorn squad with a good tuneup for what was sure to be a struggle against the Aggies a week later. Coach Stewart started his second unit, and they responded with back-to-back touchdowns to give Texas an easy 27–6 victory. Quarterback Joe King drove through the Southwestern line for 30 yards and a score, then a substitute end, Jim Boyles, took a Southwestern kickoff and proceeded to scramble,

The cover of the 1926 Texas-Texas A&M program guide at the new Memorial Stadium that had just been completed. Texas came from behind to defeat A&M, 14–5.

dodge, and twist his way through the entire Southwest team for 90 yards and a magnificent touchdown.

And now the final game in a rugged season that saw Texas with a 4–4 record—a record that had the students, alumni, and the Board of Regents discussing in not too hush-hush tones the conduct and administration of the entire football program.

But Coach Stewart was too busy to listen to the harsh voices as he prepared his team for the Aggies. He didn't intend to be the first man to coach a losing season at Texas.

The largest crowd in the history of Texas football jammed the new Memorial Stadium, some 35,000 strong. To the dismay of the rabid Texas fans the Longhorns played sloppy ball and allowed A&M to kick a field goal and to throw Texas for a safety for a 5–0 lead.

But Texas responded and began to bombard the Aggies with a series of forward passes that had the Aggies floundering. Texas completed 11 of 13 passes for two touchdowns and a 14–5 win in one of the most exciting games between the two rivals. Bill Ford caught a 10-yard pass in the second period, and then, with minutes left to play, Rufe King flipped a short, underhand pass to Clint Slover for 8 yards and a touchdown that put the game on ice.

The coveted win over Texas Aggies gave the Longhorns a 5–4 season and a 2–2 SWC league record. But it was not enough to give Coach Stewart a new contract.

1927–1933: THE LITTLEFIELD ERA

The simmering conflict within the Texas athletic department heated up once again early in the spring of 1927, and a number of coaches were burned in the raging arguments that threatened the entire department.

Athletic Director Theo Bellmont, who maintained strict unilateral control of the entire department, often stepped on the toes of the other coaches. Baseball Coach Billy Disch often argued at length with Bellmont and as the discussions and arguments flared, attention turned to Doc Stewart and his football program . . . and to his off-campus activities.

Stewart and a number of assistant coaches had opened a boys camp and then a girls camp, then followed with a resort hotel. He was often away working with his camps when he should have been attending to his football program. Stewart had been warned about spending too much time on these non-football activities, but he persisted with his camp duties until he was notified that he would not have his coaching contract renewed for 1927.

The Board of Regents, in search of a new head coach for 1927 and after much discussion and interviews with several coaches, signed Clyde Littlefield, Texas' freshman coach, to a three-year contract.

Born in Eldred, Pennsylvania, October 6, 1892, Clyde Littlefield came to Texas when the oil boom beckoned his father. Clyde attended prep school in San Antonio and the Marshall Training School, where he was an all-around star athlete. Clyde was the star of the Marshall football team, and once dashed 108 yards for the winning touchdown in the State Championship game. The following spring he scored 31 points in the State Track Championships to lead his team single-handedly to the State title. That was in 1911 and 1912.

In the fall of 1912 Littlefield entered the University of Texas and proceeded to carve out an athletic record in football, basketball, and track that has never been equalled at Texas. In the first football game he started in 1912 against the shifty, hard-running Haskell Indians team, Littlefield led his Longhorns to a 14–7 victory by throwing two touchdown passes that won the game. He then played in every game during the rest of the season, a season that saw Texas go 7–1. In 1913 Littlefield's passing created a sensation. His passes to end Pete Edmond developed into one of the great combinations in college football that year. And in 1914 Littlefield's passing and heady backfield play earned him praise from Grantland Rice, who called Littlefield "one of the great passing stars of that era."

In 1920 Littlefield was named an assistant coach at Texas, and his freshman teams were outstanding during his seven-year stint. His appointment as head coach came as no surprise, for he was one of the best-liked and respected coaches at the University.

When Littlefield took over as head coach and called his first practice, several outstanding veterans reported: Captain Ox Higgins, John McCullough, Ike Sewell, and Bill Ford, all rugged linemen; and in the backfield Joe King at quarterback, Tommy Hughes, Al Rose, Jim Boyles, and Leo Baldwin.

Texas opened the season at Austin against Southwestern Oklahoma in a game that was perfectly suited to the needs of Coach Littlefield. He

SMU, with 8 wins in 9 games, was an odds-on favorite to beat Texas in their 1927 battle, which they did win 14–0. Here Gordy Brown (without helmet) tackles an SMU back after a short gain. Texas' Harry Phillips (*left*) is ready to assist Brown.

utilized every man on the squad as Texas ran up six touchdowns in a 43–0 win. The following week Texas played TCU in rainy, sloppy weather that made any kind of footing impossible, and the two teams sloshed to a 0–0 tie. Trinity University was next on the schedule and once again the lighter, smaller Trinity squad was no match for Texas. Coach Littlefield again used most of his substitutes in a 20–0 victory.

Texas traveled to the State Fair Grounds in Dallas for the fourth game of the season against a Vanderbilt team that had scored 135 points in winning the first three games of the season. There was no doubt that Vandy had one of the most potent offensive teams in the Southwest, but Coach Littlefield had a few tricks up his sleeve and unveiled a new passing star in Joe King. King tossed two touchdown passes, and the Longhorns stunned Vanderbilt with a 13–6 win. The victory over the Commodores paved the way for another win, this time over Rice by a 27–0 count. Once again it was accurate passing by King in the final period that led to three scores and another big win.

At Southern Methodist's Ownby Stadium, in mud, wind, and a gale, SMU's top-notch eleven, with 8 victories in 9 games during the past two seasons, got off to a quick start in the opening moments against Texas. On the first play of the game SMU's Red Hume circled his right end for a touchdown

and it was 7–0 in favor of SMU. Then, late in the period, Hume tossed a pass to his great running star, Gerry Mann, and Mann dashed just 4 yards to give SMU another score and a 14–0 victory.

Against the Baylor Bears in the seventh game of the year Texas fell behind as the Bears drove for two touchdowns and a 12–0 halftime lead. Then Joe King uncorked his great passing arm and began to cut into the Baylor lead. A pass from King to Big Al Rose was good for 22 yards and a touchdown. The point after was made and it was 12–7 Baylor. In the final period, Texas halfback Potsy Allen got behind the Bears defensive backs and took a long pass from King, caught the ball in one hand, then dove across the goal line. The score gave the Horns a spectacular come-from-behind 13–12 victory in the final minute of the game.

Against Kansas State, a week later, behind the marvelous pin-point passing of Joe King, Texas simply outclassed State, jamming across 6 touchdowns on spectacular passes by King and fine runs by Rose and Jim Boyles. Rose sped 60 yards for another score, and then end Nono Rees scooped up a State fumble and rambled to another TD. Texas took the game by a 41–7 score.

In the final game of the season, on Thanksgiving Day, and before one of the largest crowds ever at College Station, the Texas Aggies were nothing less than spectacular as they outclassed Texas in an impressive 28–7 victory. Joe Hunt, the Aggies' sensational halfback, triple-threat star, and one of the great backs in football, took command of his team's offense. He completed 9 passes for 122 yards, scored two touchdowns, and threw a pass for a third score. The Aggies had too much offense for the Longhorns, who managed to drive 45 yards in the final period to give Texas their only score.

The victory by the SWC-champion Aggies gave the Longhorns a season record of 6 victories, 2 losses, and 1 tie. It was an improvement over the 1926 record, but Coach Clyde Littlefield was already looking forward to better things with an improved group of newcomers, a squad who would give Texas its first SWC title since 1920.

Coach Littlefield found to his delight that he would have a number of experienced veterans returning for the 1928 football season, including fullback Rufe King, elected captain of the team. King had fully recovered from a broken jaw he'd received in 1927. With King at fullback, Littlefield had Tommy Hughes, Ed Beular, and Pap Perkins as the halfbacks; Nono Rees, a fast-moving quarterback, as his signal-caller; and Dexter Shelley, a triple-threat newcomer who had transferred from Terrill Prep School in Dallas. The linemen included Bill Ford, Dusty Rhoads, and Big Rose at the end posts; Gordy Brown, Jack Cowley, Ike Sewell, and Harry Phillips as guards; Mac Burnett at center; plus a number of promising freshmen who would provide breathers for the veteran players as the season developed.

The opening game of the season against St. Edward's gave Littlefield an opportunity to display a classy newcomer in the Texas backfield. He was Dexter Shelley, a 180-pound speedster who broke away for touchdowns almost every time he got the ball. Against St. Edward's Dex broke away for three long runs and scored on gains of 45, 38, and 65 yards for three scores. He seemed unstoppable, and he gave one of the finest exhibitions of broken-field running ever seen at Memorial Stadium as Texas routed St. Edward's 32–0. Against a mediocre Texas Tech team, Littlefield started the game with his sec-

ond-stringers in the lineup, but Tech played inspired ball and held Texas to a 0–0 halftime score. But in the third period the varsity ran up 2 touchdowns and the Horns took a 12–0 win. In the Vanderbilt game in Dallas a week later, Vanderbilt quickly demonstrated their varied attack, one that had beaten Colgate and Alabama, by marching 66 yards for a touchdown. Then, after the Horns failed to gain ground, Vanderbilt blocked Leo Baldwin's punt and raced over the goal line for another score. The kick was good and Vandy had a 13–0 lead. Pinky Higgins, Texas' hard-running halfback (who would later play fourteen years of major league baseball, and then manage the Boston Red Sox for seven years), caught a pass from King and sprinted 19 yards for a touchdown. Later on in the third period King bucked over for another touchdown. But both of Texas' extra-point kicks were blocked, and Vanderbilt stole away with a 13–12 win.

Against the Horns in Austin the next week Arkansas fumbled the ball six times. Texas recovered the ball each time and as a result the Longhorns scored 3 touchdowns for a 20–7 victory. Rice a week later played hard, aggressive football but lost a heartbreaker against Texas when Gordy Brown tackled a Rice halfback who fumbled the ball at the Rice 26-yard line. Leo Baldwin smashed over the goal line minutes later for the winning score, and Texas took the game 13–6.

Southern Methodist had not lost a game to the Longhorns in their last four meetings and traveled to Austin confident of success. SMU's aerial-circus offense had given them five straight wins, and they had almost beaten a tough Army team that scored in the final minute to eke out a 14–13 win.

In a game at Austin, 22,000 fans witnessed a classic duel. Both teams were able to penetrate the other's defense. Texas made it to SMU's 3-yard line, but failed to score. In the second period a great Texas defense stopped a fierce SMU drive that got to the Texas 4-yard line. Then Sam Reed, SMU's passing star, tossed a 45-yard pass to end Ross Love. Then Reed tossed another great pass of 45 yards to Love for a touchdown. It was 6–0, SMU.

Texas regrouped in the final period and drove upfield in a determined attempt to score. With the ball at midfield, King passed to Bill Ford, who danced to the 30-yard line. Here the Horns attempted a trick play, developed for just such a situation. King faked a line buck, then passed to Rees, who flipped a lateral to Milt Perkins. Perkins took the ball at top speed, burst through the line, and was stopped at the SMU 2-yard line. On the next play, SMU massed and stopped Perkins at the line of scrimmage. Then it was up to King, but he was stopped—an inch from the goal line. SMU took over the ball on downs and gave up an intentional safety to Texas. SMU then kicked out of danger and one of the classic battles of all time between these two great rivals was over, with SMU the winner by a 6–2 score.

In the locker room, King said, "There's no doubt that I scored a touchdown. But the officials were not even in the line of play. They did not see the play." "In my opinion," said Coach Littlefield, "we scored on each of the three times we carried the ball. But the officials marked it short each time."

While the argument over Texas' failure to score was still raging all over the state, Texas defeated Baylor 6–0 in a squeaker in Waco. Then it was another tough battle, this time against TCU in Fort Worth. The Horns finished in front, 6–0.

The stage was now set for the SWC title game between Texas and the Texas Aggies in the biggest game of the year at Austin.

On Thanksgiving Day more than 45,000 fans, the largest crowd to ever witness a football game in Texas, saw a hard-hitting Texas team intent on winning their first SWC championship since 1920 completely dominate a scrappy squad of Texas Aggies by a 19–0 margin. "We won that game," said Coach Littlefield, "because we were doing the best blocking all season long. We hit their ends so hard they wound up in the stands, when they tried to run off-tackle."

There was no score in the game until the third period as both teams bashed each other throughout the first half, though Texas made first downs almost every time they got the ball. But they could not score until the end of the third period. Then

Shelley cracked over for a touchdown from the 1-yard line.

Then Ed Beular tossed passes to Ford and Hughes. Then another to Ford for another touchdown. A third score resulted on a pass of 25 yards from Beular to Ford, and Texas had a 19–0 victory and their second Southwest Conference title.

Bill Ford, Gordy Brown, and Dexter Shelley were named to the All-SWC Team.

The successful 7–2 record and the SWC championship gave Coach Littlefield and Texas one of the most gratifying seasons in years. Littlefield was congratulated throughout the winter season for the success of his Longhorns.

The year 1929 will always be remembered as the year of many great college football teams—Knute Rockne's greatest club, winners of 9 straight games; Pittsburgh's great squad, with 10 wins; Purdue and Tulane, both unbeaten; Tennessee, with its third straight unbeaten year; and in the Southwest, Texas Christian University, with one of their greatest teams in history.

At the University of Texas, Coach Clyde Littlefield approached his third year with ambivalence, for he was faced with a schedule that included several major opponents: the Texas Aggies, TCU, Baylor, Rice, Oklahoma, and SMU. When he looked over a list of his players for the upcoming season, it was with the realization that he had few experienced men to face a difficult season.

While all of this was taking place the nation was facing one of the stormiest periods in history. The stock market, which had been churning out profits for years, making bootblacks and financiers tons of money, suddenly went into a tailspin. The nation quickly slid into the worst depression in history. So 1929 was to be the last tremendous year of sports, a year in which new attendance records in football were attained. It was a red-letter year, a year of marvelous teams, great players, of drama on the gridiron and in the economic life of the nation as the Golden Twenties, the most fabulous decade in sports history, closed with a crash that left Wall Street and thousands of alumni in mourning.

When Coach Littlefield and his aides appraised the players who reported for practice, they noted with dismay the thin line of class players on hand. Most of the 1928 backfield and much of the great line had either graduated or left school for one reason or another. There were a couple of bright lights as they discovered at the end of a week's practice, and they were heartened by the magnificent display of ability shown by Dexter Shelley, who had fully matured and now was a triple-threat star, good enough to match the best in the nation. Tackle Gordy Brown also showed vast improvement and would prove to be a most valuable tackle who could play almost any line position.

Some two weeks into his practice sessions, Littlefield was delighted with the return of quarterback Nono Rees, who had two previous years of experience. He also welcomed back two big, tried-and-true ends in Big Rose and Rut Vining; Hank Mills, a tough 190-pound tackle; Curt Beaty, a fine guard; Mac Burnett at center; and halfbacks Jim Beard and Milt "Pap" Perkins.

In the opening game of the season at Austin, St. Edward's University was defeated by a 12–0 score. It was a game that saw a stuttering offense and a sloppy defense by Texas, and the Longhorns barely managed to pull the game out. In the next game, against Centenary College, Texas played much more like a team. The offense looked sharp as they ran up a 20–0 score over Homer Norton's eleven. The next week Texas met a true test against Arkansas in the third game, a contest played in a sea of mud in Fayetteville. The horrible footing kept both teams from scoring until the final period, when Texas finally began to make some big plays and scored four times to win convincingly, 27–0. Texas' next opponent, Oklahoma, would test the mettle of the Longhorns, for Texas had not met the Sooners since 1923 and had little knowledge of Oklahoma's offense. But for the first time this season, the Longhorns played well the entire game. They scored three times and went on to a 21–0 win as Dexter Shelley, Bull Elkins, and Andy Brown all scored touchdowns for Texas.

A week later a vastly improved Longhorn squad, playing like a well-oiled machine, romped by a five-touchdown margin over Rice in a field that was ankle-deep in mud. Texas scored in the first period as Nono Rees took a punt, raced to his right, and sped 78 yards through the entire Rice team for a brilliant touchdown. The next time Texas had possession, Rees again burst through the Rice line for 22 yards and another score. In the third period, Dexter Shelley on a fake reverse cut off his tackle and outran all pursuers in a beautiful 65-yard touchdown run. Curt Beaty and Frank Cheatham recovered blocked punts, and Texas converted for two more touchdowns as the Longhorns won 39–0 going away. This was Texas' finest offensive and defensive exhibition of the entire season.

At Ownby Stadium a week later Southern Methodist, owners of a 3–2 record, played their best game of the year and held the vaunted Longhorn offense to a 0–0 tie. Quarterback Nono Rees almost broke the game open in the opening moments of the game as he took the kickoff and raced by and through every member of the SMU defense . . . except one man. That one man, Speedy Mason, caught Rees from behind after a magnificent 78-yard sprint to the 18-yard line. Texas failed to score, and missed on four field goal tries.

In the seventh game of the season, on a gridiron soaking wet from a three-day downpour, a stubborn Baylor team held Texas scoreless again in a game that saw both teams miss several scoring opportunities. Final score, 0–0.

Texas Christian University, with a record of seven wins in a row including a 3–0 win over the Texas Aggies, charged into Austin for a game that would decide the SWC championship. The Longhorns, also undefeated in seven games and unscored upon, had finally come together and were now rated one of the nation's top teams.

The big game attracted more than 22,000 fans who began to cheer their favorite team at the opening kickoff and never stopped until the final whistle. And they witnessed one of the classic battles in this long rivalry.

Texas halfback "Pap" Perkins dives over TCU's Cy Leland in a 1929 game that TCU won 15–12.

After a scoreless first period, Texas began a drive in the second period as Pap Perkins broke away in a furious dash for 48 yards to the TCU 10-yard stripe. On the next play, Perkins crashed through behind his right guard for 10 yards and a touchdown for a 6–0 lead. Shelley missed the conversion.

Years later Shelley talked to a reporter about the next play: "Captain Brown told me not to kick off to TCU's halfback, Cy Leland, who was the fastest man on the field. But if the kick should get to Leland, we should all get to him and don't let him get by you. If he does, it's a touchdown, because this guy is too fast for any of us."

"Well, I kicked off," said Shelley. "Sure enough the ball went straight to Leland and before we knew what happened, Leland was out in front of all of us, running like a scared deer. Brown was the only one in sight and he dove but missed Leland and Cy was over after a brilliant 95-yard touchdown sprint. The Leland touchdown run was the spark they needed and they kicked the extra point to take a 7–6 lead. Shortly after Leland's great run, TCU had the ball and the Frogs' quarterback, Howard Grubbs, led a drive of 65 yards for another TCU score."

Moments before the end of the half, Dexter Shelley faked a punt from his 40-yard line, and played it perfectly. He even drove his foot through the air while holding the ball in his hands. Then he

took off right through the center of TCU's line for a brilliant 60-yard dash for a Texas touchdown. Again Shelley missed the extra point and the score was 13–12 TCU. Then, in the waning moments of the game, Shelley was tackled behind his own goal line for a safety, and the game ended with the final score TCU 15, Texas 12.

The loss to TCU, after Texas had outplayed the Horned Frogs, took the heart out of the Longhorns, and they went down to a 13–0 defeat at the hands of the Texas Aggies in the final game of the season. The loss gave Texas a 2-2-2 SWC record and a fourth-place finish. It was a bitter end to a season that had started so promisingly.

The Golden Twenties had truly been the golden age of college football. It was the period of the game's greatest growth, the decade in which interest mounted to dizzying heights, with new stadiums opening in all parts of the nation. It was the period in which the college football coach won recognition and financial reward far beyond his compensation heretofore. And it was a decade of more great teams, in all parts of the nation, than football had produced in any other ten years.

In the Southwest Conference, SMU had become the league's most consistent winner under wily Ray Morrison. TCU had one of its greatest teams under Francis Schmidt; at Baylor, Morley Jennings had the Bears charging forward again;

and Rice and Arkansas were making moves up the ladder.

At the University of Texas, Coach Clyde Littlefield, with a marvelous three-year record of 18 wins, 6 losses, and 3 ties, was back on the job in 1930 for his fourth season. He had a new three-year contract and a group of players who would develop under his coaching skill and become one of the powerhouse teams in the SWC.

This despite the fact that every starting member of the 1929 team had graduated or left school except Captain-elect Dexter Shelley, a three-year veteran who could do anything in the backfield. Dex could run like a deer, had a marvelous passing arm, and could kick with the best in the SWC. He was an unselfish star who at 185 pounds would rather block for a teammate than run the ball. Littlefield was to discover two halfbacks and a number of substitutes from the 1929 team who with some game experience would prove to be valuable assets in 1930.

The two halfbacks were Ernie Koy and Harrison Stafford. Koy was a 190-pound fullback who could run through a brick wall and was called upon whenever Texas needed that extra three or four yards for a first down; Koy was the man who delivered. Harrison Stafford, who weighed just 175 pounds, astonished the coaches the very first time he carried the ball. In a practice game against the freshman team Stafford ran through the frosh line as if it were made up of papier-maché. On defense Stafford was a ferocious blocker. Nobody on the team could stop him on offense or defense and when he teamed up with Koy and Shelley in the backfield, Coach Littlefield soon found he had potentially one of the greatest backfields in Texas' thirty-eight years of football.

Texas opened the season with a semipractice game against Southwest Texas Teachers College. Actually it was more of a scrimmage, as the coaches of both teams stopped play and pointed out mistakes. Texas easily romped off to a 36–0 victory. Then, in a game against the Texas College of Mines, the Longhorns scored three times in the final period to win by a 28–0 margin. Next was Centenary, with a first-class team. They played nose to nose against Texas in a quagmire that made foot-ing practically impossible, and the teams battled to a 0–0 tie.

Howard Payne, always a troublesome foe, gave Texas fits for the first half and held the Longhorns to a 0–0 tie. But Dex Shelley broke loose for a number of big plays with two TD runs of 15 and 13 yards. Both kicks were good and Texas went on to win 26–0.

Whatever the records of the two teams, when Texas and Oklahoma faced each other on the gridiron, records were meaningless. A favored Texas team with a 3–1 record faced a Sooner eleven with 2 wins in two games played, and Oklahoma held the Longhorns scoreless in the first half. At the beginning of the second half, the Sooners broke the tie with an astonishing 50-yard pass play that caught the Texas defense by surprise. It was 7–0, Oklahoma. Then Coach Littlefield shook up his lineup. He sent Harrison Stafford in at halfback and on the first play Stafford tackled Oklahoma's star halfback Guy Warren so hard that Warren fumbled. Texas recovered the ball and Koy battered through the line to tie the score at 7–7. Minutes later Ox Blanton, a great field goal kicker, booted one from the 20-yard line. Another touchdown by Koy as the game neared its final moments put the game on ice for Texas with a 17–7 win. It was the Longhorns' fourth straight win over the Sooners.

Texas had beaten the Rice Owls five straight—but this year, in a game played in Houston, it would be different. Rice took advantage of a fumbled punt, recovered the ball, and then scored a touchdown from the 1-yard line for a 6–0 lead. In a desperate last-minute frenzy Texas launched an attack sparked by a 50-yard pass play from Perkins to John Craig that got the ball to the Owls' 14-yard line. But before the Longhorns could get off another play the gun sounded. Texas had to settle for a 6–0 loss in the biggest upset of the year.

The defeat by Rice, after four wins, brought a roar of anguish from the alumni, who thought poor strategy cost the Horns the game.

With 4 wins in 5 games, SMU was a heavy favorite to beat Texas. But Coach Littlefield kicked a few Texas butts in the locker room before game time and a rejuvenated Texas team shot into action as the game began.

From the opening gun, the Texas offense had Southern Methodist on their backs with a series of brilliant plays. On the first series of downs Shelley began several running plays. Then, just as SMU set their defense to stop the running game, Shelley opened with passes to Harrison Stafford: first a brilliant 44-yard toss for a TD, then a couple of running plays, then another pass and another Texas score. By this time SMU was so completely bewildered that when they took the ball over after a Texas score they failed to gain ground and attempted a kick. Lester Peterson, Texas' great end, charged in, blocked the kick, grabbed the loose ball, and charged to the SMU 7-yard line. On the next play Shelley scored to give Texas a 25–7 lead they never relinquished. The victory broke a 6-game winless streak against the Ponies.

The Horns continued their fine play against Baylor the next week in Waco. They won 14–0 as Stafford starred with a couple of brilliant runs, one for 55 yards through the entire defense of the Bears.

TCU, with an unbeaten record of 8 wins and 1 tie, felt confident they could eliminate the Horns to win the SWC title. But Texas was equally confident, and in a game played in Fort Worth, the Horns completely throttled TCU's great halfback, Cy Leland. Stafford, Koy, and Peterson punched through the TCU line for big gains, and then it was Koy to Stafford on a spinner play and Stafford smashing in for the only score of the afternoon. When it was over Texas had their biggest win of the season, 7–0. This was a game that meant the SWC championship for Texas, although the Longhorns had to win the final game of the season against Texas A&M and they accomplished just that.

In the Big Thanksgiving Day game at Austin, Texas blew out an overmatched Aggie team—they finished 0–5 in conference play—with a stunning 26–0 win as they smashed 60 yards on their first possession for the first TD of the game. In the second period, Pap Perkins sprinted 35 yards for another TD; then Shelley, in his last game for his alma mater, scored from the 1-yard line. On another series of downs Shelley tossed a sparkling 31-yard pass to Johnny Craig for the final score. Texas 26, Texas A&M 0.

The victory gave the Longhorns a marvelous 8-1-1 season, with Coach Littlefield gaining his second SWC title in his four years as head coach. A record six Horns were selected All-SWC: Ox Blanton, Ox Emerson, Lester Peterson, Harrison Stafford, Dexter Shelley, and Ernie Koy.

For the second time in two years, Coach Clyde Littlefield received a three-year renewal of his contract. The athletic board agreed that Littlefield deserved more money, but for various unnamed reasons—there *was* an economic depression sweeping the nation—he was given the same salary he had previously received, about $6000. But Littlefield paid little attention to the money. He loved what he was doing, he loved the University, and he was successful in developing outstanding football teams.

Now in his fifth season, Littlefield and his coaches, Bill James, Marty Karow, and Shorty Alderson couldn't be happier as they checked over the veterans and newcomers reporting for the first practice session of 1931. In the backfield was a bigger, heavier Harrison Stafford; the brilliant Ernie Koy; Bull Elkins, a Phi Beta Kappa and future Rhodes scholar at quarterback; and halfbacks John Craig and Andy Brown. The coaches thought they had as fine a set of backs as any team in the SWC. In the line, Littlefield had to settle for one top lineman, Captain and guard Maurice Baumgartner; Ed Price and Jack Sparks at the end positions; Ox Blanton and Herschel Moody at the tackles; Walt Howle, a capable center; and Roy Cooledge at the other guard position.

Texas opened the season with an easy romp over Simmons University by a 36–0 score. A week later a Missouri team limped into Austin and were beaten 31–0.

Rice, beaten by Oklahoma a week before the Texas game, was supposed to be a soft touch for the Longhorns, but the Owls took command of the game from the opening kickoff. They took a 7–0 lead and then played a tough defensive battle to win 7–0. A week later, a shell-shocked Texas team, still suffering from their loss to Rice, played listless ball, but still managed to edge Oklahoma 3–0. Ox Blanton,

Wilson "Bull" Elkins, Texas' Rhodes scholar and quarterback, carries the ball for a big gain against Missouri in a 1931 game.

despite a very sore ankle, came into the game and just managed to boot a field goal for the victory.

But on tap was the most exciting game of the year for Texas, perhaps even bigger than the Notre Dame battle of fifteen years before. It would be a two-and-a-half day journey to battle the great Harvard team at Cambridge. The Texas squad thoroughly enjoyed the travel and spent a good part of the trip in the train's luxury dining rooms. Several hundred Texas fans and alumni made the long trip along with the 45-member Longhorn Band.

The Harvard team already had the stamp of greatness, for they had won three straight games including a sensational 14–13 thriller over a tough Army team. They were coached by a former Harvard star, Ed Casey, who had played halfback on the 1916 Crimson squad. Casey had also played in 1917 and '18, and in 1919 had led his team to an undefeated season and was named to the all-American team.

The crowd of more than 35,000 fans were excited at the opportunity to witness a great Texas squad and eager to see the personal duel expected between two of the brainiest, most brilliant quarterbacks in college football, Barry Wood of Harvard and Bull Elkins of Texas. Both men were honor students and Rhodes scholars, and sportswriters had

been playing up the quarterback rivalry. Stories about the expected brilliant duel plastered the front pages of all the Eastern papers.

Instead of a fast, even-handed game, they saw a rip-roaring Harvard team that came out like a heavyweight champion, smashing and battering their opponents with one kayo punch after another. Harvard's offense overwhelmed the Texas defense as they rushed for 21 first downs and 387 yards. It was never a contest, and Harvard won by the score of 35–7.

Discussing the game with reporters after the contest, Coach Littlefield said he thought his team was simply worn down after spending the better part of two and a half days on the train that took them 2000 miles to Cambridge. "And my fellows were in that dining car hour after hour, eating and eating. I think they were just too sluggish to play Harvard."

Back in Austin on Tuesday, the Longhorns had only three days of practice before meeting a Southern Methodist team that was undefeated in 5 games with wins over Rice, Centenary, and Arkansas. It was a game that Texas had to win to remain in the SWC race. In a nip-and-tuck battle, SMU scored first as their great back, Speedy Mason, sped 35 yards for a TD. The kick was good

**Captain Dutch Baumgartener makes a diving tackle and stops SMU's back
Speedy Mason in a 1913 game won by SMU, 9–7.**

and SMU led 7–0. In the third period, Texas came to life with a dazzling 67-yard play that had the crowd roaring. Halfback Jim Burr tossed a great 45-yard pass to end Dause Bibby and then Bibby flipped a lateral pass to Bull Elkins just as he was tackled. Elkins raced 15 yards for the tying touchdown. It was 7–7 in the final quarter when Texas halfback John Craig attempted to punt, but Al Delcambre of SMU blocked the kick and recovered the ball behind the Texas goal line. The two-point safety meant a 9–7 win for the SMU team.

Injuries to several key players hampered the Longhorns for the Baylor game, but sensational sprints by Harrison Stafford who dashed 65 yards for a score after intercepting a Bears pass, and Ernie Koy, who also intercepted a pass and sprinted 55 yards for another score, proved to be too much for the Bears. They were beaten 25–0.

Texas Christian University, with a great record of 7–1, including a 6–0 win over the Texas Aggies, stormed into Austin confident that they would beat the Longhorns. But Ben Lewis' 13-yard

field goal in the first period and Ernie Koy's smash into the line for a touchdown in the third period were enough to destroy the hopes of TCU as Texas took the game 10–0.

On the Saturday before Thanksgiving Day, Texas traveled to Shreveport and defeated the always troublesome Centenary 6–0. Once again a brilliant Ernie Koy saved the day for the Longhorns. His accurate pass in the second period to end Ed Price for a touchdown gave Texas the game for their sixth victory of the season.

The Thanksgiving Day game against A&M was at College Station. The Aggies had beaten Iowa, Baylor, Rice, and Centenary, and lost to Tulane, TCU, and SMU. Inspired by their hard-running halfback, Frenchy Domingues, they overcame a 6–0 lead in the second period on Domingues' 38-yard dash for a score and the conversion to take a 7–6 lead which they protected to the final whistle. It was a well-deserved 7–6 win. The season ended with a record of 6 wins and four defeats for Texas. "With just a bit of luck," said

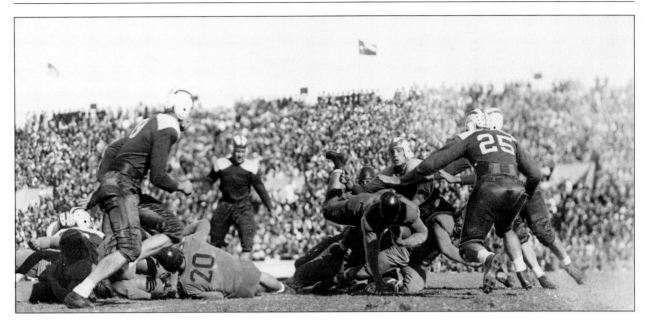

Texas center Charley Coates tackles SMU halfback Harry Schuford in a 1934 game that ended in a 7–7 tie.

Coach Littlefield, "we could have had an 8–2 season. The game against SMU we lost by two points. In the Aggies game it was 7–6. Those two games would have meant another great season. As it was a season like this one will make us tougher and harder for the next one coming up."

Texas backfield coach Marty Karow, who had assisted Clyde Littlefield in developing some of Texas' finest backs during his five years as Littlefield's top aide, made a number of amazing comments about one of his new players on the 1932 team, Bohn Hilliard. Karow, who had been a standout member of the Ohio State football teams of 1924 and '25, and had captained the 1926 team, had played against Red Grange when Grange was the most talked about star in the nation. "Bohn Hilliard can do a lot of things that Grange couldn't do," said Karow to a newspaper reporter. "Although Bohn is shorter than Red at five-nine and 170 pounds, Hilliard is just as fast, shifty, can run, pass and kick hell out of the ball, and he can block and tackle. I think before he is through here, he will go down as one of Texas' greatest backs."

"Along with Hilliard, who will be a team leader," said Littlefield to the same reporter, "we've got Harrison Stafford and that tremendous Ernie Koy and a great blocking back in Hank Clewis. It's an all-star backfield.

"We'll also have some experienced linemen," said Littlefield, "including Ox Blanton, Wilson Cook, Charley Coates, Sears Earle, Dause Bibby, Ed Price, Herschel Moody, Cliff Braly and Bill Smith."

Opening the season against Daniel Baker, Texas ran up a 26–0 win as Stafford and Koy did all the scoring. But against Centenary in the second game, with the score 6–6, Centenary's Ralph Murff smashed through the Texas line in the final moments of the game to score a touchdown, then kicked the extra point to defeat Texas 13–6.

Evidently the tongue-lashing administered by Littlefield all week long paid off, for in the next game Texas went to war against Missouri and handed the tamed Tigers a humiliating 65–0 beating on Missouri's own field. Ernie Koy played the greatest game of his career at Texas, ripping the Tigers for 4 touchdowns. Koy scored on sprints of 36 and 40 yards and two other touchdowns as the Longhorns scored 46 points in the first half against the former Notre Dame all-American Frank Carideo, the new Missouri coach. It was the most points scored by a Texas team since the 72–0 win over TCU.

Against Oklahoma the following week, Hilliard fulfilled his promise. In the first period a brilliant double pass play went from Koy to Stafford to Hilliard, and then Hilly threaded his way through the entire Sooner line for a touchdown.

In the third period, Hilliard caught a punt on his 5-yard line, spun away from two tacklers, burst through two more defenders, and outran two backs for an incredible 95-yard dash and another touchdown. The partisan Dallas crowd cheered him for five full minutes. Blanton booted a field goal from the 25-yard line in the final period to nail down a 17–10 victory over the rugged Sooners.

Under the brilliant coaching of former Notre Dame star Jack Meager, Rice had won its first four games of the season and was a favorite to beat the Horns in Houston the next week. In the dressing room before the game, Coach Littlefield talked to his players: "I don't care if we lose a couple of games after the Rice game, but this is one game we can't lose. I want this one. Now, we all got our ears blasted for losing to Rice last year, and I don't want a repeat. Now dammit, let's go get 'em."

The Longhorns, full of fight and fury, dashed out onto the field so excited and anxious to win that they wrapped up the game in the first period, scoring 18 points while holding Rice to 6 points. Hilliard again was the star of the game as he burst through the Rice line for 9 yards and the first score. Then, Hilliard sprinted for another touchdown on a 57-yard pass play from Koy to give Texas revenge and an 18–6 victory.

SMU had dropped four of its five games played this year, but they plowed into Texas in their first series as if they were going to crush the Longhorns. But after they scored a touchdown to lead 6–0, Texas took over and proceeded to cut down the SMU offense. SMU halfback Whitey Baccus attempted to pass the ball to his end, but Harrison Stafford, who had his eyes glued to the ball, charged in, intercepted the ball, and dashed 92

yards in a brilliant display of broken-field running for a Texas score. In the third period, Hilliard broke loose for 25 yards and another score as Texas took the game 14–6 for their fifth win of the year. Against Baylor at Waco a week later, Hilliard again sparked the Horns with a sprint of 66 yards as Texas won its sixth game by a 19–0 margin.

Texas Christian University, under the direction of Francis Schmidt, welcomed Texas to Fort Worth on Armistice Day for their annual battle. It was a game that is still talked about by those lucky to have been there, for the Frogs had one of their greatest teams ever. TCU, with wins over Texas A&M, Baylor, and Arkansas, had won 7 of 8 games and earned a 3–3 tie against LSU. Texas had won 6 out of 7 games and had reached the peak of their game. But TCU completely thwarted a Texas offense based around Hilliard and Koy; when the Horns could not score on the ground, they resorted to a passing attack, but only completed 6 of 23 passes without a score.

In the first period, Texas fumbled on their 30-yard line and the Frogs took over. On two driving line plays the Frogs got to the 2-yard line. But Texas, in a defiant goal-line stand, held the Frogs, then took over the ball. Hilliard punted, a short kick that barely got to the 25-yard line. TCU took over, and Red Oliver sped over left end for the touchdown and a 7–0 lead.

In the final period, with both teams battling furiously, a Texas kick went out of bounds on the Texas 10-yard line. Then Oliver passed for a touchdown that gave TCU a 14–0 lead.

Now it was Texas' turn, and the Longhorns tore up the field in a hurry. They reached the Aggie 25-yard line with Koy and Stafford battering the TCU line. Texas made it to the TCU 2-yard line, but before they could get another play off, the gun sounded, ending the game, and the Frogs had an amazing 14–0 win.

Five days later at Fayetteville, it was Arkansas' turn. In a complete reversal of form and behind the brilliant passing of Ernie Koy, the Horns battered the Razorbacks to the tune of 34–0.

The Texas Longhorns were at their very best in the Thanksgiving Day game against the Aggies and defeated A&M in a game that saw Hilliard, Stafford, and Koy all have great games. Koy's marvelous passes registered two touchdowns: one to Stafford and another to Hilliard. In the final moments of the game, Hilliard flashed 65 yards and scored the final touchdown as Texas went on to a well-deserved 21–0 victory over their rival.

It was Harrison Stafford and Ernie Koy's last game as Longhorns, and both players, along with Hilliard, were honored on various All-Star teams. Texas ended the season with a record of 8 wins and 2 losses, good for second in the conference behind TCU. For Coach Littlefield, it was one of the most satisfying of his six years as head coach at Texas.

Clyde Littlefield approached his seventh season as football coach in 1933 with mixed feelings. When he met with his coaches, Bill James, Marty Karow, and Shorty Alderson, they discussed plans for the upcoming season. All agreed that with the loss of some sixteen varsity players from the successful 1932 squad, including such stalwarts as Ernie Koy, Harrison Stafford, Ox Blanton, Dause Bibby, Ed Price, Cliff Braly, and Hank Clewis, it would be a difficult season. And when the 1933 schedule of games was released, with such major opponents as Nebraska, Oklahoma, Missouri, Rice, SMU, Baylor, TCU, Arkansas, and the Texas Aggies and Centenary, the coaches realized they were in deep trouble.

"Gentlemen," said Littlefield, "with the exception of the two opening games against Southwestern and Texas Mines, I don't see a soft spot any place in the entire schedule. Week after week we're going to have to compete against the best teams in this section of the country, and a couple of them are among the best in the nation. Now, we're going to have to be smarter, trickier, if we're going to stay alive. It's not going to be much fun, but let's give it a hell of a try."

In the opening game of the season against Southwestern, in the first night game ever played by Texas, Ron Fagan, the third-string quarterback in 1932, directed the Longhorns offense to an easy 46–0 win as every member of the squad had an opportunity to play. Fagan again led the team to

another win in the second game of the year, against the Texas College of Mines, as his accurate passes accounted for 3 touchdowns and a 22–6 win.

The third game, at Nebraska, proved to be the first real test for the 1933 Longhorns, and they met one of the great Nebraska teams. Coached by one of the nation's top coaches, Dana X. Bible, and led by three all-Americans in George Sauer, Bernie Masterson, and Larry Ely, the Cornhuskers proved too strong and too smart for Texas and handed them a 26–0 beating. Sauer, a 195-pound fullback, smashed and hacked through the Texas line for two touchdowns.

In Dallas a week later Oklahoma scored a touchdown and a field goal to defeat Texas 9–0 as halfback Bohn Hilliard sat out the game due to injuries. Then Texas suffered its third straight shutout as Centenary held the Longhorns to a 0–0 tie.

In an abrupt change of tactics, Texas resorted to an air attack against a Rice team as quarterback Ron Fagan threw for 2 touchdowns to defeat Rice 18–0. Bohn Hilliard was back in action for the SMU game at Ownby Field in Dallas and scored all 10 points as the Longhorns defeated SMU 10–0. Then, in windy, rainy weather, on a gridiron ankle deep in mud, Texas and Baylor battled until the final two minutes of play with neither team able to score. But with thirty seconds on the clock, Baylor kicked a field goal to upset Texas, 3–0. It was Baylor's first win over Texas since 1926.

Texas Christian University, with one of the most aggressive teams in years, traveled to Austin for the Texas game with a record that included wins over the Aggies and Arkansas. TCU handed the Longhorns a 30–0 defeat in a game that saw Texas make only 5 first downs.

Several days after the TCU game, Littlefield handed in his resignation as football coach effective at the end of the season.

When Arkansas came into Austin for their annual game against Texas, it was already known all over town that Coach Littlefield had handed in his resignation. The resulting poor morale of the team had a great deal to do with another defeat as Arkansas, taking advantage of a number of Texas miscues, defeated the Longhorns 20–6. It was Arkansas' first win over Texas in fifteen games.

In the season-ending contest against the Aggies, Texas played what was probably their finest game of the year. But it was not enough to win, as the Aggies and the Horns played to a 10–10 tie.

The tie game left Texas with a season record of 4-5-2—their first losing record ever—and the 2-3-1 SWC record was good for fifth place in the conference.

Clyde Littlefield ended his seven-year stretch as football coach with a record of 44 wins, 18 losses, 6 tie games, and two SWC championships.

Littlefield was retained as track coach, and remained in that post at Texas until ill health forced him to quit in 1961.

As track coach, Littlefield produced some of the greatest runners in the history of track. His 440-yard relay team held records in all the relays and was the national champion for three years. Among the national collegiate champions developed by Littlefield were Jim Reese in the mile run; Rufe Haggard and Garlan Sheppard in the high jump; Jud Atchison and John Robertson in the broad jump; Charlie Parker and Earle Collins in the 220-yard dash; and Jerry Thompson in the two mile run.

1934–1936: THE NOTRE DAME CONNECTION

1934's incredible 7–6 victory over the famous Notre Dame eleven had the Texas Longhorns and Coach Jack Chevigny on a high they were never able to recapture during the rest of the season. They did, however, finally come down to earth following the all-out celebration in Austin that topped any previous victory fête. This one was led by Governor Jim Allred and lasted for several days. The Horns were now 2–0 after their 12–6 opening win against Texas Tech.

Following a week of festivities, Texas still had enough verve to defeat a rugged Oklahoma team in Dallas by a 19–0 score. But the victory was a costly one, for Hilliard, the star of the Irish win, had been injured and would miss several important games.

Centenary came to town and ruined what should have been a great day for the Longhorns. Jack Chevigny was given a day in his honor, but Centenary spoiled the party by holding Texas to a 6–6 tie until the final minute of play, when Buddy Parker of Centenary kicked a field goal from the 13-yard line to defeat Texas 9–6. Parker later on in his career became an outstanding professional star and coach with the Detroit Lions.

Rice Institute, with a new head coach in Jim Kitts, scored first against Texas and were on its way to a second score when Jake Verde intercepted a pass and raced 90 yards for a Texas TD. Hilliard came off the bench to kick but missed the conversion, and Rice led 7–6. Texas drove downfield after they had taken over the ball on downs and reached the Rice 15-yard line. Once more Hilliard limped in and this time kicked an 18-yard field goal to make it 9–7, Texas.

In the third period, the Owls scored on a 67-yard pass play to give Rice a 13–9 lead. With just thirty seconds left to play, Rice scored their third TD on an intercepted pass to win the game 20–9 on the way to their first SWC championship.

A week later, SMU and Texas battled to a 7–7 tie. Then Bohn Hilliard, fully recovered from his injuries, led the Longhorns to a 25–6 victory over Baylor. Just a week later, it was Hughie Wolfe who dashed 65 yards against TCU for a touchdown. But Sammy Baugh came back with 2 touchdowns for a TCU lead. But Hilliard scored on an 18-yard drive and then booted the conversion to give Texas a thrilling 20–19 win.

Texas defeated Arkansas in Fayetteville a week after the rugged TCU battle. Hilliard once again proved his brilliance, scoring twice and then tossing a touchdown pass for an exciting 19–12 victory over the Razorbacks. Hilliard picked up 125 rushing yards in this bruising battle.

In the final game, against rival A&M, with a crowd of more than 20,000 on hand, Hilliard put on the performance of his young life as he passed for a touchdown, and set up another as Texas defeated the Aggies 13–0.

There were just two minutes left in the game when Coach Jack Chevigny removed Hilliard and Charley Coates from the game and the crowd stood and cheered these two stars who had performed so nobly for Texas throughout their careers. Along with Bill Smith they were both named All-SWC.

Texas ended the season with an outstanding 7-2-1 record, and Coach Jack Chevigny was given a nice salary increase for his marvelous work. But it was all downhill after Notre Dame.

Jack Chevigny had thought that his recruiting job would be an easy one in 1935, as the great win over Notre Dame and wins over such top teams as Baylor, Oklahoma, and Texas A&M would surely bring a host of promising recruits to his team. For the win over the Irish had resulted in nationwide press for Texas. But he was sadly mistaken, for outside of a fine track star in Jud Atchison he had to rely on his 1934 second-stringers after losing most of his veterans. His new backfield consisted of Atchison along with Duke Gilbreath, Jim Hadlock, and Ney Sheridan. Chev knew that the newcomers would be unable to offset the loss of such stars as the incredible Bohn Hilliard, Charley Coates, Phil Sanger, and Hughie Wolfe.

In the first game of the season, Texas defeated Texas A&I University in what was more of a warmup than anything else, as Texas ran up a total of 5 touchdowns in a 38–6 victory. In a night game against LSU at Baton Rouge, Texas quarterback Jim Hadlock broke away for 65 yards to the Tigers' 4-yard line. On the next play fullback Bill Pitzer banged through the LSU line for a touchdown. The extra point was missed, but Texas had a 6–0 lead. LSU came back quickly and marched right downfield and scored to tie the score at 6–6. In the fourth period, LSU suddenly found new life and scored 2 touchdowns to put the game on ice by an 18–6 margin. One week later, following the loss to LSU, Texas sophomore Morris Sands took the opening kickoff against Oklahoma and returned the ball 45 yards to the Sooners' 22-yard line. On the next play Sands went to the OU 2-yard line, then scored on the next attempt. Oklahoma, not to be denied, came back quickly and scored a TD and kicked the extra point to lead by a 7–6 margin. Jud Atchison then tossed a 38-yard pass to Duke Gilbreath, who scampered in for the winning touchdown. Final score: Texas 12, Oklahoma 7.

Texas always had problems with the tough Centenary squads and this year was no different as the two teams battled each other up and down the gridiron until late in the fourth period. With the score tied at 13–13, Texas punched down the field in the last two minutes and scored the touchdown that gave Texas a 19–13 win. Then in the game

against the Rice Owls, with the score 22–19 in favor of Rice, the Owls mounted a late drive of 73 yards and scored another touchdown for a 28–19 victory in as tough a battle as Texas had all season.

A week later at SMU, the Ponies' sensational sophomore halfback, Bobby Wilson, scored a touchdown and was personally responsible for two additional scores. His long, booming punts forced Texas deep within their territory, where SMU easily scored 3 touchdowns and a 20–0 win on the way to the SWC championship. Texas quickly rebounded a week later, played their finest game of the season to cop a 25–6 win over the tough Baylor Bears. But in this up-and-down season for Texas, TCU and Sammy Baugh were in fine form. Sammy tossed just 3 passes, but all 3 resulted in TCU touchdowns, and they took a 28–0 win over the Horns. Then, Arkansas halfback Jack Robbins scored two touchdowns to lead the Arkansas Razorbacks to a 28–13 win over Texas.

In the final game, the Thanksgiving Day battle, Texas was determined to salvage the season with a win over A&M. A victory would give Texas some respectability and a 5–5 season. But A&M took a 7–6 halftime lead, then turned on the offense, adding two more touchdowns to defeat the Horns 20–6.

The loss to A&M gave Texas a 4–6 season and set off a howl of anguish by alumni and fans. As the months flew by, their voices grew louder and louder and were finally answered by the Athletic Association.

By the time the 1936 football season arrived in Austin, coach Jack Chevigny was at the center of a storm of controversy that threatened to depose him before the season began. There were reports that Chev had lost interest in coaching the team and was more interested in his law practice and the oil business. Some of his players were fed up with his weekly pep talks, and many felt that his fast talking had outlived its usefulness and was not what a coach should display. Whatever the criticism, Texas officials and alumni were hot under the collar for his losing season in 1935, the poorest showing ever by the Horns.

To add to his problems, Chevigny's out-of-state recruiting had not met with success at all. As a matter of fact there were only two new players who would be any help at all in the upcoming campaign—two quarterbacks, Hank Mintermayer and Bill Forney. He had lost ten outstanding players from the 1935 unit, including Nick Wheeler and Harris Van Zandt, two fine ends; tackles Jim Tolbert and Nick Frankovic; guards Joe Smartt and Moreland Chapman; and Hal Griffin, a capable center. In the backfield, Jim Hadlock, Charlie Johnston, Bill Pitzer, and Mike Collie were gone.

To add to Chevigny's woes, the 1936 schedule consisted of 9 games and every game was against a major opponent. There was not a single soft touch in the entire schedule. As a matter of fact, the Texas schedule-makers had added a new opponent, the Minnesota Gophers, one of the nation's top teams.

Texas opened the season at home against a favored LSU team but fullback Hughie Wolfe sprinted 37 yards in the second period to give Texas a 6–0 lead. LSU fought back; in the third period they capitalized on a Texas fumble and banged in from the 17-yard line to tie the game at 6–6. And that was the final score.

The following week, at the Dallas Fair Park stadium, Texas and Oklahoma battled up and down the field with neither team able to score until the final two minutes of the game. Then halfback Bill Pitzer tossed a magnificent 50-yard aerial bomb to end Homer Tippen for the touchdown that gave Texas a 6–0 win.

The Baylor Bears trooped into Austin for their game against Texas and the Longhorns ripped into the Bears with a vengeance. The Longhorns scored two touchdowns and added a third when Jack Collins, the big Texas end, intercepted a Baylor pass and galloped through the entire Baylor team for a 95-yard touchdown dash. Texas had an 18–0 lead at the half. But late in the third period the entire complexion of the game changed in Baylor's favor. Halfback Bill Patterson and Lloyd Russell led the Baylor march to the Texas 7-yard line as the period ended. In the fourth period, Russell scored to give Baylor its first TD. On the next sequence of

Fullback Hugh Wolfe (*left*) and coach Jack Chevigny pose alongside a float before the A&M game in 1936. Texas won 7–0.

plays, Baylor drove for 75 yards to score their second TD. Now the score was Texas 18, Baylor 14. Injuries to key Texas players forced Chevigny to make a number of substitutions, and the subs could not stem Baylor's drives. A late Patterson-to-Russell pass gave Baylor a touchdown and an incredible come-from-behind 21–18 win.

One week later, still haunted by the loss to Baylor, the Longhorns lost 7–0 to Rice in a game that had the alumni howling for Chevigny's scalp. Back home in Austin, Texas again found itself on the short end of a 14–7 loss to SMU. The following week TCU and their great star Sammy Baugh shocked the Longhorns with another loss, this time by a 27–6 score.

A few days before the team was to leave for their game against the Minnesota Gophers, Jack Chevigny revealed to some friends and associates that he had asked the Texas athletic officials not to re-appoint him as coach when his contract ran out at the end of the season.

At Minneapolis, Bernie Bierman had developed one of Minnesota's great teams; as a matter of fact, the Gophers were on their way to a National Championship in 1936 and they ran roughshod over Texas. Jules Alphonse, the great Gopher halfback, scored the Gophers' first two TDs, then fullback

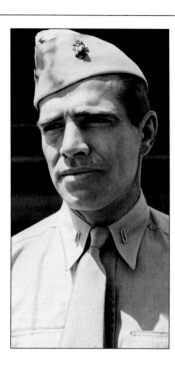

Marine Corps Captain Jack Chevigny, former star halfback at Notre Dame and football coach at Texas, was killed in action February 13, 1945, in the battle of Iwo Jima while leading a charge.

Larry Buhler scored two more as the Gophers moved, mostly on the ground, to a humiliating 47–19 victory. It was the fourth straight loss for the Longhorns on their way to the poorest season in Texas football.

Then on Thanksgiving Day, with Texas A&M favored to win at home, the Longhorns completely outplayed the Aggies and scored a touchdown in the first period, when Ney Sheridan took a 39-yard pass from Atchison and tore through the entire Aggies line like a man possessed for the only score of the game to give Texas their biggest win of the season, 7–0. In the second half the Aggies attempted several times to cross the goal line, but great defensive play by the entire Texas line halted A&M at least three times and Texas had the ball game.

In the final game of the season, against Arkansas in Little Rock on a field ankle-high in mud, Texas was stopped on three occasions within the 10-yard line and failed to score. In the third period, Dwight Sloan intercepted a Texas pass and ran it to the Texas 34. Four plays later Sloan's toss to Jim Benton gave Arkansas a 6–0 win in a hard-fought battle.

The loss to Arkansas gave Texas a season record of 2-6-1, the most disastrous season in the 44-year history of Texas football.

At the conclusion of the season, the Texas Athletic Council announced they had accepted Chevigny's verbal resignation offered just prior to the Minnesota game.

Jack Chevigny then served briefly in the army before taking a commission as a first lieutenant in the Marine Corps during World War II. As a first lieutenant, Jack led his Marine company into the thick of some of the fiercest fighting on Iwo Jima in one of the bloodiest campaigns of the Pacific War. During one attack against the Japanese, a shell dropped right upon his command post and Chevigny and several of his men were killed.

Wherever and whenever Texas and Notre Dame football men get together, the name of Lt. Jack Chevigny is recalled with honor and reverence, as a great player at Notre Dame, as a great Texas coach, and a true American hero.

1937–1946:
BIBLE THUMPERS

t is to Dana Xenophon Bible's eternal credit that he was able to become a man among men, born as he was into surroundings of a genteel nature. His father, Jonathan (his mother's name was Cleopatra), taught in the public schools of Jefferson City, Tennessee, and was a student of the classics. (Xenophon was a great Greek general.) He grew up in Jefferson City and played quarterback for Carson-Newman College. There was no football coach and the players furnished their own equipment. Bible was a great improvisor; he once scored on a play that he borrowed from a Rover Boys book.

Upon graduation, Bible became the football coach at Brandon Prep in Shelbyville, Tennessee. In those days coaches often permitted each other to play; in one game against Chattanooga Academy, Bible played halfback. Bald at twenty-one, he had to listen to the jeers of "grandpa" from the rival student section.

Even as a high school coach, Bible dogged the heels of the game's great coaches—Fielding Yost, Zuppke, Pop Warner, and Amos Alonzo Stagg—and he imitated some of their coaching techniques.

In 1912 Bible was endorsed by a Shelbyville minister to Mississippi College as Latin teacher, football coach, and athletic director. Bible presented himself to Dr. J. Provine, president of the college, who led him to the chapel and told the students, "Here is Mr. Bible, an applicant for our coaching post. Mr. Bible will now conduct chapel exercises."

Caught unawares, Bible read the Scriptures, talked about them, and asked Dr. Provine to give the benediction. Bible got the job.

Bible was only twenty-one. But success did not wait. In 1915, his third year at Mississippi, he beat bigger, tougher Tulane 20–8 and won the majority of his games. Then Texas A&M decided they needed a new coach to help head coach Jigger Harlan. Bible accepted the job and was assigned to

Dana X. Bible, who coached Nebraska to one of the most remarkable records from 1929 to 1936, winning 50 games and losing only 7, was named head football coach at Texas for the 1937 season. Bible signed a 10-year contract.

the freshman team. He proceeded to develop a frosh unit that could play on even terms with the varsity.

After his first year, Bible was promoted to head coach; he took a year out in 1918 as an Air Corps officer teaching flying although he hated the task. Bible returned to A&M in 1919 and his teams won ten games without a loss. All told, his 1917, '19, and '20 teams won 26 games against one defeat. Dana Bible did not have a losing season during his entire eleven years at A&M.

Joel Hunt, one of the Southwest's greatest halfbacks under Bible in 1927, called him "as confident as a banker, as astute as a schoolmaster." Hunt recalls in particular the aftermath of a Texas Christian-Texas A&M scoreless tie in 1927. The Aggies were tired, dirty, disgusted, and anxious to leave the stadium. Speed was not among the bus driver's attributes, and he was slow in driving the squad home. Hunt and several players asked him to step on it, and the driver drawled, "Take it easy, bub, we got all night."

Bible stepped in and shouted, "Get this darn thing going, or I'll jerk you out of your seat and take it in myself."

"We drove out in a hurry on to the championship," Hunt remembered.

From 1929 to 1936 Bible was head coach at Nebraska and his teams posted a remarkable record, winning 50 games, losing 15, and tying 7.

Early in 1937, Bible was approached by the Texas Athletic Council. The council had interviewed a number of coaches and athletic directors, and all agreed that Bible would be the ideal coach to boost the sunken football fortunes of the Longhorns, who had suffered two losing seasons in a row under Jack Chevigny.

But Bible hesitated at the Texas opportunity. He had the job of a lifetime at Nebraska. But he was struck by the great challenge at Austin. For one thing, he knew that he had to split state-of-Texas football material with six other Texas teams. At Nebraska he had the state all to himself.

Finally, after much talk, much discussion, and much soul-searching Bible accepted a ten-year contract, worth anywhere from $15,000 to $20,000 per year. That was more than twice what the school president made.

In short order, Bible hired on as his chief aides Blair Cherry, Bully Gilstrap, Clyde Littlefield, Ed Price, and Jack Gray. Cherry's Amarillo High School team had just won a third state championship and Gilstrap had been a constant winner in twelve years at Schreiner Institute, a junior college where a number of top Texas players had been developed and shipped to Austin.

Coach Bible's first squad was built around the all-around talents of the 185-pound, All-SWC Hughie Wolfe, who had been outstanding in two previous seasons. Wolfe had set a Texas record in the 1936 game against the undefeated Minnesota Gophers, flashing to a 95-yard TD through the entire Gopher defense for a sensational score. Bible also had some ten lettermen from the 1936 squad, including tackle Park Myers, center Glenn Jackson, ends Stan Neely and Ned McDonald, and Lew "Bullet" Gray, B. F. Bryan, and Charley Haas. But this group did not have the depth or experience to challenge such teams as LSU, Oklahoma, Rice, SMU, Baylor, TCU, and the Texas Aggies.

Coach Bible's first game against Texas Tech was a winning one, but Texas had to run up two touchdowns in the final period to clinch a 25–12 victory. LSU, with one of their strongest teams, shut out the Longhorns 9–0 in a night game that was mired in mud. Then Texas and Oklahoma tangled in a fierce defensive battle that wound up a 7–7 tie. A week later fullback Hugh Wolfe scored a touchdown and kicked a field goal for 10 points, but it was not enough as Arkansas took a 21–10 victory.

The rest of the season was grim. In a battle that was a bitter defensive struggle throughout, Rice took a 14–7 game from Texas in a game that was protested bitterly by the Longhorns. The game was tied at 7–7 in the final period. Rice took over and began to drive from the 35-yard line. On an 11-yard pass from halfback Ernie Lain to Frank Steen, Steen dove for the ball in the end zone and caught it just before the ball hit the turf. Texas players protested that Steen had trapped the ball. But the referee signaled a TD and that was the game. The following morning, photos in the *Austin*

American-Statesman showed Steen holding the ball slightly above ground. At any rate, the official verdict was a Rice TD and a 14–7 victory.

Frequent errors by the Texas halfbacks in a game against SMU paved the way to a 13–2 loss in a game at Dallas. Texas faced undefeated Baylor next. The Bears had won six games in a row and seemed headed for the Rose Bowl. In an amazing reversal of form, Texas upset Baylor 9–6 as Hugh Wolfe kicked a 26-yard field goal with the score 6–6 to shock Baylor with its first defeat.

Davey O'Brien, the sensational TCU quarterback, scored two touchdowns in a 14–0 win over Texas. It was the Longhorns' sixth defeat. TCU went on to beat Marquette in the first-ever Cotton Bowl.

In the season's finale, on Thanksgiving Day, the Texas Aggies scored in the first period to take a 7–0 lead before a large home crowd of more than 32,000 thrilled spectators. The game, like every other Texas-Texas Aggie game, was brutally fought, and after the Aggies scored their lone touchdown, they waged a cautious defensive battle and played for the breaks. Texas on the other hand was only able to reach the Aggies' 25-yard line, and could advance no further.

The defeat gave Coach Bible a 2-6-1 record, the first losing record in his coaching career.

Coach Bible surveyed his football prospects for the 1938 season, slowly shook his head in protest in a meeting with his coaches, and said, "Gentlemen, I can't wait until next year when we get the best of some 125 freshman prospects that you fellows have recruited from all over the state. But this year's pickings have been mighty slim. We'll just have to do it on guts and brains."

The Longhorns were especially short on experienced backfield performers. Only Bill Forney, a fine quarterback; halfback B. F. Bryan; and Walley Lawson and Bullet Gray, two solid fullbacks; had returned. Halfback Charley Haas and end Stan Neely were injured and would be lost for the greater part of the season.

Texas, who had never lost an opening game in its forty-six seasons of football, did just that in

1938. A Kansas Jayhawk team pounded out 19 points in the first half to take a 19–0 lead. In an amazing turnabout, Texas came out throwing the football in the second half, completing 27 of 46 passes for 3 touchdowns. But failure to convert after each touchdown cost Texas the game, as they lost a thrilling 19–18 struggle to Kansas.

In the opening home game, a week later, LSU's strong Tigers clawed their way to a 20–0 victory. Texas had outplayed the Tigers in the first half, which ended in a scoreless tie. In the second half, LSU's all-American, Ken Kavanaugh, led the way with a thrilling 65-yard pass play, and LSU pulled away to a 3-touchdown victory by a 20–0 score.

On their way to a Sugar Bowl championship, Oklahoma held Texas to just 9 yards rushing and punched out a 13–0 victory over the Horns. Against Arkansas in Little Rock a week later, Texas end John Peterson blocked an Arkansas punt, recovered the ball, and sped 48 yards for a Texas score. But Arkansas came back, and in rapid succession halfback Neil Martin scored 2 quick touchdowns and sparked them to a decisive 42–6 win.

Then a strong Rice team scored the winning touchdown with just three minutes to play in the game to wrap up a hard-fought 13–6 win. It was the fifth straight Longhorn loss. Once again, in a game against SMU, Texas failed to kick the conversion and dropped a 7–6 heartbreaker verdict to SMU. Then the big Baylor Bears, with one of their top offensive teams, decisioned Texas in another close battle, 14–3.

Davey O'Brien, one of the all-time passing stars who would win the Heisman that year, led a great TCU team on the way to the national championship into Austin. His marvelous aerial attack, with four bulletlike passes for four touchdowns, gave TCU a 28–6 win. This was the eighth loss for Texas, two more even than last year's sad total.

In the annual battle against Texas A&M, the Longhorns showed true defensive ability as they stopped the aggressive Aggies time after time, never permitting them inside the 20-yard line. At the same time A&M stopped the hard-charging Longhorns. At least five times Texas penetrated within A&M's 10-yard line, but Texas failed to score. Finally, in the fourth period, Nelson Puett and Wally Lawson pounded through A&M to the 10-yard line. Then, in successive smashes, Lawson banged in for the touchdown. Bill Forney, who had failed to make a conversion all season long, kicked the most important extra point in his young life. He booted the ball straight through the crossbars and Texas had a 7–0 lead.

But in the final two minutes of play misfortune struck the Longhorns. Texas was penalized for roughing, and the penalty was half the distance to the goal line. Then A&M kicked to the Texas 5-yard line and Texas was in trouble.

There were just twenty seconds to play as Lawson handed the ball to Bobby Moers behind the goal line. Moers was hit hard and fumbled the ball, and the Aggies recovered for a touchdown. The score was now 7–6, Texas.

A&M's Dick Todd, trying for the extra point, booted the ball, but Roy Baines leaped high into the air, blocked the kick, and preserved the 1-point win for Texas. It was one of the most thrilling games of any year.

When the final gun sounded the hometown crowd of more than 35,000 cheered the Longhorns for fully 15 minutes after the game had ended. They charged onto the field and carried the players and coaches into the locker rooms and began one of the most joyous Texas celebrations in years.

Although the win over their rivals was the only one of the season, it was more than enough for Coach Bible and his aides.

In 1936, in Jack Chevigny's second year at Texas, he had initiated several notable improvements in the overall football program. He began to film all games and had a small studio set aside so that his coaches could study the films. He also made arrangements to house the football squad in a dormitory. He believed that it would make for a more unified group and would help develop a new spirit of togetherness. The players loved living together as an elite group and it boosted their campus image.

In 1939 Coach Bible further improved the film department. He enlarged and added separate film and lecture rooms and rebuilt a dressing room. A new press box was built and a new four-story dormitory was erected to house all varsity athletes.

But the most important development to Bible was the marked improvement of the sophomore class, who would prove to be the nucleus for one of the most versatile and talented backfields that Texas had seen in years. Such sophs as Jack Crain, Pete Layden, Noble Doss, Gil Davis, Nelson Puett, Bullet Gray, and John Gill would provide Bible with a set of backs who would bring nightmares to rival coaches during the next three seasons. Other returnees included guard Chal Daniel, linebacker Mal Kutner, guard Ted Dawson, tackle Don Williams, and Shelby Buck and Ned McDonald, two fine backs.

All these veterans added up to the most promising group of players in several years. Coach Bible, in a talk to the alumni, said, "We might be a year or two at the most away from great things for this team. But I can see it on the gridiron and feel it in my bones that we've finally got the horses."

It didn't take Jack Crain a long time to impress the Florida Gators. In the first few minutes of play of the opening game of the 1939 season, Crain caught a beautiful 42-yard pass from Layden, skirted left end, and sprinted by two defenders for 14 yards and a TD. On the next sequence of Texas plays, Layden made it 12–0. That was the final score. In this, his first varsity game, Crain ran for 113 yards in 14 plays. It was a sensational debut for the youngster.

Texas then traveled to Madison, Wisconsin, for a game against a tough Wisconsin team. Once again it was Crain with a beautiful 35-yard broken-field dash for a touchdown. Then fullback Bob Patrick scored in the third period to give Texas an impressive 17–7 win.

In the third game of the season, the Oklahoma Sooners had what seemed like a comfortable 17–0 lead late in the fourth period. Suddenly Jack Crain broke loose on a buck-lateral pass and sprinted through the entire Oklahoma team for an electrifying 70-yard touchdown. Three minutes later, Crain again took a lateral pass and again dashed 70 yards for a second TD as the Dallas crowd went wild with excitement. But just as the Longhorns were beginning another drive for a third score, Oklahoma stopped Texas and smashed across another touchdown to take a 24–12 victory in an exciting game.

In the first SWC game of the season, Arkansas quickly scored as Kay Eakins, their fine back, led the Sooners on a 91-yard TD drive to take a 6–0 lead in the first period. Then Crain took over. He received a punt by Arkansas on his 10-yard line and darted in and out and over and around the Sooners for 85 yards. Patrick then smashed in from the 5-yard line. The kick was good and Texas had a 7–6 lead. Arkansas scored late in the third period and had a 13–7 margin.

Then the play of the year . . . There were just 30 seconds to play, and while half of the crowd of some 17,000 fans were leaving Memorial Stadium, there was sudden pandemonium. Fullback R. P. Patrick took the pass from center, faded back, then tossed a short pass to Crain. Jack darted to his left, stiff-armed two players, ran over two others, cut to his right, and sprinted 67 yards for a touchdown that tied the score 13–13. Frantic Texas fans

jumped the rails and surrounded the team, hoisting Crain on their shoulders. But the game was not over. Police cleared the field after some fifteen minutes. Then, as the crowd held their breath, Crain kicked the extra point and Texas had pulled out the most thrilling victory in years by a 14–13 margin. The win was hailed by Texas sportswriters as the Longhorns' return to glory.

A week after the Arkansas win Crain again sparked an attack that defeated Rice for the first time since 1933. In the first play from scrimmage, Crain bluffed an end run, cut back sharply off-tackle, and sprinted 80 yards for a touchdown. As Rice focused on Crain, Jack handed off to his other backs. Gilly Davis scored two touchdowns to give Texas a convincing 26–12 win over the Owls.

SMU snapped Texas' winning ways with a 10–0 win at Ownby Field as they concentrated on stopping Crain and held him to just 55 yards rushing. Baylor had thoroughly scouted Crain and the Longhorns, and they too concentrated on stopping him in a game in Waco a week later. They held him to just 59 yards rushing and took a hard-fought 20–0 win over Texas. After shutout losses at home to SMU and Baylor, Texas was ready for a comeback against TCU. Crain startled the big home

Halfback Gilly Davis (with ball) gets some great blocking from teammates Mal Kutner (*left*) and Chal Daniel (*right*) **as he picks up 30 yards on this play against Rice in the 1939 game won by Texas, 26–12.**

crowd by taking the ball in the opening moments of the game and racing 60 yards for a touchdown. But TCU soon took a 19–14 lead, and then Gillespie of TCU gave up two intentional safeties to make the score 19–18, TCU. Then Gilly Davis, after faking a handoff, sped 64 yards for a touchdown. Crain converted and Texas had taken a 25–19 thriller.

In the final game of the season, on Thanksgiving Day in College Station, the two teams battled in the rain and the mud. Texas' offense was slowed to a walk, and the Horns were beaten by an Aggies team on their way to an 11–0 season and the national championship. "It was pouring when we got off the train," said Crain, "and it poured throughout the game and we never could get started." The final score was 20–0.

Texas ended the season with a record of 5 wins and 4 losses, but both Texas rooters and coaches were already looking toward 1939. Several returning stars would be carrying the Texas colors to a victorious year.

As Bible approached his fourth season at Texas in 1941, it was apparent that his recruiting efforts would pay off. Eighteen lettermen reported for practice and they were joined by a group of outstanding freshman prospects. And as practice continued during the early fall weeks, Bible and his coaches discovered they had at least three full squads to complement the varsity team.

The varsity backfield consisted of halfbacks Jack Crain and Pete Layden, Texas' great one-two offensive punch; Noble Doss and quarterback Vern Martin; and a 200-pound strapping fullback, Spec Sanders. This quintet of backfield men gave Bible the finest all-around offensive backs that Texas had ever had. In Crain and Layden, Texas had two of the top broken-field speedsters, and both could also kick and pass the ball. Doss, Sanders, and Martin were hard-running, versatile backs who could play any backfield position. Linemen included such stars as Ted Dawson and Chal Daniel, two fine guards; Mal Kutner and Preston Flanagan at the ends; Don Williams and Bo Cohenour, tackles; Red Goodwin at center; and a host of fine substi-

tutes who could jump in at any position to fill in when necessary.

To open the season, Colorado's Buffaloes herded into Austin to oppose Texas. They were handed a battering as Texas scored almost at will for a 39–7 victory. Spec Sanders tore loose for 2 touchdowns, Crain and Layden scored, and Layden tossed passes to Doss for two additional TDs as the Longhorns showed great power in the air and on the ground.

At Bloomington, Indiana, Bo McMillan led his Indiana team against the Longhorns in a game that Texas dominated from start to finish. But they were only able to come away with a 13–6 victory. Texas fumbled the ball on six occasions, several within scoring distance, nevertheless they slowed Indiana's ground game to a halt.

At Dallas, Texas and Oklahoma engaged in another of their life-or-death struggles for three and a half periods with the Sooners out in front by 16–7. Bobby Harkins' magnificent 67-yard broken-field run had brought the Horns back into the battle. Late in the third period, Jackie Crain finally made his move as he took a buck-lateral pass and then dashed 65 yards to score. That made it 16–13 in favor of Oklahoma. With three minutes left to play, the Sooners fumbled the ball, and it was Texas' ball on the Oklahoma 10. Then it was up to Crain. Jack took the pass from center and flashed around left end for a touchdown, and Texas won a 19–16 thriller as the gun sounded to end the game.

In Little Rock a week later Arkansas concentrated on stopping Crain. But after a scoreless first period, Texas went on a rampage. They scored 21 points in the second period as Kutner, Layden, and Crain scored touchdowns to upset the Razorbacks 21–0. On a gridiron awash in rain, mud, and ankle-high water, Rice played their best game of the season to upset Texas 13–0. Jack Crain, injured against Arkansas, was only able to play a few minutes of the game.

A week later a strong SMU squad, keying on Crain, stopped him cold. Then SMU's strong aerial attack riddled Texas air space for a 21–13 win. Then the Baylor Bears strode into Austin to tangle with Texas, but this time Jackie Crain was in fine shape and led the Horns to a convincing 13–0 win. Crain and halfback Pete Layden put together an 80-yard TD drive in the final minutes of the game to give Texas their second score and the game.

In Fort Worth, Texas and TCU furiously battled each other throughout three periods to a 14–14 deadlock. Then Layden tossed a screen pass to Johnny Gill, who cut to his right, stiff-armed a couple of SMU defenders, and sped 40 yards for the winning TD. Final score: Texas 21, TCU 14.

Next up was A&M, with one of their greatest teams. They were led by all-Americans Jarrin' John Kimbrough and Marsh Robnett, and they carried a 19-game undefeated record into the battle, confident they would easily beat Texas and go on to the National Championship.

But Texas had other plans . . . plans that were carried out in the first two minutes of the battle.

In the first series of plays, Pete Layden tossed a great pass to Jack Crain for a 35-yard gain. Then, before the startled Aggies could regroup, Layden hurled a high, arching pass to Noble Doss. It seemed Doss would be unable to get to the ball, it was far out of his reach. But with an incredible effort Doss leaped high into the air, and with his back to his quarterback, made one of those unbelievable catches that have to be seen to be believed. He caught the ball and then was pulled down on the Aggies' 1-yard line. Then Layden smashed

Quarterback Pete Layden tossed a high arching pass to his halfback Noble Doss on the third play of the game against A&M. Doss made a remarkable over-the-shoulder catch and was downed on the A&M 2-yard line.

On the next play, Layden leaps over A&M defenders to score the game's only touchdown. The 7–0 loss to Texas cost the Aggies the national championship.

through for a touchdown. Crain kicked the extra point and it was 7–0 Texas.

The Aggies tried every conceivable play . . . on the ground . . . in the air . . . but just when it seemed they might score, Texas braced and held them. When the gun sounded they had defeated a great A&M team by a 7–0 score. The defeat cost the Aggies the national title and guaranteed Texas a fine year. Texas then defeated Florida in Gainesville 26–0 in the final game of the season. The win over Florida gave Texas an 8–2 record, its best mark since 1932.

Fullback Pete Layden had his greatest year as he led his team in rushing, passing, and scoring and was selected to the All-SWC Team.

As the German Army pounded France in 1941, President Franklin Roosevelt declared in a radio broadcast that the nation faced an unlimited national emergency, and he froze all German and Italian assets in the U.S. The State Department shut down all German consulates and Nazi propaganda organizations and signed a Lend-Lease Bill that gave Great Britain fifty vintage U.S. destroyers. The U.S. congress enacted the first peacetime selective service for the armed forces. 900,000 selectees between the ages of twenty and thirty-six would be taken each year.

At the University of Texas the mood was grim as it was announced that two varsity members of the Longhorn squad, Captain Red Goodwin, an outstanding center, and David Thayer, had entered the Army Air Corps as both had low draft numbers.

When Coach Bible issued his call for the 1941 season, he expected a good turnout of varsity members from the 1940 squad. When all the players had reported, he was delighted by the fact that eighteen varsity lettermen were included in a group of more than eighty-five freshman and assorted walk-ons reporting for the first week's sessions. Only four linemen from the previous year— Ted Dawson, Don Williams, Glenn Jackson, and Red Goodwin—did not return.

A Dallas sportswriter, commenting on the players reporting in 1941, said, "The talent on this year's squad is the very best I've ever seen at Texas."

Prospects were so high that the great Grantland Rice, in his famous syndicated column, wrote that "Texas looks to be the best not only in the Southwest, but I rate Texas over the Minnesota Gophers, who won 4 straight national titles."

For the opening game of the season against Colorado, Coach Bible selected the following starting team: The backs included quarterback Vern Martin, captain and fullback Pete Layden, and halfbacks Jackie Crain and Noble Doss. Mal Kutner and Preston Flanagan at the ends, tackles Don Cohenour and Julian Garrett, Chal Daniel and Buddy Jungmichel at the guard posts, and Henry Harkins at center rounded out the squad.

A major rule change went into effect that allowed a coach to freely substitute any number of players at any time in the game. Coach Bible was delighted with this rule, for this year he had so many first-class players that he could freely substitute entire teams.

In the opening game of the season on the road against Colorado, Texas started the first team in the first quarter. Then the second team played the second quarter. Texas had only a 13–6 lead at the half. In the second half of the game, with the first team in place, Pete Layden scored 2 touchdowns in five minutes and then sat out the rest of the game as Texas easily defeated Colorado 34–6.

LSU came into Austin confident of taking their third straight game from Texas, but the Longhorn varsity, playing on a muddy field, scored at will. Although they only played eighteen minutes each, Layden scored 2 touchdowns and gained 162 yards in 10 carries and Harkins tossed a 60-yard pass to John Max Minor for a score. Layden also dashed 65 yards for another score as Texas defeated LSU 34–0.

In the first two games of the season, the Longhorns' offense had displayed remarkable power in registering 68 points, while the defense held their opponents to just 6 points. The Horns were on their way.

Against Oklahoma, husky Jack Crain electrified the crowd when he sprinted 55 yards for a score. He galloped for another touchdown and picked up 144 yards in 10 carries as Texas buried Oklahoma 40–7.

The Dallas State Fair Committee issued a new trophy to the Horns after the game. The trophy, a bronze cowboy hat, would be issued on a rotating basis to the winner of each Oklahoma-Texas game.

Arkansas next trooped into Austin and slunk out after absorbing a 48–14 drubbing by the Longhorns. Jack Crain sparked Texas in the opening minutes of the game as he sprinted 51 yards for a score. Then Doss tore off a 41-yard run for a TD and the Longhorns had a 14–0 lead with the game just three minutes old. When the varsity was taken out of the game they turned over a 28–7 lead to the substitutes, who continued to batter Arkansas, scoring three more touchdowns to give Texas a 48–14 win.

Rice Institute had defeated Texas in 1940, but in this year of revenge, Texas showed no mercy. They battered the Owls with a barrage of touchdowns by Pete Layden and Jack Crain. Crain thrilled the crowd of more than 42,000 fans in Memorial Stadium by taking a Rice punt and winding his way to an 85-yard touchdown late in the game. Texas battered Rice 40–0.

The Mustangs of SMU had not lost to Texas since 1933 and they were confident they could handle Texas on their own turf in 1941. But Crain and Layden, packing the biggest one-two punch since Jack Dempsey, put the crusher on SMU with one TD after another. Final score: Texas 34, SMU 0.

The win over SMU moved Texas into the number-one spot in the nation in a poll of the country's top sportswriters. After the game SMU Coach Matty Bell told a group of sportswriters that Texas was the greatest team in the SWC and one of the all-time great teams he had ever seen. The Longhorns had crushed their first six opponents by an average score of 38–5.

In the seventh game of the season, with injuries to Pete Layden, Mal Kutner, Noble Doss, and Julian Garrett, Texas faced a grim, determined Baylor squad coached by Frank Kimbrough, brother of John Kimbrough, A&M's all-American. Kimbrough, in his first year as a head coach, had scouted Texas for weeks, and he had set up a unique

defense to stop Texas' great runners, Crain and Layden. The stage was set for one of the biggest games of the year.

The injuries to four of his leading players forced Coach Bible to start Rob Harkins at fullback, Fritz Lobpries at halfback, Wally Scott at end, and Zuehl Conoly at tackle, and the subs were not able to deliver as Texas failed to make a single first down in the first period of play. Additionally, two fumbles forced Texas to their own goal line to stop the Baylor threat. They did, with a great stand in both instances.

In the final minute of the first half, Texas recovered a poor Baylor punt and fullback Roy McKay bulled across the Baylor goal line. Crain kicked the extra point and it was 7–0, Texas.

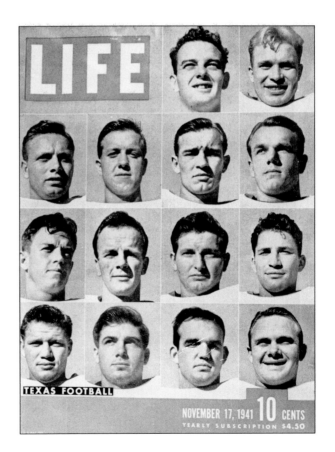

After Texas had piled up double-digit wins against six of the nation's top teams, *Life* featured the Longhorns' varsity on its cover, calling the Texas team "National Champs."

Malcom Kutner (80), Texas all-American end in 1941, handles the blocking for Pete Layden (31) on this play.

In the second half both teams battled up and down the field and threatened to score on several occasions, but failed. With but four minutes to play, Texas punted to Baylor on the Bears' 25-yard line, and the Bears mounted an offense led by halfback Kit Kittrell that reached the Texas 19-yard line. There Kittrell passed to end Bill Coleman and with thirty seconds to play Coleman scored. Baylor made the extra point and the game ended in a 7–7 tie.

"The week following the Baylor game was gloom and doom days on the campus," said Coach Bible later. "We had been knocked out. We should have gotten off the floor and started punching back. But we didn't. We didn't get ready for another tough battle against TCU and they were loaded with great talent and were on top of their game."

The week before the TCU game, *Life* magazine featured the Texas football team as the cover story and detailed the great stars in a ten-page treatment. Faces of the 14 Longhorn starters adorned the cover and there was great excitement on the campus over the magazine, as it praised Texas as "the nation's greatest football team." But

like Cinderella, Texas failed to come home before midnight.

TCU came into Austin amid all the excitement and scored a touchdown just as the half ended to tie Texas 7–7.

The teams came out for the second half like two prizefighters sparring for an opening which never seemed to appear—until about two minutes to play. Then TCU halfback Emory Nix raced 34 yards to Texas' 24-yard line. After a Texas penalty Nix tossed a bullet pass to Joe Van Hall, who drove in for a TD from the 19-yard line. The kick was good and TCU had a stunning 14–7 upset victory.

After the 7–7 tie with Baylor the defeat cost Texas a bid for the national championship and plunged the campus into even greater gloom. But after the sobbing had subsided, Coach Bible and his aides prepared to face the ultimate test—the annual game against Texas A&M at College Station. Homer Norton's squad was undefeated and edging toward the national championship that earlier had seemed to belong to Texas.

A crowd of more than 40,000 fans wild with excitement thrilled to one of the great college games of the year. The two great teams smashed into each other with unabated fury. There was no score until the final minute of the first half, when Jack Crain booted a field goal from the 19-yard line to give Texas a 3–0 lead as the teams trotted back into their respective locker rooms.

"In the second half," said Jackie Crain later, "it was a different story. They were watching my every move and three guys were on me all the time. So on the kickoff in the second half, I handed the ball to Doss at the 20-yard line and Noble, with the aid of a couple of great blocks, was not stopped until he hit the 20-yard line." Several plays later, Crain blasted in for a TD from the 9-yard line and Texas was off and running. They didn't stop until they had three more scores and a 23–0 victory. It was one of the most impressive wins of the year for the Longhorns.

Texas had nursed the hope that they would be invited to the Rose Bowl, but while they waited for an invitation, A&M accepted a Cotton Bowl game bid with Alabama. Then the Longhorns rejected an

Orange Bowl bid and then lost a Sugar Bowl bid. Texas was infuriated by the lack of interest from the Rose Bowl Committee, who finally picked Duke. Texas flatly stated that they were not interested in "any bowl bid."

In the last game of the season, against Oregon, Texas took out their frustrations and battered Oregon with a barrage of 10 touchdowns in a shattering 71–7 victory. Texas scored two touchdowns in every period, four in the final period, to win in a walk. Jackie Crain and Sanders scored twice, and Kutner, Doss, Layden, Minor, Martin, and R. L. Harkins also ran for TDs in the scoring orgy.

Texas finished the season with a marvelous 8-1-1 record, the best since Clyde Littlefield's 1930 team with an identical record. But it was disappointing after the promise of the first six games.

Just twenty-four hours after the dominating win over Oregon, the joy and happiness on the Texas campus was suddenly shattered. News of the Japanese sneak attack on Pearl Harbor plunged the entire nation into mourning for the more than 3000 U.S. servicemen killed in that treacherous attack.

On the Texas campus students and professors talked of nothing else but the attack on Pearl Harbor and what the U.S. response would be. They did not have long to wait, for several hours after the attack, President Roosevelt broadcast the answer: "The United States is at war with the Empire of Japan."

Members of the Texas football team and other athletes were already lined up at various service enlistment offices. Before the week ended, most of the athletes had decided on their branch of service.

The war hit home in 1942 as the United States buckled down to the grim task of recovering from the blow at Pearl Harbor and of holding the Japanese in the Pacific while sending aid to Britain and Russia. Coaches and players went off to war. Freshmen had to be called up to help man the depleted varsity football ranks. Dim-out regulations curtailed practice sessions under floodlights. Coaching staffs were shorthanded in many cases.

Despite the restrictions football carried on full steam. Army and Navy officers came to its support after President Roosevelt had given the green light to baseball. They stressed football's value in conditioning young men for the task of hitting the enemy hard, and in inculcating teamwork and the leadership required of officer personnel. The continuation of major sports was also a big boost to the country's morale.

At Texas, Coach Bible was faced with replacing most of the varsity with a group of rugged, hard-

The 1941 Texas team ended the season with a most impressive 8–1–1 record.

hitting men. In the backfield Bible had Jackie Field, Roy McKay, Ken Matthews, and Max Minor; Spot Collins handled the quarterback post. In the line, Co-captains Wally Scott and Joe Schwarting were the ends; Stan Mauldin and Zuehl Connoly played the tackle post; Harold Fischer and Jack Freeman were the guards; and Audrey Gill and Jack Sachse were the centers.

In the opening game of the season against the Corpus Christi Naval Air Station Texas rained 6 touchdowns upon the heads of the Navy fliers and pounded out a 40–0 win. Every member of the squad participated in the game. A week later, Texas unleashed all their weapons against a hapless Kansas State team as they trampled KSU by a 64–0 margin. The Longhorns rammed over 10 touchdowns to easily win their second game of the year. In the third game of the season, talented all-American quarterback Otto Graham, who would go on to become one of the NFL's greatest quarterbacks, led his Northwestern University team to a tough 3–0 win over Texas.

Then, in an abrupt about-face, Texas defeated Oklahoma 7–0 in a struggle that saw each team's offensive weapons throttled by superior defense. In

Coach Dana Bible discusses strategy with his backs. *Left to right:* **Max Minor, Jackie Field, Harold Collins, and Roy Dale McKay—as the Longhorns prepare for their Cotton Bowl match against Georgia Tech on January 1, 1943.**

Great blocking by Texas' Stan Mauldin (77) paves the way for halfback Roy McKay as McKay tears off a nice gain against Rice in a 1942 game. Texas won 12–7.

the final moments of the game Roy McKay flipped a 30-yard pass to Ken Matthews for a TD. Then Matthews kicked the field goal for the extra point to give Texas the victory.

At Little Rock, Arkansas, a crowd of more than 22,000 packed the stadium to watch Arkansas against Texas. It was a game that was expected to be a close, hard-fought tussle. But on the second play of the game, halfback Roy McKay broke loose for a 65-yard touchdown gallop. After that tremendous sprint, Arkansas was too shocked to respond. Texas poured on 6 additional TDs for a 47–6 rout.

A week later Rice did not make a single first down in the first three periods of play and lost to the Longhorns by a 12–7 margin. The score was misleading, for Texas was far superior in every offensive department. Texas ran up some 325 yards rushing to Rice's 110 yards.

In Austin, SMU was defeated by Texas 21–7 as halfback Jackie Field broke away for two touch-

The Texas "brain trust" on the sidelines during the A&M game in 1942. *Left to right*: Head Coach Dana Bible with assistants Blair Cherry and Bully Gilstrap.

downs. It was the Longhorns' first win over SMU in Austin in ten years. The defense proved to be the outstanding factor against the Baylor Bears a week later as the Longhorns held the Bears to just 21 yards rushing and pounded out a 20–0 victory. It was the seventh win in 8 games for Texas.

The TCU game in Fort Worth would be a battle for undisputed possession of first place in the SWC. Texas, severely battered by injuries to key players, got off to a fast start and held TCU scoreless for the first half, then scored a touchdown to lead 7–0 going into the fourth period. But two quick touchdowns by TCU in the final minutes of play meant the difference, and Texas lost to TCU by a 13–7 margin. It was their first SWC loss of the year.

Austin was the site of the final game of the year, against the Texas Aggies. Texas knew they had to defeat A&M to win their first SWC title since 1930 and they proceeded to throw up the toughest, fiercest defense A&M had met all season long. The Texas defense permitted just three first downs in the entire game. Then, with the score Texas 6, A&M 0, Aggie halfback Barney Welch returned a punt 70 yards for a TD. It was a 6–6 game going

into the final four minutes of play. Furious drives by Roy McKay and Jackie Field moved the ball to the A&M 40-yard line. Another drive by Field and then a 30-yard pass, McKay to Field, and the ball was on the Aggies' 12-yard line. Field broke through the Aggie line on the next play and scored the winning TD to give the Longhorns a hard-fought 12–6 triumph.

Immediately after the win over A&M, the players voted to accept the Cotton Bowl's invitation to play Georgia Tech, the No. 2 team in the nation.

On New Year's Day, the Cotton Bowl was host to a crowd of more than 36,000 spectators. On the first series of Georgia Tech plays, Jack Freeman and Harold Fischer tackled Tech fullback Pat McHugh and knocked the ball loose, and Joe Schwarting recovered for Texas. Several runs brought Texas inside the Tech 10-yard line; from there Jackie Field drove over the tackle for 5 yards to give Texas a first down on the Tech 4-yard line. Roy McKay lobbed a short pass to Max Minor, and Minor scrambled across the goal line for the first Texas TD. Field kicked the extra point to make it 7–0 Texas. Texas

Jackie Field is in the clear and races for 61 yards and a touchdown to beat Georgia Tech in the Cotton Bowl, 14–7.

threatened to score several times, but each time they were within range of the goal line, Tech's defense held and they took the ball over on downs.

In the third quarter, Tech punted, and Jackie Field took the ball on the Texas 40-yard line. He dodged and twisted and cut away from several Tech tacklers and sped across the gridiron for 61 yards and the second Texas score. Now it was 14–0, Texas.

Late in the fourth period Tech began a drive through the air and reached the Texas 5-yard line. Then Dave Eldridge took a handoff and raced over the goal line for Tech's first score, 14–7, Texas.

Georgia Tech's offense perked up once more and Ed Prokop, a new quarterback for Tech, shot a 35-yard pass to Tech Captain Jack Marshall, who got down to the 9-yard line. Now the crowd was standing and screaming for a score. But here the Texas defense stiffened, held Tech's frantic charges into the line, and took the ball over on downs. The game ended with Texas the winner, 14–7.

The Longhorns' brilliant defensive line, headed by Joe Schwarting, Stan Mauldin, Hal Fischer, Audrey Gill, Jack Freeman, Zuehl Conoly, and Wally Scott, had stopped the potent Tech offense

time after time. Texas had one of its greatest seasons with a Cotton Bowl championship and an SWC title.

The 9–2 season was another fine one for Coach Bible, and in his honor there were banquets, dinners, and father-and-son affairs that kept him busy around the clock.

In 1943 college football was on a wartime footing. A number of players on the Texas varsity had already entered the various services. The only lettermen reporting for Coach Bible's practice sessions were end Joe Parker, halfback Joe Magliolo, and halfback Ralph Park. Freshman and Navy V-5 players made up the balance of the squad, including Frank Butler, a guard; Ralph Ellsworth, a halfback; Harlan Wetz, a 250-pound kicker; and a tackle, Jim Plyler. At center was Kiefer Marshall, and at end was Clyde Harville. Several of Austin High School's championship team of 1942, Bobby Coy Lee, George McCall, and Jim Canady, also joined the team.

In the season's opener at Austin, Texas ran roughshod over a Blackland Army Air Force team by a 65–6 romp. But Southwestern, which had

Coach Bible talks things over with his 1943 captains. *Left to right:* Joe Magliolo, Ralph Park, and Joe Parker.

seven former members of the 1942 Texas varsity in their lineup as Marine trainees, took a hard-fought 14–7 win over the inexperienced Longhorns. The Oklahoma Sooners had one of their better teams, but the Longhorns took a 13–7 win as Bobby Lee connected on a 65-yard pass play to halfback Ralph Ellsworth for the winning touchdown.

Arkansas rambled into Austin for their game against Texas and the Longhorns ran up a 14–0 lead by the end of the third period. At this point, Coach Bible inserted his reserve team and they poured it on, scoring 20 points for a 34–0 win. Then, in the fifth game of the year, the Rice Owls came to Austin and were handed an unmerciful 58–0 pounding. Texas ran up 9 touchdowns in administering the worst beating to Rice since the Rice-Texas game in 1915. Ralph Ellsworth scored two touchdowns for the Longhorns as Coach Bible utilized every man on the Texas roster in this game. One week later SMU was easily beaten 20–0 as the Longhorns scored their third straight shutout. Jim Callahan scored twice and Ralph Ellsworth tossed a great 35-yard TD pass to George McCall for another score.

TCU trotted into Austin for their annual battle against Texas and stunned the Longhorns by

scoring a TD in the first minute of play to take a 7–0 lead. But Texas quickly broke out in a scoring frenzy as Callahan tossed passes to Ellsworth and Harville for touchdowns, and then followed with two more touchdowns on the ground to give Texas a 46–7 win over the Frogs. This game saw the debut of Billy "Rooster" Andrews, Texas' four-foot-eleven, 120-pound football manager and the team's special drop-kicking expert. Andrews, who wore Jack Crain's No. 99 jersey, drop-kicked two extra points in the game. TCU Coach Dutch Meyer was furious, thinking the act a deliberate humiliation by Bible.

At College Station, Texas met Texas A&M in the annual Thanksgiving Day game, and it appeared as though Texas would run away with the game scoring 13 points in the first period. (The 13th point was an extra point kicked by Andrews, inserted into the game in defiance of a caustic Forth Worth newspaper column.) But the Aggies struck back with two quick touchdowns to tie the score at 13–13. Just before the half ended halfback Ralph Park scooted 35 yards for a TD after taking a lateral, and then Texas scored their fourth touchdown just as the final gun sounded for a 27–13 triumph.

The win over the Aggies was the seventh win of the season for Texas and gave Texas its second

Texas' "Blonde Bomber," Bobby Layne.

straight SWC championship. Texas was again invited to the Cotton Bowl. Their opponent was the Randolph Field team, headed by star halfback Glenn Dobbs, who would go on to a great NFL career as a player and coach.

On New Year's Day the weather was so cold and rainy that the players had difficulty holding on to the ball. Both teams were handicapped on the ground and in the air.

In the first period, after several incomplete passes, Glenn Dobbs passed to his end Tex Aulds, and Aulds drove in for a Randolph Field score. In the second period Texas halfback Ralph Ellsworth tossed a 35-yard pass to end George McCall, who raced in for the Longhorns' score. The play was good for 35 yards and it was the only pass that

Texas completed all day. But it was good enough to tie the score at 7–7 and the game ended with no further scoring.

Texas finished the season with a 7-1-1 record and won its second consecutive SWC championship. Joe Parker, Jim Callahan, Ralph Ellsworth, Joe Magliolo, and Frank Butler were named to the All-SWC Team.

A slim, well-built, six-foot, 170-pound freshman entered Texas on a baseball scholarship in 1944 and when he got his chance to pitch for the Texas baseball team, he was nothing short of sensational. He won game after game. As a matter of fact, he never lost a game in the SWC in his four years at Texas.

Utilizing a tantalizing curve ball and marvelous control, the kid established an SWC record, winning 28 games and losing none. In his final year at Texas, the young pitcher led Texas to the school's first NCAA tournament with a team that consisted of such future major league stars as Jackie Jensen and Randy Jackson. The kid lost only 7 games in the 46 he pitched for Texas.

At Highland Park High, in Dallas, the kid, Bobby Layne, had been a baseball, basketball, and football star, and after he teamed with his buddy, the great Doak Walker, Highland Park's football team reached the State Finals in 1942 and '43.

In 1944, Layne entered Texas after Coach Blair Cherry had taken over as baseball coach. "It was through my association with Mr. Cherry and Mr. Bible that I decided to go out for football," said Layne.

Layne was an immediate star in his first scrimmage in 1944, passing to end Hub Bechtol for big gains. In his first practice sessions Layne so impressed Coach Bible that the boyish-looking seventeen-year-old with the arm of a Hercules became the starting fullback in Bible's single-wing offense.

That first year Bobby began a friendship with tough, high-spirited Billy "Rooster" Andrews, "the All-American Water Boy."

One night in 1942 some of the more playful football players at Texas—Jack Crain, Roy McKay, Bo Cohenour, and Buddy Jungmichel—got Billy

Rooster Andrews, Texas' all-American team manager from 1944 to 1947.

out of his bed around midnight. They demanded that he climb a tree near Clark Field to bring down a rooster named Walter perched on a tree limb. They didn't tell Billy that Walter was a fierce fighting cock and that they had planned to take him to Elgin to enter the cockfights. Billy climbed up the tree and with one hand, the other holding a flashlight, attempted to get Walter. In the struggle both bird and Billy fell from the tree. "I hit the ground, smashed my arm, scratched myself all over. Then those other guys took the bird to Elgin for the cockfights and made $300," remembered Billy.

On the football field, the feisty Andrews would don a helmet and grab his water buckets, which led the press to call him "the All-American

Water Boy." Andrews was full of fun and got a million laughs from the team because of his antics.

"But you forget his smallness pretty quick," said Layne. "And he was such an outstanding dropkicker and Coach Bible used him in a number of games and he would kick a field goal with ease. Before long," said Layne, "you'd forget his size. He became as tall as you. He was one hell of a guy, and the best roommate I ever had."

In the season's opening game, his first at Texas, Bobby Layne wasted no time in establishing himself. He threw two touchdown passes in the game against Southwestern and led Texas to a 20–0 win. Randolph Field, who had former Texas stars Pete Layden and Jack Freeman in their lineup, easily defeated Texas 42–6 in the second game as Layne sat out with an ankle injury.

In the third game of the season Layne was in the backfield against Oklahoma, and he passed for two touchdowns to beat the Sooners 20–0. Bobby also became a receiver, as he combined with his pal, Rooster Andrews, on a fake kick play. Rooster, who had entered the game to kick an extra point, faked the kick, then faded back and tossed a perfect aerial to Layne, who was wide open in the end zone.

"In the next game against Arkansas Bobby had a temperature of 102. He had tonsilitis and was weak," said Andrews. "So all he did was scramble for 44 yards and a TD. Then he tossed passes to Bechtol and Anderson and kicked the conversion for all the points in a 19–0 win over the Razorbacks."

A week later in Houston, with Rice bottling up Layne at every opportunity, the Longhorns could not come up with a single scoring play and lost to Rice in a stunning upset, 7–0. In the next game against SMU, with an injured Layne playing just the first quarter, Texas defeated SMU 34–7 as Bobby tossed passes to Hub Bechtol and Earle Anderson for scores.

Slowed down to a walk by a knee injury, Layne led the Longhorns to an 8–0 lead the next week over Oklahoma State. But Oklahoma State rallied to score twice in the final period to take a 13–8 win, scoring the winning TD as the gun sounded to end the game. Next, against a tough

TCU team in a game that developed into a kicking duel, TCU blocked a Texas punt, recovered the ball in the end zone, and took a 7–0 lead. With fifteen seconds to play, Layne, who was battered by injuries and could hardly move, lofted a desperation pass to Anderson from the TCU 45-yard line. Anderson leaped into the air, grabbed the ball, and fell across the goal line. It was 7–6, TCU. But Texas missed the conversion, and TCU took a 7–6 victory.

In the final game against Texas A&M, Layne scampered for 9 yards and a touchdown and a 6–0 victory in College Station on Thanksgiving Day.

The win over Texas A&M gave the Longhorns a 5–4 season. It was the poorest season for the Longhorns since 1939, when they had an identical record. But it was only a prelude to great seasons to come.

Hub Bechtol was named to the all-American team by the Associated Press.

On March 16, 1945, in the South Pacific, Iwo Jima fell to the U.S. Marines after thirty-six days of bloody fighting. More than 4000 Marines were killed, including Lieutenant Jack Chevigny, former Texas coach, as he led his company in an attack against a Japanese stronghold.

On April 12, President Franklin D. Roosevelt died in Warm Springs, Georgia, and was succeeded by Harry S. Truman. One month later Germany surrendered to the Allies after six years of fighting.

The surrender was signed in General Dwight D. Eisenhower's headquarters in Rheims, France. On August 6, the U.S. dropped an atomic bomb on Hiroshima. Three days later another A-bomb was dropped on Nagasaki, and on August 14 the Japanese surrendered to General Douglas MacArthur.

In the sports world Rocky Graziano was named boxer of the year after scoring five straight knockouts. Southern California defeated Tennessee in the Rose Bowl, 25–0. Army, coached by Red Blaik, won the National Championship. The New York Yankees were sold to Larry MacPhail and Dan Topping, and Army defeated Navy 32–13 in their annual battle.

And in Austin, Texas, Coach Dana Bible suffered the loss of his triple-threat halfback, Bobby Layne. Along with his boyhood friend, the great Doak Walker, he had joined the U.S. Merchant Marine.

Bible did have an abundant supply of lettermen back and a great group of freshmen and several discharged servicemen. But his almost impossible task was to find a back to take Bobby Layne's place. What he found was a slim, speedy 160-pound youngster named Fred Brechtel who had played at Rice and Southwestern. Brechtel fitted right in and led the Longhorns to a 13–7 win over the Bergstrom Field team. Then, with Brechtel handling the T-formation, Texas blitzed Southwestern

In 1945, halfback Byron Gillory (49) was sensational against Oklahoma, completing 9 of 10 attempts. Against Arkansas, Gillory passed for two scores then ran for a third.

46–0. A week later, Texas Tech was baffled by the T-formation as Max Bell tossed two long passes, a 48-yarder and another for 52 yards, for touchdowns to end Charlie Tatom. Art Sweet broke off a dazzling 75-yard run for another score to give Texas its third win of the year.

In a typically rugged battle against Oklahoma, 140-pound speedster Byron Gillory completed 9 of 10 passes, one of them to all-American Hub Bechtol for a touchdown. But in the final period Oklahoma led 7–6 until Gillory sparked a 70-yard drive that ended with George Graham scoring a TD. That gave Texas a thrilling 12–7 victory as the gun sounded ending the game.

Against the Arkansas Razorbacks in Little Rock, Byron Gillory's exceptional passing to end Dale Schwartzkopf and Hub Bechtol gave the Horns two touchdowns. To top off his heroics, Gillory ran for another score and passed for two additional long gains that led to two touchdowns and an eventual 34–7 win over Arkansas.

The Rice Owls, underdogs in their game against Texas, played their best game of the season as they outhustled the Horns in the first period. The Owls recovered a Texas fumble and scored a touchdown for a 7–0 halftime lead. In the fourth period, with only four minutes left in the game, Brechtel passed to Hub Bechtol for a touchdown to bring the Horns within one point of Rice. But Texas missed the extra point and Rice came away with a stunning 7–6 win.

The next game for Texas was with one of their great rivals, Southern Methodist and it was the beginning of another great rivalry—between two former pals who played together at Highland Park High in Dallas. Bobby Layne had been discharged from the Merchant Marine just a few days before the game, and so had Doak Walker, who had decided to attend SMU.

Now they were going to battle each other as SMU and Texas met at Ownby Field that sunny day in November.

The teams were greeted by a crowd of more than 23,000 fans, many of whom had watched Layne and Walker play for nearby Highland Park. The teams battled on even terms in the first period.

But Walker broke loose in the second period for a 30-yard touchdown sprint and kicked the extra point to give SMU a 7–0 lead. Then Bobby Layne brought Texas back with a 29-yard scoring pass to end Dale Schwartzkopf. But he missed the extra point and the score was 7–6, SMU. Late in the third period, Layne intercepted a pass thrown by his pal Walker and was finally pulled down on the Texas 30-yard line. Layne then took charge of the offense and drove 70 yards, the final score coming on a Layne pass to Peppy Blount that gave Texas a hard-fought 12–7 win.

"We didn't talk to each other during the game," said Walker. "But after the game we were sitting in my parents' home telling each other how well we had done."

Bobby Layne had been injured in the SMU game and didn't start against Baylor, but he came off the bench to engineer a 75-yard TD drive that tied the game 14–14 in the third period. Then a Baylor fumble and recovery by Texas gave the Horns the ball on the Bears' 15-yard line, and fullback George Graham smashed in for the winning TD, 21–14. Layne again starred for the Longhorns in the next week's game against TCU. Still hurting, he threw just 5 passes. But 2 of the passes went for touchdowns as Texas pounded TCU for a 20–0 victory.

On Thanksgiving Day in College Station, the Horns stunned a favored Texas Aggie eleven in the first few minutes of their big game. Fullback Ralph Ellsworth took the ball from Layne on a reverse and shot to his right. Then, as the Aggie line shifted to stop him, he again reversed his field. He was out in the clear and sped 18 yards for a touchdown. In the third period with the score tied 7–7, John Balentine of A&M kicked a field goal and A&M had a 10–7 lead. Charlie Tatom then recovered an A&M fumble on the 8-yard line and Graham blasted through for a touchdown to give Texas breathing room and a 13–10 edge. In the final period, Bobby Layne put his magic to work and tossed a 20-yard pass to Bechtol for another Texas score.

Then, to write finis to A&M, Layne and Rooster Andrews uncorked their special pet play again. Rooster went in to kick the extra point and

Halfback Ralph Ellsworth (with ball) breaks away for a big gain in the Cotton Bowl game against Missouri on January 1, 1946. Hub Bechtol (81), Texas' all-American end, gets ready to block for Ellsworth.

took the pass from center, but just as he dropped his leg to kick he faded back, sighted a wide-open Layne in the end zone, and tossed a pretty pass for the two-point conversion. The crowd howled with rage. Final score: 20–10, Texas.

With a record of 9–1 Texas was invited to the Cotton Bowl against Missouri. The Tigers sported a 6–4 record and, utilizing a split-T offense, had swept by all their Big Six opponents. But they were out of their class against Texas. This was one of those games that fans talk about forever, for it was Bobby Layne at his magical best. Layne scored 4 touchdowns, running for three and then taking an unbelievable pass of 50 yards from Ellsworth for a

Bobby Layne completes a pass to Hub Bechtol for a long gain in the Cotton Bowl against Missouri. The "Blonde Bomber" was at his magical best, scoring 4 touchdowns as Texas routed Missouri, 40–27 in 1946.

Texas end Max Baumgardner leaps to snag a 35-yard pass from Bobby Layne against Colorado as the Horns swamped the Buffaloes, 76–0, in 1946.

fourth score. Bobby also kicked four extra points and tossed touchdown passes of 48 and 25 yards. When the game was over, Texas was out in front by a 40–27 margin. Bobby Layne had completed a total of 11 out of 12 passes for 158 yards—and the incomplete pass was dropped by his receiver. It was one of the all-time great individual achievements in Texas football history.

Texas finished with a sterling 10–1 record, 5–1 in the Southwest Conference, and all-American Hub Bechtol, center Dick Harris, and the already legendary Bobby Layne were named All-SWC. Coach Dana Bible, winner of three of the last four SWC titles, announced prior to the Cotton Bowl game that the next season, 1946, would be his final year as Texas' football coach.

Dana X. Bible began his tenth and final year in 1946 as the Texas football coach. He did so with the knowledge that he had taken over a failing football program from Coach Jack Chevigny in 1936 that had lost 14 games in the three years that Chevigny had coached and by 1940 had turned the Texas program into a powerhouse that ranked with the nation's greatest teams. Now, with such outstanding stars as Bobby Layne, Hub Bechtol, Dick Harris, Max Baumgardner, Dale Schwartzkopf,

Oklahoma's star quarterback Darrell Royal breaks away from Texas' Spot Collins on a punt return for a 35-yard gain as Texas defeated Oklahoma 20–13 in 1946.

In pre-game ceremonies honoring Coach Bible before the Texas-Texas A&M game in 1946, Texas players and coaches at attention include (*left to right*): tackle Harlan Wetz, Coach Bible, Coach Littlefield, back Ralph Ellsworth, back Tom Landry, guard Charlie Jungmichel, and guard Paul Tracy.

Audrey Gill, and Byron Gillory, and a talented freshman group of more than 125 ex-high school stars, Bible was ready to meet the challenges of the strongest teams in the Southwest Conference.

In the opening game of the season at Austin, Texas met and defeated with ease the tough Missouri Tigers by a 42–0 score. Texas opened the game by marching right through the Tigers for 65 yards and a TD in only five plays. On the next sequence of plays Bobby Layne tossed a pass to Jim Canady that covered 82 yards and another TD. Then, in a parade of touchdowns, Ellsworth sprinted 52 yards; Frank Guess scored on a 48-yard dash; and sophomore Tom Landry skirted for a 30-yard TD, as the 15,000 Texas fans were thrilled by the speed and suddenness of the Texas power offense.

In the second game of the season the Colorado Buffaloes were annihilated under a dizzying avalanche of 8 touchdowns on the way to a 76–0 drubbing. Every man on the squad was used by Coach Bible as Colorado simply was outclassed. Then Texas ran through, over, and around Oklahoma A&M for an astounding 54–6 win. Bobby Layne scored three TDs in the stampede.

In a close, hard-fought battle a week later against an outstanding Oklahoma team, Bobby Layne and company pulled out a 20–13 win in a game that saw halfback Darrell Royal of Oklahoma almost pull victory out from the jaws of defeat with several splashy runs that put the Sooners in scoring range a number of times. But a 75-yard drive capped by a reverse play gave Jim Canady an opportunity to score, and he broke through the Sooners' line for the touchdown that won the game for Texas. It was the Longhorns' seventh straight win over Oklahoma.

Texas was ranked among the nation's top five teams after a 20–0 victory over Arkansas that saw Bobby Layne toss passes of 50 and 47 yards to Hub Bechtol for touchdowns to give the Longhorns their fifth straight win.

In their sixth game, Texas lost to a star-studded Rice team (that would finish 9–2) by an 18–13 margin in one of the most bitterly fought games of the season. The teams battled to a 6–6 tie at halftime. Then Rice scored two touchdowns to give them an 18–6 lead late in the game. But Longhorn Ray Jones scored to make it 18–13, Rice. Texas held Rice and got the ball back with seconds to play, but Bobby Layne's last pass was intercepted just as the gun sounded. It was Texas' first loss of the season.

In the game against SMU the following week, Layne's tremendous pass of more than 60 yards to Jim Canady and Perry Samuels' brilliant 39-yard dash in the final quarter gave Texas a 19–3 win over SMU. The following week at Baylor, Texas was behind by a 7–0 margin when Layne uncorked a 40-yard toss to Canady that closed the score to 7–6, Baylor. Then a listless Texas team suddenly came to life. Layne kicked a field goal and then Jack Halfpenny and Lew Holder scored TDs and the Longhorns had a 22–7 win.

Texas was favored to easily defeat TCU in their game played at Forth Worth. The Horned Frogs had won only one game the entire season. But the Frogs played inspired ball and centered their outstanding pass defense on effectively stopping Bobby Layne, and TCU upset Texas 14–0. It was the first time this year that Texas had failed to score a point. The defeat cost the Horns the SWC championship as Rice and Arkansas battled each other for the crown.

It was Coach Bible's tenth and last year at Texas, and in a pre-game celebration prior to the Thanksgiving Day game against A&M, "The Little General" was given a standing ovation and cheered for fully five minutes.

As the game began the tough Texas defense prevailed throughout the first half and the Aggies were able to generate just 27 yards offensively. Texas moved through the air, on the ground, and around the ends as Bobby Layne passed 51 yards, 75 yards, and 47 yards for crowd-pleasing touchdowns and added a field goal. Texas pounded A&M for a 24–7 victory in the final game of Coach Bible's ten-year reign. It was also the seventh win in a row against the Aggies.

Layne, Dick Harris, and Hub Bechtol were again named to the All-SWC Team and Hub Bechtol closed out a remarkable career as Texas' first three-time all-American.

Coach Bible retired from the football program, but he continued to function as Texas' Athletic Director for ten additional years. In 1951, Bible was accorded an additional honor as he was named to the Football Foundation Hall of Fame.

1947–1956: POSTWAR, PRECHAMPIONSHIP

A football star for three years at Weatherford High School in Texas, Blair Cherry entered Texas Christian University as a fleet-footed, scrappy, 165-pound, five-foot, ten-inch end. He was elected captain of the 1923 TCU team that was good enough to beat Oklahoma A&M and Rice, among others. But Cherry was ambivalent about football. His big love was baseball, and he dreamed of a big-league baseball career. But a broken leg shattered those dreams and in 1930 Blair was hired to coach football at Amarillo High School, a team that had never reached the playoffs in the State tournament. But Cherry changed all that, for his "Golden Sandstorms," as the team was called, won 84 games and lost only 5 and captured three consecutive State titles under his leadership.

When Cherry came to the University of Texas as an assistant coach in 1937, he was ambitious and brusque. He had always been completely consumed by the science of producing touchdowns and his lack of warmth and diplomacy primarily resulted from that preoccupation. But, in time, Cherry changed.

By 1947, after 10 years at Texas, Cherry became downright amiable. Even those who had taken a dislike to him were now drawn to the twinkle in his eyes and the richness of his voice.

Although Cherry's demeanor changed with time, he never lost the careful eye of an artist, constantly evaluating the results of his labor. His thoroughness remained consistent and when Dana Bible resigned in 1947, it was Blair Cherry who was named to replace him.

Cherry had studied the intricate T-formation used so successfully by Chicago Bears quarterback Sid Luckman and had actually used some parts of the T as he knew it back in 1946. Cherry had drilled his freshman team in some of the basic T-patterns and he was fascinated with this dazzling new offense.

Now in 1947, Cherry decided on a gamble—he would install the new offense with his varsity.

Blair Cherry, at forty-seven years old, was appointed Texas' football coach in 1947, when Dana Bible resigned after 10 years.

"The T-formation was an amazing style for us to utilize in 1947," said Bobby Layne. "But when we got it set, we beat everybody in sight in 1947."

The team worked on some basic patterns in spring practice and he liked what he saw. Before the season began Cherry, accompanied by quarterback Bobby Layne, went to Chicago to the Bears training camp and had Luckman, a former all-American at Columbia University, teach the T-formation in all its intricacies to Layne. The Blond Bomber fit into the T like a glove.

Layne worked with Luckman for several days while Cherry made copious notes and diagrams of the new offense. Then they returned to Austin and the coach and the quarterback continued their work in earnest.

Within ten days Layne and his teammates began to utilize and understand the incredible phases of the T-formation. As practice continued they began to smooth out the rough edges.

Cherry drilled his team hour after hour, day after day. He was constantly at Layne's side, stop-

ping each play, discussing what was wrong or what went well. Step by step, painstakingly, the players began to take to the new formation. Cherry ran his players through drill after drill. He would shout, "Harder you work now, the easier the big games will be. You're going to love coming to the park on Saturday. Now get your tail moving."

"We worked harder than at any time I've ever played," said Layne. "The T-formation was a complete departure from the offense we had used under Coach Cherry. The T-formation took minute timing and great speed and great hand speed. In addition, we had to do plenty of running and running and running. But it all paid off, for when the season started we were in much better condition than most of the teams in the Southwest Conference, and we had a new and dazzling offense."

In the opening game of the season against Texas Tech, Cherry opened with a backfield consisting of Randy Clay, Joel Williams, Billy Pyle, and Bobby Layne. Tom Landry and Jim Canady were the backup defensive backs. The linemen included Co-captain Max Baumgardner and Dale Schwartzkopf at end; Dick Harris and Ed Kelley at tackle. The guards were Joe Maglioli and Joe Mitchell, and Dick Rowan was at center.

It was immediately apparent in the first game that Texas Tech was out of its class, for the Longhorns scored touchdowns on each of their first three possessions. The first TD came after a 75-yard drive, and was followed by sprints of 47 yards and 53 yards by Billy Pyle and Byron Gillory. Two additional scores gave the Horns a surprisingly easy 33–0 victory.

Texas made their first plane trip ever to play the University of Oregon, and Bobby Layne put on a demonstration of passing accuracy that had the Oregon team floundering. Bobby tossed two passes to Gillory for 25 and 13 yards for TDs, and one to end Max Baumgardner for 48 yards. Then quarterback Norm Van Brocklin, who would go on to a great pro career as player and coach, tossed for two Oregon TDs and Texas' lead was down to 20–14. But Layne and company turned up the heat and scored 18 additional points. Perry Samuels' 41-yard

Halfback Byron Gillory, behind perfect blocking, flashes for 53 yards and a touchdown against Texas Tech. Texas won 33–0.

touchdown on a punt return gave Texas a 38–13 win.

A star-studded North Carolina team traveled to Austin for the Longhorns' third game of the season and came out on the short side of a 34–0 beating. Layne opened the scoring with a picture-perfect 45-yard toss to Gillory, who caught the ball over his shoulder and never broke stride as he crossed the goal line. But the big surprise was the play of halfback Tom Landry after Coach Cherry moved him into the fullback post. Landry gained 91 yards on 12 carries to spark a 34–0 rout of Carl Snavely's Tarheels.

After the North Carolina game Cherry was named Coach of the Week by the United Press and Texas was ranked behind Notre Dame and Michigan as the No. 3 team in the nation.

In a furious battle against the Oklahoma Sooners, and with the score 7–7 late in the first half, Texas was at the Oklahoma 1-yard line. Time was called to end the half. But the referees gave Texas one more play and the Longhorns scored to give Texas a 14–7 lead. Oklahoma protested, but the TD counted. Another protested play by Texas brought a shower of pop bottles, so much so that quarterback Darrell Royal, playing defense for

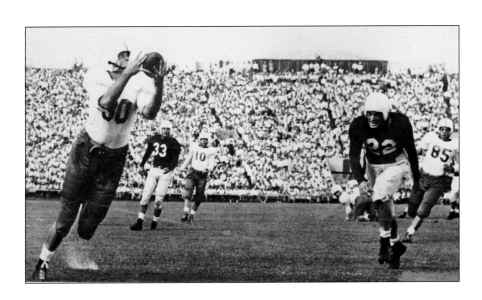

"Peppy" Blount catches Bobby Layne's 25-yard pass and beats Charley "Choo-Choo" Justice (22) to the end zone to score against North Carolina.

Oklahoma, retreated to the center of the field to avoid being hit by flying Coke bottles. When play was resumed, Layne continued his great passing and connected with George McCall for another TD. That score gave Texas a 34–14 victory.

The following Saturday in Memphis, an all-star Arkansas team gave Texas some nervous moments as they scored in the opening moments of their game on Clyde Scott's great 47-yard sprint to give Arkansas a 6–0 lead. But the Texas defense toughened and held Arkansas without a first down for the remainder of the game, and the Longhorns came back for three touchdowns and a 21–6 victory, their fifth of the season.

Coach Jess Neely's tenacious Rice Owls came close to springing another upset over Texas. But Bobby Layne's pass to Baumgardner for a TD in the next sequence of plays, and Byron Gillory's punt return of 35 yards, gave Texas a hard-fought 12–0 victory in a game that went right down to the final whistle.

The next week's game against an undefeated SMU team in Dallas was a showdown for the SWC title. Doak Walker led his Mustangs into battle against best friend Bobby Layne. After a bitter knock-down-and-drag-'em-out battle, SMU outlasted and outran Texas and came away with a 14–13 victory that had everything that a championship match should have: great hitting, great passing, and superb running. Walker gained 125 yards rushing and passing, while Layne picked up 141 yards, 121 of them through the air. Texas battled for that extra score until the final seconds of the game. With time running out, the Horns had a fourth-and-one at the SMU 32-yard line. Layne took the center snap and turned to hand off to Landry. But Landry had slipped, and Layne was tackled behind the line of scrimmage. That was the ball game, and Texas' undefeated season.

Baylor's Bears scored first against Texas in the Longhorns' eighth game of the season and it looked, for a few moments, as if Baylor, under Coach Frank Broyles, had Texas' number. But fullback Ray Borneman broke through for an 11-yard run and the game was tied 7–7. Later in the game, with just fifteen seconds left in the half, Layne tossed a 40-yard pass to Peppy Blount. Blount leaped high into the air over the outstretched arms of two Baylor defenders, caught the ball with one hand, and fell over the goal line, and Texas had another score. The play by Layne and Blount spurred Texas to two additional scores and a 28–7 victory.

In their ninth game of the season, Texas faced TCU in Austin with the realization that they simply had to win after last year's humiliating 14–0 shutout. Dick Harris intercepted a pass and set up the first in a series of 3 TDs. Then Peppy Blount scored on a 31-yard pass from Bobby Layne. The final touch was made by Dale Schwartzkopf, who blocked a punt, scooped up the ball, and raced 45 yards for another touchdown and a 20–0 victory.

On the Friday before the big Thanksgiving Day game at College Station vs. A&M, Coach Cherry was rushed to the hospital for an appendectomy and assistant coaches Ed Price and Eck Curtis directed the team to a 32–13 win over their arch-enemy. The Longhorns registered five touchdowns in scoring their ninth win of the year against one loss.

Texas was invited to meet Alabama in the Sugar Bowl in a game that brought together two of the nation's greatest college quarterbacks in Bobby Layne and Harry Gilmer of Alabama.

On New Year's Day some 73,000 wide-eyed, frantic fans filled New Orleans' Sugar Bowl but did not see the game they expected. Alabama was practically helpless against the tough Texas defense. Harry Gilmer managed only four completions for 31 yards. Layne, on the other hand, was nothing short of sensational, completing 10 of 24 passes for 183 yards and a 27–7 victory, and was named the game's outstanding player, just as he had been in the Cotton Bowl game two years before.

The victory over the Crimson Tide brought to an end what became known as the "Bobby Layne era" at Texas. Bobby had played for the Longhorns from his first day at Texas four years earlier. In his four years, Layne set records that were not surpassed by a Texas back for many years. He completed 210 passes in 400 tries for 3145 yards and was named to the all-American team by *The Sporting News*, UPI, and the Football Writers Association.

In the Sugar Bowl, Alabama's great star Harry Gilmer (52) carries the ball for a short gain against Texas in the 1948 battle. Texas won 27–7.

When the game ended Layne, Rooster Andrews, and a horde of players and fans formed their own victory band. They grabbed some mops, brooms, and plungers and took off marching through the French Quarter of New Orleans for the rest of the night.

Bobby would recall his years at Texas by saying, "Just being there with those great guys was one of the great experiences of my life. I enjoyed playing baseball, but not like I came to love football. Dana Bible was like a father to me. And it was exciting when Blair Cherry took over and switched us from the single wing to the T-formation. Those were wonderful years."

The professionals thought more of Layne than the football writers, for the AAFL Baltimore team

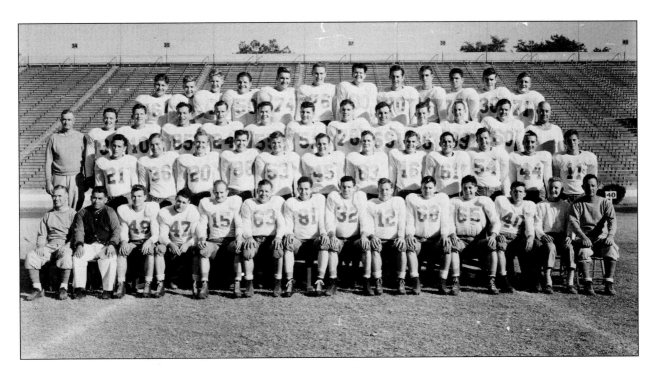

University of Texas Longhorns, 1948 Sugar Bowl champs.

Why I Quit Coaching

Blair Cherry

"Just a year ago I was occupying a hot seat as the coach of a football team at Texas that was supposed to easily win its conference championship. We made it too. Texas won the Southwest Conference title and beat every team in the league for the first time. We finished the season with a 10–1 record and the single loss to SMU by 14–13 concluded the best season Texas had since 1945.

"In 1948 my toughest problem was that of replacing Bobby Layne, our great quarterback. I was roundly criticized by just about everybody in Texas, alumni, former players, some in the administration, for using a boy, Paul Campbell, at Layne's old post, quarterback. Admittedly Paul suffered by comparison with Layne. But he was the best quarterback we had.

"In 1948 we lost games to North Carolina, Oklahoma and SMU, and tied our rivals the Aggies, but we got an invitation to the Orange Bowl, where our 'third-rate team'—so described by sportswriters displeased with the choice—walloped Georgia 41–28 as Tom Landry rushed for 117 yards on 17 tries.

"But throughout the year I received letters and phone calls that were of the most worrisome kind of thing. An example: a letter that said, 'Boy, you're on the spot. If you don't win you'd better not come home.' Signed by a group of Texas Exes. Another letter from a well-known attorney who ranted about my use of Campbell at quarterback. When I told him that it was not easy to replace an all-American like Layne with an inexperienced youngster, he said, 'I never thought Layne was so hot either.'

"In 1949 we were positively 'snake-bitten,' as we lost four games to Oklahoma, Rice, SMU and TCU by a grand total of 10 points. These narrow defeats created a climate of dissatisfaction and anger that spread throughout the state. In 1950 when we lost games to Oklahoma by a point and Tennessee by a touchdown, there was a general feeling that 'Cherry can't win the close games.' After one game I received three calls at about 2:30 A.M., and 3:00 A.M. Mrs. Cherry handled some of these calls so I could get a little sleep. But they continued right along for days and for nights. It was murder.

"Admittedly the Oklahoma game was a crucial one. But our fans didn't realize that the Sooners had a great team and had piled up a 23-game win streak. All our people wanted that game. We went in the final five minutes of the game with a 13–7 lead. Then our punter fumbled a snapback. Oklahoma took over and then their star back Billy Vessels bulled across for the TD and the extra point made it 14–13, Oklahoma.

"There was terrific criticism and at all hours for weeks to come and I couldn't stand it. Didn't have to.

"Following the Oklahoma game, a two-touchdown win over Arkansas failed to soothe my unhappy constituents. We

One of the main reasons Oklahoma defeated Texas in 1949 was the all-around passing and kicking of their star quarterback, Darrell Royal.

Texas players, Tom Landry (*left*) and Dick Harris (*center*) receive the Orange Bowl trophy from Governor Beauford Jester. Texas defeated Georgia 41–28 in the game on January 1, 1949.

got no credit for coming from behind in the last quarter to win. Instead we were blamed for playing such a close game. The following Monday one Texas newspaper carried a headline—IS CHERRY ON HIS WAY OUT?

"My decision to quit at the end of the 1950 season was made after the Oklahoma defeat. But I wasn't going to quit under fire. If we won the SWC title, I would step down and out. If things turned out badly and we lost a few games then they could come and get me . . . fire me.

"The first stepping stone was laid out at Houston the following week just before we met Rice.

"Young Ben Thompson came through magnificently at quarterback as we blasted Rice, 35–7. And overnight the tide of public opinion began to turn. Then in a terrific battle with SMU at Austin we stopped that great triple threat of theirs. Kyle Rote fended off Fred Banner's passes for a thrilling 23–20 victory that knocked the Mustangs off the pinnacle and broke their backs. They lost three of their next four games.

"Never was there a better object lesson in the folly of evaluating teams too early. Until midnight Texas was a 'disappointment,' SMU a won-

der team. My T-formation was outmoded, old-fashioned.

"Now with Rice and SMU in the bag, we were assured a successful season. The night after the SMU game I had a long talk with my wife and my brother. We had talked about going into business together, now I made it certain. I was through at Texas.

"The next day I asked Ed Price, my top assistant, over to my house and told him. 'There's going to be a vacancy in the head coaching job here. I hope you get it—if you want it.'

"Ed did want it, and he finally got it.

"My feeling was one of vast relief. But I had no intention of revealing my plans until the end of the season. However, several people knew about my plans and the word began to leak out. By Tuesday morning the papers were printing the rumors. I called in Weldon Hart, a sportswriter on the governor's staff, and Wilbur Evans, publicity director of the University, and asked them to come to my house. When they arrived I asked them to help me with a release that would detail my leaving. I then went over to Dana Bible's office and informed him of my decision. Bible was the athletic director. And that was that.

"But back on the gridiron we still had some games to play for the championship. And Baylor gave us a real battle.

Bobby Dillon, our fine half-back, had to return a punt some 84 yards in the last quarter to give us a 27–20 win after a fierce battle.

"TCU was a lot of trouble, too, but we finally beat them 21–7. Meanwhile Rice was beating the Aggies and that gave us a clear shot at the title, even before our Thanksgiving Day game against the Aggies. We completed our conference games with a clean sweep by beating the Aggies 17–0. Then we wound up the regular season by thumping LSU, 21–6.

"Then in my final game we encountered a Tennessee team in the Sugar Bowl that blocked better, tackled harder than we did, and they beat us in a crackerjack of a game that was not won until the final quarter, and we lost 20–14. But we tried until the very end and we got to their 12-yard line, but were stalled there as time ran out on us. But we battled like hell.

"Football was good to me. I don't know of another profession in which I—starting out as a penniless lad compelled to make his own way—might have risen to the top of his profession and had as much fun doing it. On the other hand I don't know of any profession that demands more of a coach. Football coaching nowadays is an around-the-clock, around-the-calendar business. While much is made of the fact that most coaches are paid more than college presidents, the financial rewards are an insufficient attraction when the hazards are all considered. You never heard of a history teacher getting fired, even in the South, because Lee didn't win at Appomattox."

(In his six years as head coach Texas amassed a 32-10-1 record and one SWC championship.)

selected Bobby as their number-one pick in the draft and in the NFL, Pittsburgh selected Layne as their number-one choice. After much consideration, Bobby signed to play for the T-formation Chicago Bears.

Ed Price had been an assistant coach under Jack Chevigny in 1936 and when Dana Bible assumed the mantle of head coach, Price was retained on Bible's staff. When Blair Cherry was named as Bible's replacement in 1947, he continued to utilize the services of Ed Price, who had worked with the freshman squad and then handled the backfield coaching chores. During the war Price took some time off from his duties at Texas to enlist in the navy and, in a short period of time, rose to the rank of Lieutenant Commander and was the officer-in-charge of the aircraft carrier *Kadashan Bay*. He was responsible for the catapult on the ship, and recalled his years in the navy "as the most arresting, most dramatic" of his life.

As Texas' new head coach in 1951, Price installed the split T-formation instead of the T-formation utilized for several years by Blair Cherry, and he found a fast-moving, quick-thinking youngster, Tom Jones, for the important quarterback post. The rest of the lineup for the opening game included Don Barton, Byron Townsend, halfback Gib Dawson, fullback Dick Ochoa, and end Tom Stolhandske. The defense featured Bob Dillon, safety; June Davis, linebacker; Don Monesko and Paul Williams at the ends; Jim Lansford and Bill Wilson at tackle; and Harley Sewell and Sonny Sowell at the guard spots.

The Kentucky Wildcats furnished the opposition for the Longhorns at Austin in the opening game of the season. Coached by Bear Bryant, the Wildcats featured two all-Americans in quarterback Babe Parilli and his top receiver Steve Meilinger. Texas pulled off a surprise as they outplayed the Wildcats to take a thriller of a victory by a 7–6 margin. Texas scored in the first period when quarterback Jones passed to Don Barton and Gib Dawson kicked the extra point—a point that meant the ball game.

Coach Ed Price was appointed head football coach in 1951 to replace Blair Cherry, who resigned. Price is shown with two of his players, guard Herb Gray (66) and tackle Buck Lansford (70).

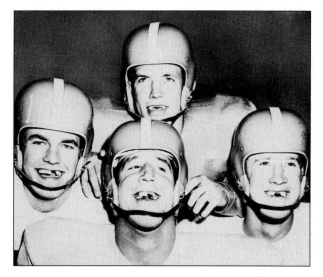

Practice had been pretty rough on these four Texas football stars in 1951. They showed up one day and a staff photographer snapped this toothless group. *Left to right*: guard Jim Pakenham, tackle Ken Jackson, and linebacker Jack Barton. *Rear*: quarterback T. Jones.

In Lafayette, Indiana, the Longhorns continued their fine play as they pounded out a 14–0 win over the highly rated Purdue Boilermakers. Halfback Gib Dawson, whose extra-point kick won the Kentucky game, also starred against Purdue with touchdown runs of 8 and 10 yards. Gib also kicked the two extra points to account for all 14 points and the win. The third game of the season in Austin against North Carolina saw the Longhorns explode with their new split-T offense as they raced for 7 touchdowns and a 45–20 victory over the Tarheels. Gib Dawson again starred with a smashing 56-yard TD spectacular and fullback Dick Ochoa, a rugged 205-pound battering ram, blasted right through the center of the Tarheels' line for 48

yards and a TD in an explosive second-period splurge that netted 18 points for Texas.

Against Oklahoma, substitute halfback Carl "Red" Mayes starred for Texas in a 9–7 win for the Longhorns as they played a tough defensive battle throughout the game. The win boosted the Longhorns into fourth place in the national rankings reported by the Associated Press.

But the Longhorns sagged when they met a rugged Arkansas team in the fifth game, played at Fayetteville. Texas simply seemed to run out of steam. Arkansas was led by a husky six-foot, 190-pound tackle named Pat Summerall who calmly booted the winning field goal from the 15-yard line to give Arkansas a surprising 16–14 victory. Years later Summerall would help win many games for the New York Giants in the NFL, then would go on to become one of the nation's premier play-by-play football announcers.

Quarterback Jim Dan Pace sparked the Texas attack in a much-needed win against the fast-moving Rice eleven. In a slashing last-minute series of

Team captains June Davis (*left*) and Bobby Dillon pose in front of the team slogan for 1951.

Harley Sewell, Texas guard in 1951 and 1952, was a tough, rugged, and aggressive lineman who was named to the all-American team in 1952.

plays, Texas, led by Jim Dan Pace, marched 75 yards to score a TD and come away with a hard-fought 14–6 victory. The following week in Dallas, SMU went down to defeat as Texas, on a victory roll, piled up three touchdowns to take a 20–13 win.

But after victories over Rice, SMU, Arkansas, and Oklahoma, the Longhorns stumbled against the Bears of Baylor, losing 18–6. In the final period, four big fumbles by Texas led to two scores by Baylor. Coach George Sauer's Bears went on to an 8-2-1 record.

In the game against TCU Jim Dan Pace directed the Longhorns in a valiant comeback as they played near-perfect ball to defeat TCU 32–21. Pace called a flawless game and completed 6 of 7 passes for two touchdowns. The high point of the battle was a 61-yard TD toss to Gib Dawson that clinched the game.

In the annual Thanksgiving Day classic vs. the Texas Aggies in College Station both teams were in contention for a bowl invitation. But the Aggies played their best game of the year and handed Texas a 22–21 beating. It was the Aggies' first win in the series since 1939 and it was a costly one. The turning point occurred in the third period as the Aggies piled up 15 points via Yale Lary's 68-yard sprint for a TD; Darrow Hooper's 37-yard field goal; and Hooper's pass for 37 yards and another score.

The loss to the Aggies cost the Longhorns a certain Orange Bowl invitation, which went to Baylor.

With the loss to the Aggies, Coach Ed Price, in his first season as head coach, fashioned an impressive 7–3 record. "In 1951," said Price sadly, "we beat the tough teams, but got beat by the weaker ones."

With nineteen lettermen returning for 1952, Coach Ed Price had some outstanding, experienced players in his two-platoon system. "But," he said, "we still have a problem at quarterback. And it has been a problem since the days of Bobby Layne." Bunny Andrews, brother of the famous Rooster Andrews, was the favorite during spring practice, but eventually Bunny was replaced by T. Jones, a frail-looking 150-pound speedster who had improved his running and passing skill. More important, he had a sixth sense when it came to running the split-T formation, where the quarterback had complete control of the offense.

Price had an outstanding cadre of players returning from the 1951 unit, including Harley Sewell, Tom Stolhandske, two fine runningbacks in Dick Ochoa and Gib Dawson, and Bill Quinn and Jim Dan Pace. Linemen included Alex Lansford, Carlton Massey, Phil Branch, Bill Georges, Jack Barton, Bill McDonald (co-captain with Ochoa), and Charley Genthner.

Texas opened the season on a wet, slimy LSU gridiron, and quickly scored on a flashy 52-yard pass play from Jones to Stolhandske. They took a 7–0

Three marvelous all-Americans: Bobby Layne (*front*), SMU star Doak Walker (*center*), and Harley Sewell get together during a coaching seminar at Texas in 1953.

In the 1952 SMU game, quarterback T. Jones leads the interference as Billy Quinn drives to a score in the final seconds of the game.

lead into the locker room at halftime. After a verbal drubbing by Coach Price, the Longhorns quickly mounted a 21-point scoring spree in the third period to easily beat LSU, 35–14. At Durham, North Carolina, a week later, Texas picked up a total of 193 yards and easily defeated North Carolina 28–7.

But those were just warmups for the next game. Frank Leahy brought his Notre Dame eleven to Austin in a game that Texas dedicated to their coach of the thirties, Jack Chevigny, the former Irish star, and they held a 3–0 lead at halftime. But in the second half the Irish turned the tables on Texas and outplayed them in an extremely physical contest, scoring two touchdowns as backs John Lattner, Neil Worden, and Ralph Guglielmi battered the Texas line for a 14–3 victory. In a game against Oklahoma the following week, the Longhorns, not yet fully recovered from the Notre Dame defeat, were sent reeling and rocking by Oklahoma, whose offense racked up 28 points in the first period and easily defeated the Longhorns 49–20.

But the Longhorns used those two defeats as positive motivation. A week later, led by Ochoa, Billy Quinn, and Larry Graham, the Longhorns took no pity on an outclassed Arkansas team and slugged them into a 44–7 defeat. Against Rice a week later, Ochoa and Quinn again sparked the Texas offense to three touchdowns and a 20–7 margin over a feisty Rice squad. Now, playing its finest football of the year, Texas battered SMU with a 21-point first period and then romped to a 31–14 win.

In a game in Waco that produced a spectacular scoring spree by both Texas and Baylor, a game that saw 68 points chalked up, Texas came from behind in the final sixty seconds of play. Sparked by Billy Quinn and Ochoa, the Longhorns drove 69 yards to score and seize a thrilling 35–33 win. A huge crowd came screaming onto the field to lift Texas players onto their shoulders as the final gun sounded.

Then, in a close-to-the-vest defensive battle at TCU, Texas edged out the Horned Frogs in the last period to take a 14–7 win and clinch a Cotton Bowl matchup against Tennessee.

Before the bowl game, Texas punched out a 17–0 win over the Aggies and a 21–6 victory over LSU. Then it was another thrilling battle against Tennessee in the Cotton Bowl as Cliff Polk recovered a fumble and bulled his way into the end zone to give Texas a 7–0 halftime lead.

In the final period a safety gave Texas a 9–0 lead. Then Quinn, Ochoa, and Dawson drove downfield and Quinn dove in for another TD, and Texas had a hard-fought 16–0 victory, the Cotton Bowl championship, and a measure of revenge for their 20–14 loss to the Vols two years earlier.

Eight members of the Longhorn squad were named to the All-SWC Team—Sewell, Stolhandske, Dawson, Ochoa, Jones, Quinn, Branch, and Georges—while Harley Sewell and Tom Stolhandske were also named to the all-American squad.

Coach Ed Price's 1952 Longhorns had closed out the year in a blaze of glory.

One big question faced Coach Ed Price as he appraised the squad of eighty players who reported for practice at the start of the 1953 season. Where was the quarterback who could handle the complicated Texas offense? A week into the practice Price settled on Bunny Andrews. Bunny was a three-year veteran who could pass and run with the ball. Once that position had been set, Price selected the rest of his starting lineup. It included ends Carlton Massey and Menan Schriewer, Buck Lansford and Gil Spring at tackle, Phil Branch and Kirby Miller at the guard posts, and John Tatum at center. In the backfield with Andrews were Delano Womack, Doug Cameron, and Charley Brewer.

In the opening game of the season at LSU, Texas was upset by a 20–7 margin. It was only the second season-opening loss in the sixty-two years that Texas had played football. Against Villanova a week later Price juggled his lineup and the team responded with a smashing 41–12 win. Bunny Andrews came into his own in the next game against Houston. With Houston leading 7–2 at the half, Andrews sparked the Longhorns in a 26-point drive in the third period to give Texas a 28–7 win.

In a nationally televised game, Oklahoma drove to a 19–0 lead before Texas awakened and quickly ran up two touchdowns. Just as it looked as if the Longhorns would score again time ran out and Oklahoma escaped with a 19–14 victory.

In the first period against Arkansas in Fayetteville, Texas fumbled the ball three times but managed to eke out a 16–7 win. Bunny Andrews started the Texas scoring with a bullet pass to Womack good for 30 yards and a TD. Another Andrews TD pass to Womack cemented a 16–7 win. The following week in the game vs. Rice at Austin, Texas scored in the first period after a brilliant 52-yard drive. Rice stopped another Texas drive, then took over the ball and proceeded to churn out 76 yards and a TD. The extra point made it 7–6, Rice. Texas came back in the third period to score on a TD pass from Brewer to Schriewer good for 27 yards and it was Texas 13, Rice 7. But in the final period, Rice picked up 11 points—a TD and 2 safeties—to win by an 18–13 margin.

In the seventh game of the season SMU got off to a 7–6 halftime lead at home. But Andrews, Texas' slick ball-handling quarterback, led a 62-yard drive for a Texas TD as Cameron scored from the 7-yard line. Then in the fourth period Buck Branch booted a 10-yard field goal in the final period for a 16–7 victory for Texas.

In a slashing, physical battle against Baylor that had the Memorial Stadium crowd on its feet cheering throughout, Texas and its fine backfield of Massey, Brewer, and Branch gave Texas a close 21–20 victory as the Longhorns slowly ground up time and yardage in the final period. A week later against TCU, with the score 3–0 TCU late in the fourth quarter, Bunny Andrews came off the bench and in five plays marched the Longhorns 60 yards for a touchdown. Then Andrews' 49-yard touchdown pass to Schriewer gave the Longhorns another squeaker, 13–3.

Coach Ed Price was feeling good as the Texas varsity began their practice sessions for the start of the 1954 season. In his first season, Price's team had finished third in the SWC; in his second year, Texas won the SWC title; and in 1953 Texas had a share of the title. Now in 1954 the aura of winning was so strong that Grantland Rice, writing on football for *Collier's* magazine, rated Texas No. 4 in the

Charley Brewer's (21) pinpoint passing was responsible for two touchdowns against A&M in the final game of the 1953 season. Brewer also rushed for a third score while Delano Womack (44) rushed for 103 yards to give Texas a 21–12 win over A&M and the SWC championship.

nation. With some 22 lettermen reporting that opinion appeared to be well-founded.

In the opening game of the season at Austin, Texas easily defeated LSU by a 20–6 score. The following week was the big game, the game that had nationwide press attention—Notre Dame at South Bend. Texas was shut out by the Irish 21–0 as Ralph Guglielmi, the Notre Dame quarterback, led the Irish to three quick scores. This was Terry Brennan's debut as Notre Dame coach and the young 25-year-old proved he was a worthy successor to Frank Leahy, who had retired.

Following the Notre Dame debacle, Texas switched gears and ran up 5 touchdowns against Washington State to give the Longhorns a 40–14 victory before a hometown crowd of 35,000. Then Oklahoma, the No. 2 team in the nation, played errorless football and pounded out a bruising 14–7 win over Texas in a game that saw both teams battle tooth-and-nail. The two TDs by the Sooners in the second period, long drives of 73 and 58 yards,

Notre Dame backs, in their final practice session before meeting Texas in 1954, take the Texas hurdle at full stride. Irish backfield (*left to right*): Don Schaefer, Jim Morse, Tom Carey, and Nick Raich with co-captains Paul Matz (*left*) and Dan Shannon (*right*) holding the Texas sign. The Irish won 21–0.

Johnny Tatum has just intercepted an SMU pass and heads for the goal line and a touchdown that tied the game at 13–13 in 1954.

earned the win over Texas. Then it was Arkansas' turn to take on Texas and they defeated the Longhorns by a 20–7 margin. Arkansas outweighed Texas by at least fifteen pounds per man, and managed to outplay and outfight the Longhorns for the win on the way to an 8–3 season and the Cotton Bowl.

In the Texas dressing room after the game a number of local sportswriters and critics commented that they thought the Texas players, particularly the linemen, were not in shape. Additional stories in the local press also commented on the poor condition of the players, and other stories panned Coach Price for Texas' second straight loss.

For the game against Rice the following week, Price juggled his lineup. Although the changes improved the team, the result was no different as Rice rammed over the winning touchdown after intercepting a pass by Brewer to give the Owls a hard-fought 13–7 victory. This was Texas' third straight loss and the alumni's complaints could be heard throughout the state.

In a vain attempt to put some spit and fire into the Texas attack Price dropped several players and suspended some others for a few days. He had the guilty players move out of the dorms as part of their punishment. Against SMU the following week, Texas still played as if they were sleepwalking and SMU drove to two touchdowns and a halftime 13–0 lead. But after a dressing-room tongue-lashing by Price, Texas rebounded to score two quick TDs

Halfback Billy Quinn (15) races to the goal line in the 1953 A&M game.

and tie the score at 13–13. The Longhorns were breaking through the SMU line in the fourth period and had reached SMU's 14-yard line when the gun sounded. The game ended in a 13–13 tie.

Texas was back at full strength for the Baylor game and scored a quick TD to take a 7–0 lead. But the Bears tore into the Texas line in the third and fourth periods for two TDs and defeated Texas 13–7. In Fort Worth a week later in the game against TCU, the Texas players again appeared to be bored with football as they allowed TCU to score 4 touchdowns for a 27–7 lead.

Then all hell broke loose. The Longhorns fought back to score a quick touchdown and it was 27–14. Then TCU scored to pull ahead, 34–14. But the Longhorns put together 2 exciting touchdowns in the final ten minutes of play. Then, with two minutes to play, Del Womack piled through the TCU line for another score. Lansford kicked the extra point. The kick was slightly to the right of the crossbars, but veered and just hit the top of the post and fell in for the extra point. It was the margin of victory in an incredible come-from-behind 35–34 win, one of the most exciting games Texas had ever played.

In the final game of the season at Austin, the Longhorns played another inspired game to take a

21–12 victory from the Aggies. The Bear Bryant-coached A&M squad had a chance to win or tie the game in the final period, but failed to do so. With the score 19–12 Texas, Elwood Kettler, A&M's fine quarterback, led the Aggies in a drive that reached the Texas 10-yard line late in the period. But tackle Herb Gray then made a diving tackle of Kettler and dropped him in his tracks, and Texas took over the ball on downs as the final minute ticked away and Texas moved further in front, 21–12.

The win over the Aggies gave Texas a 4-5-1 season, and provided Ed Price with some breathing space, for the alumni had been howling for his scalp. As a matter of fact, the day before the Aggie game, the Longhorn Club was planning to ask for Price's ouster. But the meeting broke up with a policy statement supporting Price and all the Texas athletic programs.

Beginning his fifth season as the Longhorns' football coach, Ed Price realized that he could not withstand the pressure of the Texas alumni if his 1955 team did not have a winning season. But his team would have to go all out to better the 4-5-1 mark of the 1954 squad.

With that in mind, Price revamped his entire offense. He brought in several new assistants, including the great Bobby Layne, now a professional star with the Detroit Lions. He had Bobby work with his quarterback prospects.

Thirty-two lettermen reported for the fall practice, plus some fine substitutes and walk-ons, and Price went to work with a vengeance to develop a Texas team that had to be successful.

In the opening game of the season, a night game against Texas Tech, the Longhorns were beaten by the Red Raiders at home for the first time since they began to play football in 1893. Texas halfbacks Walt Fondren and Joe Clements, tackle Garland Kennon, center Louis Del Hommee, and end Menan Schriewer were outstanding in the 20–14 loss. Against Tulane in the second game, Coach Price started Walt Fondren at quarterback but then switched to Joe Clements. Clements was sensational. He tossed 17 passes, three of them for touchdowns, to give Texas a dazzling 35–21 win.

The Longhorns then traveled to Los Angeles for a game with the University of Southern California and the Trojans quickly rolled to a 12–0 halftime lead. But Dick Miller at quarterback tossed a 40-yard pass to Fondren that reached the 5-yard line. On the next play Fondren scored to close the margin to 12–7. But the Trojans quickly scored their third TD and took a hard-fought 19–7 win.

In a game against Oklahoma, Joe Clements, once again back at the quarterback post, tossed 31 passes in an attempt to defeat a dazzling Oklahoma team on its way to a 10–0 season. The Bud Wilkinson team shut out Texas 20–0. The following week it was another defeat, this time at the hands of Arkansas by the score of 27–20. The Razorbacks had a 27–6 lead in the fourth quarter, but Texas clicked for two touchdowns and were on their way to another when time ran out. The loss to Arkansas was the fourth defeat for Texas and brought their midseason record to 1–4.

In the Rice game, Coach Price inserted Charley Brewer at quarterback, his fourth different starter at that spot. Brewer guided the Longhorns to an impressive 32–14 upset win over the Owls. Walt Fondren scored two touchdowns and gained 145 yards in 11 carries to spearhead the Texas attack.

The following week against SMU the difference again was the play of Walt Fondren, who scored two touchdowns in the final four minutes of the first half to give Texas a 13–12 lead. SMU scored in the third period to go ahead 18–13, but with two minutes remaining in the game, Delano Womack sprinted in for a TD from the 11-yard line to give Texas a 19–18 thriller.

In another one-point heart-stopper, Texas the following week took a 21–20 victory over the

Quarterback Walt Fondren (24) scored two touchdowns in the final 4 minutes of the first half against SMU to give the Horns a 13–12 edge. Then the Mustangs scored to move ahead 18–13 in the final period. But Delano Womack won the thriller as he scored a last-minute TD for a 19–18 win. Fondren is at the goal line, while Womack (44) has just thrown a block for him.

Baylor Bears as Ed Hawkins and Walt Fondren starred for Texas. A win against TCU the next week would mean a Cotton Bowl game for Texas and a share of the SWC championship, but TCU had ideas of their own. In a dazzling individual performance, halfback Jim Swink scored three touchdowns to lead the TCU squad to a 47–20 romp over Texas that extinguished any title hopes.

The final game of the season was the Thanksgiving Day war against rival Texas A&M. The Longhorns came into the game as underdogs and promptly played their finest football of the season in handing the Aggies a 21–6 beating. Texas held the vaunted Aggie offense to just three first downs and just 30 yards rushing. Texas slammed in two last-period scores to win the final game of the year and to assure the Longhorns an even 5–5 season.

The victory over the Aggies in the final game of the 1955 season again gave Coach Ed Price some breathing room. But he knew 1956 had to be a winning season or he was out as the Texas football coach. He set out to institute the most massive recruiting campaign of his tenure as head coach.

With an eye fixed on the opening game of the 1956 season at Austin, a return contest against USC, Price had just three veteran players who had

started in the A&M game in 1955. They were quarterback Walt Fondren, who'd had several tremendous games a year ago, tackle Garland Kennon, and guard Louis Del Hommee. Tackle J. T. Seaholm, halfback Joe Clements, and Vince Matthews also were experienced players whom Price counted on for a successful season.

The Southern California Trojans were surprised by the fierceness of the Texas offense as Clements ripped off a 36-yard reverse to score Texas' first TD in the first period. But the Trojans, led by Charley Roberts, who scored three touchdowns on spectacular sprints, tore and ripped and clawed at the Longhorns to win by a 44–20 margin. Joe Clements gave the Longhorns two scores late in the game, but it was too little, too late.

Tulane was the next Texas opponent and the Green Wave put up a tough battle in New Orleans but just managed to lose by a 7–6 margin. Walt Fondren's conversion was the margin of victory. But the following week, the gods of football looked the other way as West Virginia three times halted the Longhorns within their 15-yard line and came away with a tense, thrilling 7–6 win.

Oklahoma University, sporting a remarkable 32 straight wins, made it 33 in a row as they romped to an incredible 45–0 win over Texas. It was Texas' worst defeat since a 50–0 beating by

Quarterback Walt Fondren attempts to pass in a game against TCU in 1956 as Joe Clements (28) blocks for him. TCU battered Texas 46–0.

Oklahoma in 1908. OU's all-American Tommy McDonald scored 3 TDs, including a 54-yard sprint on the opening kickoff.

On successive weekends, Texas lost to Arkansas by a 32–14 margin and then to the Rice Owls, who scored 4 touchdowns to romp over Texas 28–7. The howls of anguish and late-night phone calls to the coach asking him to resign began in earnest.

But in a game against SMU at Austin, after being battered by the Mustangs to the tune of 20–0 at halftime, the Longhorns struck back with a vengeance. They scored three TDs and came within two minutes of winning the game, but time ran out and SMU came away with a 20–19 thriller. Then it was another loss, this time to Baylor. Del Shofner, who would later play for the New York Giants, dominated the game on brilliant runs of 55 and 47 yards as Baylor triumphed 10–7.

Jim Swink and his TCU gladiators marched into their home grounds and ran roughshod over Texas. Swink scored three times and was responsible for a fourth TD as TCU battered Texas by a 46–0 score.

Bear Bryant led his undefeated Texas Aggies into Memorial Stadium and marched out with a stunning 34–21 beating of their Texas rivals. A&M's all-American, John David Crow, scored on a slashing 37-yard sprint in the first period and from then on the only question was, How many points would A&M score? Texas tried vainly to pull the game out and Joe Clements, Walt Fondren, and Carl Wylie did give A&M some anxious moments. But it was to no avail and the Aggies came away with a great 34–21 victory to keep their undefeated string intact.

With the loss to Texas A&M, Ed Price looked back on a 1–9 season and sent in his letter of resignation. Price's record in six years consisted of 33 wins, 27 losses, and 1 tie. It was time to find another head coach, one who could lead Texas out of the wilderness.

1957–1976:
THOSE CHAMPIONSHIP
SEASONS

As a small boy growing up in Hollis, Oklahoma, in the 1930s, Darrell Royal's dream was to play football for the University of Oklahoma and then to become a football coach.

Royal went through quite a lot before he found a home at Texas. He was one of six children in the midst of the dreaded Dust Bowl during the depression.

"We had a tiny house on the edge of Hollis and we had a milk cow and chickens and a garden," he recalled, recently. "The house was right by Highway 62 and I used to stand by the front yard watching the cars and trucks race by with people jammed in and water jugs hanging from the sides. They were all heading the same way—west. I must have been about thirteen or fourteen then."

His father, Burley Royal, drove a gas truck for a farmer's co-op in the day and at night was a watchman. Darrell's mother died when he was six.

In the summer after his freshman year in high school, his father loaded the family in an old blue Whippet and they set out for California to pick fruit.

That was a miserable summer. The Royals lived in a tiny migrant shack and the entire family worked the harvest. At the end of the summer, Darrell packed his baseball glove and ball and all the clothes he owned and told his dad he was going back home to live with Grandma Harmon. He washed cars, shined shoes, and quarterbacked the Hollis High team to an undefeated season his senior year. He also found time to court his future wife, Edith, in between work, school, and football.

Darrell's older brother suffered a broken arm playing high school football. It was about the time that Darrell began playing.

"I was out for the football team for a long time just scared to death that Papa was going to find out I was playing and make me quit because my brother had his arm broken," he laughed.

His father did not make him quit. Royal began working on his punting with an old rubber football he got for Christmas one year. "I still remember how excited I got the first time I kicked a spiral." By the time he was in high school, Royal could punt, pass, and run with the ball, and nobody was better on offense or defense than Darrell.

Royal had to put his dreams on hold for a few years as he enlisted in the Army Air Force during World War II, but an emergency appendectomy kept him in the States.

"I played service basketball and made the football team, then got a tryout with the 3rd Air Force football team in Florida. I went down there and made the squad and played basketball while I was waiting for football to start." Royal and the basketball team traveled to Stillwater to meet the powerful Oklahoma team coached by Hank Iba. Iba offered Royal a scholarship.

"There were about 500 prospects out for the team," said Royal. "But I just knew I had to make that team. It was part of my dream to play football for Oklahoma and it just had to be."

Royal was a star halfback and quarterback at Oklahoma and the next year in 1947, when Bud Wilkinson took over as the Oklahoma coach, Royal soaked up every bit of football knowledge possible from Wilkinson and his assistants. He never slowed

In 1949, all-American quarterback Darrell Royal led Oklahoma to an outstanding 11–0 season.

down in his pursuit of his dream to become a football coach . . . and a good one.

In 1948 he directed the Oklahoma offense from his quarterback post and guided the team to 11 straight wins. His play calling was superb and his punting amazing. In a game against Oklahoma A&M, Royal kicked a wet, soggy ball 81 yards and out of bounds on the 4-yard line, and his all-around brilliance led to his being named to the all-American team.

Royal graduated from Oklahoma during the midterms and took a coaching post at El Reno High School. But two months later North Carolina State offered him a coaching job and El Reno officials allowed him to leave. Following NC State there were coaching stops at Tulsa and Mississippi State, and in 1953 Royal took over as head coach at Edmonton in the Canadian Football League.

Mississippi State offered Royal his first head coaching post in the states and he compiled identical 6–4 seasons in 1954 and in 1955. Then he moved to Washington, where he chalked up a 5–5 record.

Then one bright, sunny day—a day Royal would never forget—he received a phone call from the legendary Dana X. Bible, Athletic Director at Texas. Bible asked Royal a few questions, and mentioned that Texas was looking for a new coach to replace Ed Price. Then Bible said, "Would you like to come in and be interviewed for the job?"

A score of football's great coaches had been queried for the post, and the great Frank Leahy of Notre Dame asked about the situation. But every time Bible talked to a coach, the questioning invariably got down to, "Why not talk to Darrell Royal?"

Bible made arrangements, all very hush-hush, for Royal to fly into Austin to be interviewed by the Board of Regents. "He made such a marvelous impression on every board member," said Bible, "and he had such intimate knowledge of our situation, that within four hours after he had landed at the airport he was informed that he was Texas' new head coach—and with a five-year contract."

When Royal phoned his football staff at Washington that evening and told them he had the Texas post, two of his top aides—Mike Campbell, a very successful high school coach and his top aide at Washington, and Jim Pittman, another fine aide—told Royal, "Our bags are packed, we're ready to leave for Texas with you." Royal gave them the go-ahead, and both men and several others—Ray Willsey, Jack Swarthout, Bob Schultze, T. Jones, and Charley Shira—were added to his staff. Royal was ready to take on the enormous job of taking over a squad that had just posted the worst seasons of Texas football on record—1–9—and turning the entire football programs around.

What Darrell Royal was about to accomplish at Texas would make football history.

That first spring training session under Royal demonstrated why Texas football, which had floundered for so many years, would once more rise to the top. For Royal's practice sessions were so well-

When Darrell Royal was officially introduced as Texas' new head coach, he brought his top aides, Mike Campbell and Jim Pittman, with him. Royal is shown with his new coaching staff. *Left to right*: Royal, Ray Willsey, Jack Swarthout, Mike Campbell, T. Jones, Bob Schultze, Jim Pittman, and Charley Shira.

planned and organized that not a minute was wasted. He was an outstanding teacher of the game and every player on the squad was taken in hand and thoroughly taught to understand every play in Royal's system. Players would walk through plays on offense and defense, and if a question arose about the movement on a certain play, the coach was on hand ready to answer the query. No time was lost in standing around, every drill was efficiently timed to the minute. Practice sessions lasted one hour and forty-five minutes and the players responded with enthusiasm.

In the opening game of the season against Georgia, in Atlanta, Royal fielded a lineup that included Louis Del Hommee at center; tackles J. T. Seaholm and Garland Kennon; at guards, the twins Will and Wes Wyman; and Bobby Lee, Don Wilson, Bob Bryant, and Maurice Doke. The backfield consisted of Max Alvis, George Blanch, Rene Ramirez, Don Allen, Mike Dowdle, Walt Fondren, and Joe Clements. Vince Matthews and Bob Lackey were the quarterbacks.

Texas got off to a fast start, racking up two touchdowns to take a 13–0 halftime lead. Georgia scored in the third period to make it 13–7. Then Walt Fondren sprinted 60 yards for another TD. The final touchdown came when Texas recovered a fumble and scored from the 17-yard line. Final score: Texas 26, Georgia 7. The Longhorns continued their winning ways by defeating a tough Tulane squad 20–6 as Rene Ramirez, an unheralded halfback, sprinted for big gains, caught several passes, and sparked the Texas offense to victory.

Next on the slate for Texas was South Carolina. The Gamecocks proved to be a major problem and Royal's first loss at Texas as they fought back from a 21–7 deficit. They scored 20 points in the final five minutes of play to win a 27–21 thriller that featured a 98-yard scoring dash by South Carolina's King Dixon.

Oklahoma came to Dallas favored by 21 points over Texas and riding a 42-game winning streak. But they were jolted in the first period of the game when Walt Fondren, improving with every

Coach Darrell Royal with his 1957 co-captains, center Del Hommee (50) and quarterback Walter Fondren (24).

game, quick-kicked the Sooners to their 6-yard line. Then, Texas took possession of the ball on an interception and Fondren flipped a short pass to Monte Lee to give Texas a 7–0 lead. But Oklahoma came back quickly with two touchdowns to take a 14–7 halftime lead. A third TD in the final period gave the Sooners a hard-fought, tense 21–7 win.

The next week Texas received all the breaks in a battle in Fayetteville against Arkansas and came away with a stunning 17–0 shutout over the favored Razorbacks. A week later against Rice an electrifying 80-yard dash by Ramirez proved to be the key score in another upset win for the Longhorns as they edged the Owls 19–14.

Bob Lackey and Walt Fondren alternated at the quarterback spot in a key game in Dallas against Don Meredith and his SMU Mustangs. Texas moved into scoring position on six occasions—at the 21, 3, 7, 33, and 35—without scoring, and SMU with Meredith pitching TD passes managed a 19–12 victory. Walt Fondren shone in a tight defensive battle against Baylor. He completed 11 of 12 passes, but was only able to manage a 7–7 tie against Baylor. But by winning at home over TCU 14–2, Texas was back in the SWC title race as Rice beat Texas A&M. Then it was the big Thanksgiving Day battle vs. the Aggies. The win-

ner of the Texas-A&M game would receive a Sugar Bowl invitation. The rivals collided under the eyes of millions of fans on national TV in a game that had all the earmarks of a title match.

In one of the thrillers of the year, the Longhorns and the Aggies fought each other tooth and nail up and down the gridiron. Finally Bob Lackey scored to give Texas a 6–0 lead. Then, near the end of the final period, Lackey kicked a field goal to make it 9–0. It looked like a safe lead. But not for A&M's Heisman winner and great all-American halfback, John David Crow, who took a short pass from quarterback Rod Osborne, fought off several Texas tacklers, and raced 57 yards to the 1-yard line. On the next play Crow scored, then kicked the extra point, and it was now a 9–7 squeaker. But before any further damage was done the game ended with Texas still in front. Texas had nailed down a Sugar Bowl trip and a chance to play Mississippi just a year after a 1–9 record.

Coach Johnny Vaught's 8-1-1 Mississippi team had outstanding offense and defense capabilities and were a veteran team. They simply had too much power for the Longhorns and pushed across six touchdowns in a 39–7 win over Texas. It was a game high on Coach Royal's list of embarrassments.

For Texas and Dallas Royal it was a strong first season as the Longhorns finished with a 6-3-1 regular-season record and second place in the SWC championship scramble.

Royal was named Texas Coach of the Year by the sportswriters of the state and it marked Texas' best record since 1953. The season left no doubt that Texas football under Darrell Royal was on the rise—and nobody knew it better than Royal himself.

If the University of Texas football fans were jubilant at the success of their 1957 team, they became absolutely ecstatic when Coach Royal unveiled a 1958 squad that racked up five straight victories over some of the top teams in the country. Texas was victorious over Georgia, Tulane, and Texas Tech. Those victories were followed by a titanic 15–14 win over Oklahoma that broke a six-year losing streak and a strong 24–6 thumping of

Coach Darrell Royal is carried from the Cotton Bowl after the Longhorns snatched a 15–14 thriller from Oklahoma. Royal is on the shoulders of guards H. G. Anderson (*left*) and Dan Petty.

by Rice, Texas shook off its lethargy to take a 10–0 lead over SMU in the third period. Then quarterback Don Meredith un-hitched his great passing arm and scored two quick TDs to send Texas reeling to a 26–10 defeat.

In Waco the following week, Baylor jumped to a 15–14 lead with just ten minutes left to play. Then Larry Cooper, a Texas substitute quarterback who had not thrown a pass in weeks, connected on four straight passes. The final toss was for 25 yards and a touchdown produced a 20–15 win for Texas. The ninth game of the season was at TCU, the SWC leader with four wins in a row. The Frogs played a ragged first half against a hopped-up Texas team that built up an 8–0 lead via a touchdown and a safety. But the Frogs held Texas in the second half and drove to three touchdowns and a 22–8 win.

Before a national TV audience on Thanksgiving Day, Texas pounded A&M for 4 touchdowns

Oklahoma had dominated Texas, winning every game for seven years. But in 1958 as the game neared its end, Bobby Bryant (85) caught a great pass from quarterback Bob Lackey and scored a touchdown to give Texas a come-from-behind 15–14 victory.

Arkansas. After the win over Oklahoma, Texas fans charged onto the field and carried Royal off on their shoulders.

Royal was named Coach of the Week and Texas' great end, Bobby Bryant, was named Lineman of the Week. To cap off the celebration, the plane carrying the squad back to Austin had to circle the airport for more than fifteen minutes while police moved several thousand fans off the field for their own safety. The Texas win streak had captivated the entire state.

But a scrappy Rice Owls squad caught Texas off-balance a week later and stunned the Longhorns with two quick touchdowns in the second period. Before Royal could get his squad down from the clouds, Rice quickly put another 20 points on the scoreboard to bury the Longhorns by a 34–7 margin. One week later, still in shock from the beating

In 1958, Royal's second season as head coach, Texas returned to its winning ways with an outstanding 7–3 record, including a streak of 5 victories and a smashing 15–14 win over Oklahoma. *Front row, left to right:* Wells, Muennink, Shillingburg, Bryant, Parkhurst, Doke, Ramirez, Allen. *Second row, left to right:* Bergen, Pittman (assistant coach), Dowdle, Blanch, Branch, Schulte, Matthews, Stephens, J. Padgett, Anderson, Dreymala, Lackney, Newman, Willsey (assistant coach), Knicker. *Third row, left to right:* Fincher (senior manager), Swarthout (assistant coach), Jones (assistant coach), Murray, Rivers, Biasatti, Kruse, Grubbs, Jones, Morris, Dyer, Williams, Ehl, Cayce, Goodwin, Halm, Wetzel, Schultz, Mabra, Royal (head coach), Shira (assistant coach). *Fourth row, left to right:* Moffett, Gurwitz, Rose, Cooper, Harwerth, Petty, Laughlin, Hollon, Neffendorf, Gott, Matocha, Stolhandske. *Fifth row, left to right:* Bednarski, Jennings, Fitts, Young, Crutsinger, Jackson, O'Brien, Goodman, Talbert, Gates, E. Padgett, Blasingame.

Texas halfback Rene Ramirez (46) outraces four Maryland defenders to score a TD in a 1959 game that Texas won 26–0.

and a field goal to defeat the Aggies 27–0 in rainy, muddy Austin weather that hampered both teams. Rene Ramirez was a phenom, scoring three touchdowns, and guard Bob Harwerth was a stone wall on defense as time after time he single-handedly wrecked the A&M offense.

Royal finished on a high note with a great win over Oklahoma and A&M and a marvelous 7–3 season record. Darrell Royal's 1958 season was another big step on the way back for UT football. Wins over Oklahoma and Texas A&M and an improving group of young players pointed to even bigger things.

A talented group of sophomores and some twenty-three varsity lettermen reported to Coach Darrell Royal as he began his third season as head coach at Texas. Fifteen seniors who had struggled through two years of the toughest training that any Texas squad would endure were the backbone for what every Texas fan expected would be one of the most successful seasons in years.

Two outstanding veterans were made co-captains of the Longhorns: Don Allen, an explosive defensive fullback, and end Monte Lee, a hustling player, who could block, tackle, and catch any ball thrown his way. Other key veterans included quarterback Bob Lackey; Jim Bob Moffett, a strapping 215-pound tackle; guards Maurice Doke and Babe Dreymala; and Don Talbert and David Kristynik, two solid linemen. In the backfield Royal had Jim Saxton, a flashy, 165-pound speedster who could run the 100-yard dash in 9.9 and was to provide Texas fans with some of the most brilliant plays in Texas football history.

The opening game against a veteran Nebraska team was an eye opener, for Royal's speedy backs and ends just ate up the turf, scoring on runs of 50, 23, and 33 yards in a 20–0 win. Jack Collins served notice that he was just as fast and flashy as teammate Saxton by sweeping for 85 yards and a TD in the opening moments of a night game vs. Maryland. Before they could recover, Texas scored 19 additional points in the third period courtesy of Ramirez and Dave Russell. That gave Texas a sweet 26–0 victory.

After the Maryland win, the Board of Regents gave Coach Royal a new five-year contract. But the Regents did not increase Royal's $17,500 salary.

A national TV audience that tuned in to the Texas vs. California contest the following week saw the Longhorns' splashy stars—Jim Saxton, Jack Collins, Rene Ramirez, and Mike Dowdle—stun California with long runs of 42, 44, and 40 yards and Saxton's 55-yard TD run gave Texas five touchdowns and a surprising 33–0 win over Cal.

Next was Oklahoma. The Sooners gave every indication they would rout the Longhorns, scoring two quick touchdowns in the first period, but Ramirez sparked a 72-yard Texas drive that gave Texas its first score. The half ended with Saxton, Lackey, and Dowdle driving 61 yards for a second TD. Texas was out in front by a single point, 13–12.

The Sooners threatened on several occasions but could not crack the tough, determined Texas defense led by Doke, Monte Lee, and Jim Bob Moffett. Then midway in the final period Mike Cotten tossed a screen pass to Collins and Jack sprinted past three Sooner tacklers on a 61-yard TD jaunt that gave Texas a 19–12 lead they never relinquished. It was a thrilling win over the tough Sooners.

With eight wins in a row Arkansas was ranked No. 5 in the nation, and they proved to be as good as their rating. They scored with four minutes gone to go up 7–0, and had a 7–6 halftime lead. The Razorbacks scored again to go out in front by a 12–6 margin. But in the fourth period Texas scored and managed to hang onto a 13–12 victory for its fifth straight win.

Rice rolled into Austin for a night game vs. Texas confident that they could repeat their 1958 34–7 victory over Texas, but the still-smarting Longhorns completely outplayed and dominated the Owls from start to finish. Collins and Ramirez sparked the Longhorns to a 28–6 win. SMU's all-American Don Meredith, whose great passing had twice defeated the Longhorns, was stymied and throttled by the Texas line as Texas scored a 21–0 win.

A week later, the Baylor Bears quickly passed for two long TD drives and took a 12–7 lead over the Longhorns. It looked as if Texas' hopes for an undefeated season would go by the boards when Baylor drove to the Texas 13-yard line. But Baylor fumbled, and Texas recovered and scored a TD as Cotten pitched to Collins to give Texas another thriller, 13–12.

Texas, now rated No. 2 in the polls and the first 8–0 Texas team since Berry Whitaker's great team of 1920, was a slight favorite to beat a very good TCU squad. But this time the gods of victory were in TCU's corner and the Frogs took a convincing 14–9 win over the Longhorns in a bruising, scrappy defensive battle. Baylor permitted Texas just one first down in the final two periods to win the game and knock the Longhorns from the undefeated ranks.

Against the Texas Aggies, the Longhorns were now playing for a shot at the SWC title and a Cotton Bowl invitation. But they were still shocked by their tough loss to Baylor, and fell behind A&M by 10–0 at halftime. The second half saw a resurgent Texas team, though, fighting with a fury that could not be contained. In the third period, Texas drove 90 and 35 yards for two touchdowns. But the Aggies came back to score a TD for a 17–14 lead with 7½ minutes left to play. Texas began to operate. A pass from Bob Lackey to Collins. Then a drive by Collins, then another pass from Lackey to Cooper for the winning TD. Final score: 20–17. Texas had won a trip to the Cotton Bowl and a contest against undefeated Syracuse.

It was Texas' seventh visit to the Cotton Bowl. They had won four, lost one, and tied one. The Longhorns were meeting a Syracuse team that to this day is called the greatest in Syracuse history. The Orangemen led the nation in scoring and in defense. Texas Assistant Coach Mike Campbell said of the Syracuse line, "I have never seen a college line as big and strong as this one is. And this halfback they have, Ernie Davis, is a worthy successor to the great Jim Brown."

On the second play of the game, Syracuse back, Gerhard Schwedes tossed a long pass to Ernie Davis, who caught the ball at midfield, outran three Texas tacklers, and sped in for a touchdown. The play covered 87 yards, a record for the Cotton

Talking about the Syracuse team meeting Texas in the 1959 Cotton Bowl, Texas Assistant Coach Mike Campbell said, "I've never seen a bigger college line than this Syracuse line." Syracuse won 23–14.

Bowl. Texas reached the Syracuse 23-yard line, then punted. The Orangemen drove 80 yards for another score. In the second half, Texas struck back as Lackey hit Collins on a pass and Jack sped 35 yards for the first Texas TD. But Syracuse quickly struck back and scored its third TD, giving them a 23–6 margin. Midway through the fourth period, Texas scored on Branch's dash up the middle for 35 yards and a touchdown to make the score 23–14, Syracuse. Texas recovered a fumble and then drove down to the Syracuse 1-yard line. But they could not cross the goal line and the game ended with Syracuse on top, 23–14. The win cinched the national championship for Syracuse.

The 9–2 season chalked up by Coach Royal and his Longhorns—in particular the great wins over Nebraska, California, Oklahoma, and A&M—

and their tremendous all-around play in the Cotton Bowl—marked the return of Texas as a national football power.

Guard Maurice Doke was named to the all-American team and Monte Lee, Jack Collins, Rene Ramirez, and Doke were named to the All-SWC Team. And once again Coach Darrell Royal was awarded a new contract. This time it was for ten years.

Texas Freshman Football Coach Bob Schultze left on the morning of December 10, 1955, to scout the high school talent in the state playoff game between Baytown and Reagan. Schultze had received glowing reports about a fast, rangy end who was the best player in the area. But in watching the exciting high school contest, Schultze's eyes were glued to the performance of a young giant who roamed all over the field of play, stopping the Baytown backs time after time before they could get started. He was in on almost every play and his tackling was so fierce that he jarred every player he hit. His name was Jim Bob Moffett, and after the game Jim Bob was named to Houston's All-City High School team.

Moffett will never forget the final days of his high school career. There were a few coaches who showed some interest in the six-foot-three, 195-pound tackle and three-sport letterman. "But," said Moffett, "Mr. Schultze was the only coach who kept coming back again and again to see me play and to talk about a scholarship."

The other players who made that All-City team abandoned football and are forgotten, but Moffett got that Texas football scholarship and made the team. Now, in 1960, he was a senior and in his fifth year of eligibility was performing in a manner that thrilled Darrell Royal.

Moffett was bigger and tougher. He weighed 225 pounds and had played every position in the line except center, and he had performed like the veteran that he was.

"Over a long period of time," said Royal, "Jim Bob was one of the biggest surprises we've ever had. He was almost the forgotten man. For two years he suited up for every practice and every game but sat

"Jim Bob Moffett was one of the biggest surprises I've ever had at Texas," said Coach Darrell Royal. "For two years he suited up for every practice and every game. But he persevered, stayed with it, and by 1960 was one of our top linemen. In a sense, Jim Bob typifies the true spirit of the Texas Longhorns."

on the bench. But he persevered and stayed with it. He had a perfectly solid excuse for not playing. He had so much work to make up in the geology lab that he could not devote all his spare time for football, and he failed to make the traveling squad his first couple of years."

But he hung on, and in 1959 he made his letter and got to play in a couple of games.

"Even though I didn't play that much the first three years, I never had any idea of quitting the squad. That football scholarship meant a whole lot to me. Not too many people got scholarships back in those days," said Moffett, now CEO of Freeport McMoran in New Orleans.

He rapidly improved his blocking and tackling and by 1960 was counted on as a starter. In addition Jim Bob was a top candidate for the All-Southwest Conference scholastic team. An A and B student, Jim Bob was in the top 3% of the 5800 students in the arts and sciences department.

Texas' Larry Cooper has just caught a pass and is off for a 54-yard touchdown against Texas Tech, as Tech defender Bake Cooper misses the tackle. Texas defeated Tech 17–0.

In the first three games of the 1960 season, a 14–13 loss to Nebraska and shutout wins against Maryland and Texas Tech, Jim Bob Moffett was a key man in the Longhorns' invincible defense—a defense that held Tech to just 85 yards.

"In a sense," said Coach Royal, "Jim Bob Moffett typifies the true spirit of the Texas Longhorns. He stuck it out in the pits for three years, then became an honors student and was one of my top players in his fifth year. Not too many people would have that much courage and stick-to-itiveness."

Against Oklahoma, Texas shocked the Sooners with a 24–0 upset as Jim Saxton, Dan Petty, and Ray Poage starred for Texas. Poage scored two touchdowns in the victory. A strong Arkansas team looked vulnerable, as they had lost to Baylor 28–14 just a week earlier. But the game was nip and tuck. Texas scored two quick touchdowns, and Arkansas came back with one of their own. At the half it was 14–7, Texas. Arkansas rallied and quickly tied the score in the third period, but Texas halfback Jerry Cook broke through the

Arkansas line for several big gains to the 15-yard line. Then tackle Dan Petty booted a field goal to give Texas a 17–14 edge. Texas quickly scored another touchdown and it was 23–14. The Razorbacks bounced back with a touchdown and it was now a 23–21 margin with Texas in the lead.

There were just 38 seconds to play when Mike Cissell, Arkansas' ace place kicker, booted an easy 15-yard field goal to win the seesaw struggle 24–23.

A week later, it was Rice's turn and the Owls defeated the Horns in a defensive battle, 7–0. But the Longhorns rebounded with a good effort against SMU and took a 17–7 victory over the Mustangs despite having two scores nullified due to penalties. Baylor was defeated next, 12–7. One week later, against TCU, Texas scored a field goal and held the Frogs to just one first down through the first half and took a 3–0 lead into the locker room. In the final period, with both teams still waging a cautious, defensive struggle, Saxton was tackled in the Texas end zone for a safety to give TCU 2 points. The game ended with Texas out in front by a remarkable 3–2 score.

Texas quarterback Mike Cotten (12) tosses a flat pass to Tommy Lucas (84). Lucas then picks up a nice gain against SMU in this 1960 game. Texas won 17–7.

In College Station in the final regular game of the season, Texas completely outplayed the Aggies and scored three quick touchdowns in the first half. Then, in a complete reversal, A&M pulled their offense together to score 2 touchdowns, but the game ended without any further scoring. Final score: Texas 21, A&M 14.

An invitation to play Alabama in the Bluebonnet Bowl was accepted by Texas, and Darrell Royal began plans to defeat his good friend, Bear Bryant. The Alabama legend's Crimson Tide had ended their regular season with an 8-1-1 record.

The game, played before 75,000 fans at Rice Stadium, was as close as expected. Both teams played cautiously, and it was strictly a defensive battle by both teams. One big pass play by Alabama from Bob Skelton to end Bill Rice was good for 49 yards, but Rice was tackled on the 7-yard line by David Russell and the only threat of the half ended.

Coach Darrell Royal (*right*) and Alabama's Bear Bryant (*left*) have a quick chat before their teams battle in the 1960 Bluebonnet Bowl.

Texas halfback James Saxton (dark shirt) was voted the Most Valuable Texas Player in the 1960 Bluebonnet Bowl against Alabama. The game ended in a 3–3 tie.

Texas quarterback Mike Cotten (12) picks up 10 yards on this run before being downed by two Alabama tacklers in the 1960 Bluebonnet Bowl.

In the third period, a poor Texas punt set up Alabama at the Texas 39-yard stripe. However, Alabama's ground game was shut down by a great defensive stand by Texas. Then, on fourth down, Tom Brooker of Alabama booted a 30-yard field goal that was just barely good. Alabama had a 3–0 lead. But Texas fired right back with a Mike Cotten pass to Jim Saxton, and Saxton sped down to the Tide 23-yard line. Dan Petty missed the field goal from the 35-yard line. The Tide took over but could gain little ground and once again Texas had the ball. Drives by Saxton, Collins, and Russell brought the ball down to the Tide's 5-yard line. With three minutes left in the game, Petty booted his name into the Longhorn Hall of Fame with a perfect three-pointer to tie the score.

As the bruising 3–3 contest ended, Coaches Royal and Bryant met at midfield and walked off the field with their arms around each other's shoulders.

Jim Saxton was voted the Most Valuable Texas Player, and the entire defensive unit was acclaimed for their fine work in the trenches.

"All things considered," said Royal, "after we had a 3–3 record in the first six games, I look upon our last four games as one of our finest accomplishments. It was remarkable to wind up with a 7-3-1 season after a poor start."

In his fifth season as coach of Texas football, Darrell Royal could look back on four successful years in Texas football with a record of 29 victories, 12 losses, and 2 ties. The Longhorns had twice captured SWC titles, had shared the title in another season, and had been invited to the Sugar Bowl, the Bluebonnet Bowl, and two Cotton Bowls. The record spoke for itself. Any other coach would have been delighted with that record. But Royal wasn't like any other coach. He wanted a championship team—a national championship team. He worked like a horse in 1961 to reach that lofty goal.

To prepare his team for the 1961 season, Royal completely revamped his "grind-'em-out type offense." "We've got to have a new offense and come up with a break-away runner, a guy who can give us a big play every once in a while." And in 1961 Jim Saxton was the man Royal was seeking. Saxton, a fleet, 164-pound senior, was the key man in Royal's new "flip-flop" offense. With Saxton in the ball-carrying slot, he would handle the ball on almost every play. This meant that the halfbacks and linemen, everybody but the quarterback, center, and fullback, would have to learn half again as many blocking assignments on every play.

In the lineup for the opening game Royal had Saxton and Mike Cotten alternating as the quarterbacks, Jack Collins and Ray Poage at halfbacks, and Pat Culpepper at fullback. Linemen included Tom Lucas, and Bob Moses at end; Marv Kubin and Don Talbert at tackle; guards Ed Padgett and John Treadwell; and center Dave Kristynik.

In the opening game of the season against California, Jim Saxton broke away for two fine runs that led to a score. But poor ballhandling led to several Texas fumbles and it was 7–3 at the half. Texas pulled away in the second half, scoring three times to give the Longhorns a 28–3 victory in a game that Royal called "most unimpressive."

Against Texas Tech, the Longhorns needed just twenty-eight plays to strike for 5 touchdowns in the first half, then ran the score up to 42–14 over a good Tech squad. Against Washington State, the new Texas offense sputtered in the first half of the game, but came to life as they ran up 27 points in the second half to beat the Cougars 41–8. Jimmy Saxton was outstanding, and his 56-yard touchdown run sparked the second half scoring.

Oklahoma had played tough games against Notre Dame and Iowa State. But Saxton, Culpepper, and Poage provided the spark to overcome the Sooners 28–7. The Longhorns were made a six-point favorite to beat Arkansas the next week. Led by fullback Tom Ford, they marched 51 and then 74 yards for two quick scores, then ran up a 33–7 win to make it five straight.

Now the Associated Press poll boosted Texas into the No. 3 spot in the nation. Suddenly the Texas football program, Coach Royal, and the Longhorns were front-page news on the nation's sports pages.

In the game against Rice, the Texas offensive machine put together sparkling drives of 75 and 80 yards, led by Saxton, Cotten, and Culpepper, to pile up several scores. But above all it was the sensational play of a newcomer, linebacker Scott Appleton, that anchored the Texas defense. Appleton was all over the gridiron, spilling Rice backs and upsetting plays before they could get started. Texas easily defeated Rice, 34–7.

An SMU eleven primed to defeat Texas held the powerful Longhorn offense to just 88 total yards in the first half to claim a 0–0 tie. But late in the third period Jim Saxton faked a pass, then ducked under an SMU tackler, burst through tackle, shot to the sidelines, and raced almost the entire length of the field for a scintillating 80-yard touchdown. Then the power and timing of the Texas offense

Texas quarterback Mike Cotten on his way to a touchdown against Washington State in 1961. Don Talbert (72) attempts to block for Cotten.

showed in the next sequence of downs. A great TD pass followed by two touchdown sprints gave the Horns 20 points and a 27–0 win over SMU. An easy win over Baylor the following week by a 33–7 margin vaulted the Horns into the No. 1 spot among the nation's collegiate teams. Now it was up to Texas to win its final two games.

TCU was rated a 15-point underdog as Texas tried for its ninth straight win, but the Frogs played like they were No. 1. On one of the first plays of the game, TCU tried a long pass that was intercepted by Jim Saxton and he was away like a flash. But after a 20-yard gain Jim was hit by a TCU tackler who slammed into his head, and Saxton went down and remained unconscious for a few moments. He was taken off the field, and that was the end of the Texas offense. TCU scored in the second period to take a 6–0 lead, then played heroic defense to win in the biggest upset of the year by a 6–0 score.

Texas' great halfback, Jim Saxton, on the bench after being injured in a 1961 TCU game. A teammate consoles him.

"I don't believe I'll ever forget this game," said Coach Royal in the dressing room after the most crushing loss of his career.

But a victory over the Texas Aggies would mean a Cotton Bowl game, and another chance at a strong national rating. And the Longhorns with Saxton, back in the lineup, and Jerry Cook and Jack Collins racked up four TDs and a resounding 25–0 win over the Aggies. That meant a Cotton Bowl matchup with Mississippi.

Before a crowd of more than 75,000 fans on New Year's Day, Texas had to be at their best to defeat Mississippi, who boasted a 9–1 record. The Longhorns played their very best to score two touchdowns to defeat Ole Miss in one of the most spine-tingling contests of the year.

In the second period, halfback Tommy Ford intercepted an Ole Miss pass on the 34-yard line. Then Pat Culpepper, who had not carried the ball many times this season, ran for 13 yards. Then it was Russell, Poage, and Saxton, who carried the ball over for Texas' first TD. Later in the period Mike Cotten passed to Collins and Collins raced in for Texas' second score.

In the Cotton Bowl against Mississippi on January 1, 1962, Jackie Collins (49) takes a pass from Mike Cotten and races in for a Texas touchdown to win the game for the Horns 12–7.

Late in the third period, Ole Miss scored a touchdown to narrow the score to 12–7. Again Ole Miss took possession of the ball and drove downfield to the Texas 20-yard line. Three bruising drives into the line failed to gain and on fourth down, Ole Miss was stopped an inch short of the goal line as the gun sounded to end the battle.

Texas' marvelous 10–1 season earned them the No. 3 ranking in the nation, behind Alabama and Ohio State.

Jim Saxton averaged 8.3 yards per carry, had TD runs of 80, 79, 66, 56, 49, and 45 yards, and was a consensus all-American choice, while Cotten, Talbert, Moses, Kristynik, and Saxton were named to the All-SWC team.

Coach Darrell Royal was honored by the Football Writers Association of America as Coach of the Year. The city of Austin further added to Coach Royal's glory by declaring a Darrell Royal Day. It was quite a year for the Texas coach and his team.

The graduation of some of his finest players convinced Coach Darrell Royal that in 1962 he would have to concentrate on his defense. "Rather than bemoaning the loss of Saxton, Collins, and Cotten, we ought to be grateful that we had those great kids for three years," said Royal.

"Replacing Saxton was practically impossible," said Royal. "Jerry Cook and Tommy Ford will give us more runningbacks. Then we've got Ernie Koy, whose father was a great Longhorn star in the 1930s, and in John Genung and Duke Carlisle we've got two promising quarterbacks with star potential. In the line there's John Treadwell and tackle Scott Appleton, two fine defensive guys." Tommy Lucas at one end, Sandy Sands at the other end, tackle Ken Ferguson, guards Marv Kubin and Dave McWilliams fleshed out the squad.

In the season's opener, Texas, rated No. 2 in the nation, was a two-touchdown favorite over Oregon and trailed the Webfoots 6–3 at halftime. In the second half, Oregon quickly increased their lead by scoring a second TD and led 13–3.

But Texas came to life in the third period when Genung drove the Longhorns 80 yards for a score, then added a two-point conversion to make it 13–11, Oregon. Texas then recovered an Oregon fumble on the 5-yard line and quickly scored their second TD. Johnny Genung, who completed 8 of 13 passes, sparked Texas to still another score with a 60-yard TD pass to wrap up a hard-fought 25–13 win.

Texas Tech was easily defeated in Lubbock 34–0 and then Tulane was trounced 35–8. Ernie Koy, Johnny Genung, and Tommy Ford were outstanding in both games as the entire team performed flawlessly.

Texas' outstanding field goal kicker, Tony Crosby, booted a 26-yard field goal in the second period of a bruising contest against Oklahoma, then Perry McWilliams battled three Sooners for a fumbled pitchout. McWilliams came up with the ball in the end zone for a touchdown and Texas wrapped up its fourth win of the season. The 9–6 thriller had the crowd of 60,000 screaming with excitement.

Then it was another down-to-the-wire thriller against Arkansas. The Razorbacks took a quick 3–0 lead. But Texas kept on banging away with savage drives into the line for 4 and 5 yards on each play. Then Duke Carlisle rifled several short, fast passes to Tommy Lucas and Sandy Sands. With just two minutes left to play, Ford took a pitchout on the 3-yard line, then savagely battered his way into the end zone with three tacklers on his back for the touchdown that won the game for Texas, 7–3. The Associated Press voted the Longhorns the nation's No. 1 football team.

At Houston the following week, Rice burst Texas' national championship hopes as the Owls played a stubborn defensive game to tie the Longhorns 14–14. It was a game that Texas could have won. With 3½ minutes to play, Carlisle drove downfield to the Rice 39-yard line. Tommy Wade took over at quarterback and tossed three passes that just missed; then, on fourth down, halfback Jerry Cook was stopped by a diving tackle on the 30-yard stripe, just a foot short of a first down. Rice took over and ran out the clock.

In the second period against SMU, Duke Carlisle caught a punt on the Texas 5-yard line, then sprinted upfield, aided by some of the greatest blocking of the year. He was brought down on the SMU 1-yard line. Duke's brilliant 94-yard run was all that the Longhorns needed. On the next play Texas scored, then held on to win by a 6–0 score. A week later a tough Baylor team played position ball, scored two touchdowns, and threw a scare into Coach Royal and his Longhorns. But the Horns came back fighting as Wade riddled the Bears defense with pinpoint passing, scoring two TDs. Two more scores late in the third and fourth periods and Texas chalked up another win, 27–12.

In the locker room just prior to the kickoff for the game at TCU, Coach Royal stressed the importance of a defensive game that could mean a win and the SWC championship. The Longhorns responded by holding the Frogs to just 70 yards and took a well-earned 14–0 verdict from TCU. Fullback Ray Poage blasted for the two scores as the Longhorns posted their eighth victory of the season. All that was left were the Texas Aggies . . . just five days later.

In Austin before a record crowd, the Aggies played a smart, aggressive, consistently steady game. They outplayed Texas and took a 3–0 lead into the locker room at the half. In the second half, led by quarterback Johnny Genung and Ernie Koy, who had been injured for a couple of weeks, Texas

pounded out two scores to completely halt the Aggies and win by a convincing 13–3 margin.

The win over the Aggies was the ninth of the year for Texas and gave the Horns the No. 4 ranking in the nation. It also put them in the Cotton Bowl against 8-1-1 LSU, the fifth bowl game in six years for Coach Royal.

Both LSU and Texas were geared up for the game, but both teams played a cautious, defensive battle. Late in the second period LSU's Lynn Amadee booted a 23-yard field goal and LSU had a 3–0 edge at the half.

Texas had come from behind five times during the season, but in this game they never got started. Halfback Jerry Cook fumbled the kickoff to open the second half and LSU recovered. Three plays later Jim Fields of LSU sped 22 yards for a TD and a 10–0 LSU lead. Late in the game LSU added another field goal, and upset Texas in a stunning 13–0 win.

The loss to LSU put a damper on the Longhorns' season, although it was the second best for Coach Royal, who said, "I have to be real happy with our season. That's all I have to say."

Despite the loss of eight starters from the 1962 team that had only lost to LSU in the Cotton Bowl, Darrell Royal had a feeling that his 1963

team would be among the best in Texas football history. He had some forty-two lettermen returning for his sixth season. Included in this array of veterans were such standout performers as tackle Scott Appleton whom Royal called "the best defensive lineman I've had since I've been coaching football. Scott makes tackles from sideline to sideline and he's like blocking a wall on one play and smoke the rest." Other veterans who would start the 1963 season against Tulane included end Ben House and Charley Talbert and Stanley Faulkner, tackles. At guard were George Brucks and a young man named Tommy Nobis whom Royal called "a one-man wrecking crew." At center was one of the team's three captains, Dave McWilliams. In the backfield was Duke Carlisle, a smart, cool passing fiend, at quarterback; Tommy Ford and Tony King at halfback; and Ernie Koy at fullback.

On the road against Tulane, Texas had to fight off the Green Wave for three periods and were only able to register two field goals by Tony Crosby. But in the last period, halfback Phil Harris cracked through for two touchdowns and Texas came away with a 21–0 victory.

In the second game of the season the Texas offense came alive and polished off Texas Tech with a 6-touchdown deluge and a 49–7 rout as Duke

Carlisle, Tommy Ford, Phil Harris (who darted 80 yards for a score), and Marv Krystynik scored TDs. The Longhorns showed future opponents just a hint of their speed on offense, and demonstrated tremendous defensive power.

Oklahoma State was next, and the Cowboys suffered the misfortune of five costly fumbles as they were routed by Texas 34–7. Quarterback Duke Carlisle, Ernie Koy, and Tommy Ford led the way, though Koy suffered an injury that sidelined him for the season.

In a game in Dallas that was called "The Game of the Century" between the No. 1 team, Oklahoma, and the No. 2 team, it was all Texas from the beginning. Texas took the kickoff and Carlisle and Ford slashed through the Sooner line

Left to right: **Texas quarterback Duke Carlisle (11) takes the ball on an option play, then cracks into the Oklahoma line and scores to give Texas a 7–0 lead over OU in 1963. Texas blockers Ben House (83) and Gordy Roberts (76) knock down three Oklahoma defenders as Carlisle scores the touchdown. Oklahoma defenders are George Stokes (79), Rick McCurdy (80), Dave Voiles (57), and Jacky Cowen (32).**

Charley Talbert (89) crashes into Oklahoma quarterback Rick McCurdy in a 1963 battle won by the Longhorns.

with ease for gain after gain. Carlisle scored from the 1-yard line, and from there it was simply no contest. The Longhorns played like a well-oiled machine, and efficiently mowed down the Sooners by a 28–7 margin. Appleton and Nobis were the outstanding linemen, and Appleton (with eighteen tackles) was selected as Lineman of the Week by the United Press. Texas was voted the No. 1 team in the nation. It was Bud Wilkinson's final game in the Cotton Bowl with Oklahoma.

In the game in Little Rock against Arkansas, Texas quickly scored two touchdowns. Then a field goal by Tony Crosby made it 17–0, and it appeared as though Texas had a walk-away win. But with fifty-three seconds left in the half, Arkansas half-

back Jackie Braswull took Crosby's kickoff and scampered 59 yards to the Texas 6-yard line. On the following play the Razorbacks scored to make it 17–7, and that was the score at halftime. Texas threatened on at least three occasions in the second half, but each time Arkansas held the Longhorns. In the final period Arkansas took the ball on its own 10-yard line and drove upfield. It was a furious drive of 5 yards, then 7, then 10 more, and finally Arkansas hit paydirt and scored a TD. Texas had a 17–13 lead but with five minutes to play it seemed anything could happen.

Arkansas got the ball back on the 46-yard line. Twice the Razorback quarterback barely missed on long passes that could have been a touchdown and the ball game. Then on fourth down he tossed a long pass that looked right on the money. But at the last second massive Scott Appleton leaped high in the air, tipped the ball, and Timmy Doerr intercepted it for Texas. That was the ball game. Texas ran out the clock for a smashing 17–13 victory.

It's called ball control. It consists of precision blocking, no mistakes, smart ball-handling, and sustained ball possession. And nobody ever coached it better than Darrell Royal. That kind of hard-nosed football stole a 10–6 tussle from Rice the following week in a battle that had the Memorial Stadium crowd of 55,000 standing and cheering until they were hoarse. Once again it was the accurate toe of Tony Crosby who booted a field goal to guarantee Texas the win.

Halfback Tommy Ford, moving like a runaway express train, got Texas going at the very start of next week's SMU game in Dallas. He took the ball on the first play of the game, burst through tackle, and kept going to the SMU 28-yard line before he was stopped. It was a magnificent 50-yard jaunt. Then it was up to Phil Harris and he cracked through for Texas' first TD. Then an SMU fumble was recovered by Texas on the SMU 6-yard line and again it was Ford up the middle for another TD. Now it was 14–0. SMU then settled down and put together a 60-yard drive for a TD to make it a 14–6 game. Tony Crosby kicked a field goal near the end of the half and Texas had a 17–6 lead. In

David Royal, 10-year-old son of Coach Darrell Royal, shows his dad a toy football player dressed in Baylor Bears' colors that he stuck full of pins during the Baylor-Texas game. Perhaps it was David's black magic, but undefeated Texas won their eighth straight game in a 7–0 squeaker to remain the No. 1 team in the nation.

the third period SMU scored to make it 17–12, but that was as close as they came and Texas had another squeaker and its seventh straight win.

Both Texas and Coach John Bridgers' Baylor Bears played a defensively pitched battle in Memorial Stadium a week later. But neither team could pull off a haymaker play that would give them a TD and the lead until the third period. Texas marched 50 yards and it was halfback Tommy Ford who bulled across the goal line for a TD and the only score of the game in a nail-biter 7–0 victory in a game that was not certain until the final 45 seconds of play. That's when Duke Carlisle deflected a pass from Larry Elkins of Baylor to his end, Don Trull. Carlisle saw the play develop, then leaped high into the air to knock the ball down on what looked like a certain tie-breaking touchdown as the game ended.

Fullback Harold Philipp, injured in the Baylor game, was replaced by Tommy Stockton for the TCU game. Stockton was brilliant. He carried the ball 21 times for 89 yards, scoring one TD, and his power drives up the middle set the stage for another score to give Texas a 17–0 win over the Frogs. Tony Crosby kicked a 42-yard field goal to add to the Texas win.

In a game that had national championship stamped all over it, on a cold, dreary day in College Station the Longhorns and Aggies battled each other tooth and nail in a tremendous defensive struggle. With only seventy seconds remaining on the clock, seventy seconds that spelled glory or despair, Duke Carlisle prevailed. The score showed A&M 13, Texas 9. On a smash into the line from the 5-yard line, Carlisle burst through for a touchdown and snatched victory from certain defeat by a 15–13 margin.

Texas was 10–0, ranked No. 1, and Cotton Bowl-bound. Their opponent was a Naval Academy team that was being called the finest in history. It would be a battle for the national championship, since the 9–1 Midshipmen were ranked No. 2.

The Cotton Bowl game had an aura of sadness, for President Kennedy had just been assassinated in Dallas and the entire nation mourned his untimely passing. Bringing additional personal sadness to the team, Tri-captain David McWilliams' mother suddenly passed away just a few days before the game.

For weeks the nation's sportswriters were unanimously in favor of Navy and its incomparable quarterback, junior Roger "the Dodger" Staubach, who had been terrorizing every team he faced. Staubach's marvelous passing and great ability to move "out of the pocket" and spot his receivers or take off on a touchdown sprint was sure to give Texas problems. Of course, the Cotton Bowl was the site of Navy's only loss, a 32–28 upset by SMU.

But Darrell Royal had planned a perfect defensive alignment to stop Roger before he could get started. The plan was to have the Texas ends charge in on every play to stop Roger's scrambling and keep him in the pocket, where he would have

In their last practice session before the Cotton Bowl game against Navy for the national championship, Coach Royal positions team captain David McWilliams and quarterback Duke Carlisle. Texas defeated Navy 28–6 to capture their first national championship on January 1, 1964.

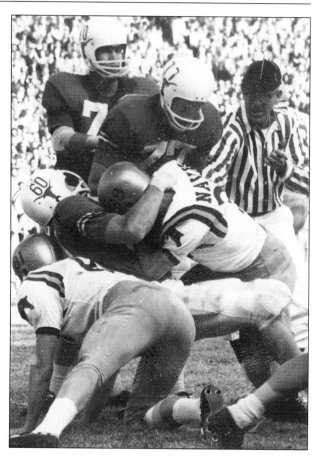

In the national championship battle at the Cotton Bowl, Texas' great lineman Tommy Nobis (60) and Scott Appleton (70, far left) were outstanding as they halted Roger Staubach's running and passing game. Both Nobis and Appleton are shown jamming the Navy defense as Texas went on to beat Navy 28–6 for the national crown.

to pass or go down. And the plan worked to perfection. Time after time, Staubach was hammered in the pocket, unable to pass, unable to scramble. And Navy was in a quandary.

In the first period, Duke Carlisle tossed a perfect, high-arching pass to Phil Harris, who caught the ball over his shoulder and streaked across the goal line for a TD. The sensational 58-yard pass play stunned Navy.

In the second period, Carlisle shot another pass to Harris. Pat Donnelly of Navy tipped the ball, but it bounced into Harris' hands, and Phil raced away for a 63-yard touchdown. The half ended with Texas in front of a shocked Navy team 21–0.

In the final period, Texas scored again on a Carlisle-to-Harris pass that Harris flipped to Tommy Wade. Wade brought the ball to the 2-yard

line. Phillips scored and it was 28–6 Texas the rest of the way.

The Longhorns of Texas had beaten "Navy's greatest football team." They were voted the National Champions by a unanimous vote of the nation's top sportswriters to cap off a dream year. Scott Appleton and Tommy Ford were named all-Americans.

Seventy years after Texas' first football game, the Longhorns were the best team in the nation, and their coach, Darrell Royal, was saluted and feted as the Coach of the Year.

1957–1976: THOSE CHAMPIONSHIP SEASONS

An undefeated Texas team ended the 1963 season with an incredible 28–6 win over Navy to capture their first national championship. *Front row, left to right:* Olen Underwood, Scott Appleton, Clarence Bray, Stanley Faulkner, Charles Talbert, David McWilliams, George Brucks, Ken Halm, Jim Besselman, Bobby Gamblin. *Second row, left to right:* Assistant Coach Jim Pittman, Manager Lane Zunker, Ken Ferguson, Gordon Roberts, Duke Carlisle, Tony Crosby, Bo Price, Frank Bedrick, Joe Dixon, Lee Hansely, Hix Green, Anthony King, Tommy Ford, Assistant Coach Bill Ellington, Senior Manager Roy Jones, Trainer Frank Medina. *Third row, left to right:* Assistant Coach Art Davis, Assistant Coach Bob Schultze, Manager Bill Vogt, Assistant Coach Pat Culpepper, Jim Hunson, Mike King, Sandy Sands, Harold Philipp, Tim Doerr, Marvin Kristynik, Dan Mauldin, Tommy Mankin, Ben House, Clayton Lacy, Pete Lammons, Tom Currie, Tommy Wade, Charles Buckalew, Assistant Coach Russell Coffee, Head Coach Darrell Royal.

Quarterback Duke Carlisle (11) is chased by three Navy players, but picks up a nice gain of 15 yards in the 1964 Cotton Bowl.

Coach Royal faced a major rebuilding job in 1964, for 16 seniors had graduated and left Texas with just three veteran players on the offense. But after three weeks of practice, Royal was enthusiastic about his new players and was beginning to feel that his '64 team was equal to the task of again challenging for the National Crown.

For the Tulane game that opened the season, Royal started a Texas backfield that consisted of Harold Philipp at fullback, Marv Kristynik at quarterback, and Ernie Koy and Phil Harris as the halfbacks. Linemen included Sandy Sands, Pete Lammons, and George Sauer at end; Gene Bledsoe and Clayton Lacy at tackle; all-American Tommy Nobis and Frank Bedrick at the guard; and Olen Underwood at center.

The opening game of the season against Tulane, a night game in Austin, provided a solid test for the 1964 Longhorns. Tulane, playing a tough defensive contest, held the Longhorns to just 10 points in the first half. Fumbles by Texas backs kept the score down, but the Longhorns tallied 21 points in the second half and took a 31–0 win over the Green Wave. Next, Texas Tech was beaten 23–0.

Then Coach Paul Dietzel and his strong Army team came into Austin for the first-ever battle between Army and Texas. Army's Rollie Stichweh struck paydirt in the first period as Army recovered a fumble and Stichweh scored on a 48-yard pass play. With Army in front by a 6–3 margin, Ernie Koy scored two touchdowns in the third period to give Texas an explosive 17–6 victory.

Oklahoma scored a quick 7 points in the first period of the yearly OU-Texas war, but Texas came right back to tie the score on a 49-yard pass play that enabled Ernie Koy to score from the 9-yard line. Phil Harris scored for Texas in the third period to make it 14–7. Then Texas jammed over two quick scores in the final period for a convincing 28–7 win. It was the seventh straight Texas win over its Red River rivals.

The big game of the season pitted Texas against Arkansas in the 59th annual game between these two undefeated rivals and it turned out to be worthy of the buildup. The Razorbacks scored when

Texas quarterback Marv Kristynik (12) does a two-step to elude an Arkansas tackler and picks up a 10-yard gain in 1965.

Ken Hatfield, their great punt return artist, broke loose for an 80-yard beauty to give Arkansas a 7–0 lead. In the third period, Kristynik tossed a perfect pitch to Phil Harris and Harris battled over for the touchdown that made it 7–7. Arkansas went ahead with a late fourth-period TD and it was 14–7 Arkansas with ten minutes to play. But Texas picked up two fine runs by Krystynik and Green and had the ball on the 8-yard line. Then with 85 seconds to play Ernie Koy found a spot inside tackle and burst through for a Texas touchdown. Texas tried a two-point conversion . . . but it failed, and Texas' 15-game winning streak was over. Arkansas had won a 14–13 heart-stopper that had the crowd on their feet throughout the entire game.

David Conway kicked two field goals to beat Rice 6–3 in a thriller of a game, and then SMU bowed 7–0 as Tommy Nobis, playing the game of his life, intercepted a pass in the second period. Texas then smashed 38 yards to score the game's only touchdown.

Baylor, playing inspired football in Waco, forged ahead of Texas by a 14–13 margin with five minutes left in the game. Then Ernie Koy made two of the greatest catches of the season for TDs to give Texas one of the most exciting wins of any season by a 20–14 margin.

Putting on their best offensive show of the year, Marv Kristynik, Pete Lammons, and Harold Philipp combined to score 4 touchdowns in a 28–13 defeat of TCU. Kristynik sped for two great runs of 41 and 21 yards, both for touchdowns, Philipp gained 109 yards and two scores, and Lammons caught several spectacular passes to spark the Longhorns to victory.

Texas was slow starting against the Aggies and only managed a 7–7 halftime tie. Then Conway kicked a field goal and the Longhorns added two fourth-period scores to win the annual Thanksgiving Day game by a 26–7 score.

Undefeated, top-ranked Alabama accepted an Orange Bowl bid to face Texas in a game that pitted the 1963 champions, Texas, vs. the 1964 Champions, Alabama. It was a game that had the entire country glued to their TV screens. It pitted Alabama's great quarterback Joe Namath against Koy, Kristynik, Lammons, and company, and the game was one of the most brilliantly played of the year. The two teams pushed each other up and down the field with Texas QB Jim Hudson connecting on a 69-yard TD to George Sauer and Namath completing 18 of 37 passes for two TDs. But Royal's defensive plan, with Tommy Nobis leading the way, stopped Alabama just as the Tide seemed ready to take control. Time after time Nobis stormed in to block passes and tackle runners just when they were on the verge of turning in a big play or a score. He led a defense that stopped the Tide four times inside the 5-yard line. Final score: Texas 21, Alabama 17.

For Darrell Royal 1964 was another magnificent season with a 10–1 record, an Orange Bowl victory, eight All-SWC selections, and in Tommy Nobis a unanimous all-American. The 1-point loss to Arkansas prevented the Longhorns from a winning streak that could have reached 22 consecutive games in a row.

Darrell Royal says he has never had a better or more dedicated football player than Tommy Nobis. Army Coach Paul Dietzel learned about Tommy when the Cadets were beaten by Texas, and he said, "Nobis is the best linebacker I've ever seen in college football." And SMU's Hayden Fry said,

"Tommy Nobis is a once-in-a-lifetime player. He's a perfect type of a kid. One player like Nobis can make the difference between a winning team and a losing one."

Nobis looked every bit the part in 1965, when his teammates voted him captain of the team. At six-three and 235 pounds, he was still growing. He had added more than twenty pounds to his frame since he had first reported to Royal in 1963, just out of Jefferson High in San Antonio. From the very first day in practice the Texas coaches knew they had someone special in the big, fast-moving redhead who shook the turf with his ferocious blocking and tackling. "He was the most unselfish team player I've ever had the pleasure of working with at Texas and he loved to hit," said Mike Campbell, Royal's chief aide.

"I just always followed Texas football as a kid," said Nobis, "and had dreams of someday making the team, of being an all-American and playing with a Texas team that won the championship. I keep pinching myself about all the great things that have happened to me here under Coach Royal and his staff. But I can't quite believe it all. And now this year, 1965, I'm captain of a team that won the national championship. It's a far cry for a kid from Jefferson City who weighed 140 pounds and worried about making the high school team."

In the opening game of the 1965 season, Royal started a lineup consisting of Pete Lammons and Kelly Baker at the ends; Gene Bledsoe and Howard Goad, tackles; Nobis and Frank Bedrick at guard; and Jack Howe, center. In the backfield, co-captain Marv Kristynik at quarterback, Phil Harris and Les Derrick at the halfback position, and Tom Stockton at fullback were the heart of the offense.

In the season's opener at Austin, Tulane fumbled the ball away seven times, three of them setting up Texas scores, and the Longhorns came away with a 31–0 triumph. In the game against Texas Tech, one of the highly rated teams in the Southwest, Texas shot into a 13–0 lead behind the superb passing of Marv Kristynik and then continued on a 20-point scoring spree in the second half to chalk up a 33–7 win. Then a strong Big Ten team, Indiana, was beaten 27–12, and the

Texas player Joel Brame (61) is the lone pursuer attempting to stop Arkansas' Tommy Tranthom, who's on his way to a 77-yard touchdown sprint in a 1965 game.

Longhorns vaulted into second place in the nation in the United Press poll. Injuries to half a dozen players slowed the Texas attack against Oklahoma, but the Longhorns had enough reserve power to pound out a 19–0 victory.

Suddenly and without warning Dame Fortune caught up with the Longhorns. They dropped a dra-matic seesaw battle in Fayetteville to undefeated Arkansas, 27–24. The Razorbacks scored the winning TD with 90 seconds left to play in a game that was called one of the greatest ever in college football.

The following week Rice, a 20-point underdog, took another thriller from Texas, 20–17. The Owls booted a field goal with 43 seconds of play to win. For the third time in three weeks an injury-plagued Texas team was battered hard. SMU took a 31–14 game from the Horns, whose ragged play, especially on defense, continued to haunt them.

Texas charged out of their three-game slump with a vengeance over Baylor a week later as Marv Kristynik tossed three superb touchdown passes all in the first period to swamp the Bears, 35–14.

But next week against the Horned Frogs Texas committed four glaring errors and TCU turned the errors into touchdowns to take a sloppy 25–10 win. It was the fourth loss of the season for the Longhorns.

In the annual Thanksgiving Day battle against the Aggies, Texas, still unable to avoid their sloppy play, allowed the Aggies to pound over and through their line for 17 unanswered points before the two teams trudged into their respective locker rooms as the first half ended.

Quarterback Marv Kristynik gets perfect protection as he tosses a beautiful flat pass to Pete Lammons for a touchdown in the 1965 game against Baylor to give the Horns a 35–14 win. Kristynik passed for 3 touchdowns.

In the locker room, Coach Royal addressed his team:

"Fellas, it's just a matter of whether we want to win or not." Royal then put some numbers on the blackboard: 21–17.

Then he again looked at his squad.

"Now, look at these numbers. That's what this team can do. Now go on out there and win."

Back on the field, inspired by Royal's confidence, Texas began a furious attack. Behind the sparkling passion of Kristynik, who bombed A&M with three sensational touchdown passes to Pete Lammons, Les Derrick, and Jim Helms, the Longhorns took a 21–17 lead and held off a determined A&M drive to win a sensational 21–17 battle against their age-old rivals—just as their coach predicted.

Pete Lammons, Frank Bedrick, Jack Howe, Diron Talbert, and Tommy Nobis were selected to the All-SWC Team.

Tommy Nobis was awarded the Outland and Maxwell Trophies and was once again named an all-American. He was drafted by Atlanta and offered a multi-year contract to play professional ball.

The season was not a happy one for Coach Royal, as the former National Champions dropped to a three-way tie for fourth place in the SWC Conference.

Back in the 1930s, young Darrell Royal, growing up in the Dust Bowl along the Oklahoma-Texas border, had a dream. He would grow up, become a great football star, and get a scholarship to the University of Oklahoma. He would quarterback and captain a great Oklahoma team, win a championship, and be named to the all-American team. Then he would learn to be a great football coach, return to Oklahoma and each year turn out great teams.

In 1966, Royal had an opportunity to realize the last part of his boyhood dream. His alma mater, Oklahoma, offered him a generous contract to return and take over the head football post. And for two heart-tugging weeks, Royal battled with himself to come to a decision. But his heart and soul

were now buried deep in Longhorn tradition, and he finally informed Oklahoma officials that he would remain with Texas. It was the hardest and most painful decision of his life.

Once that decision was made, Royal turned to the task of rebuilding the Longhorns after the rather dismal 6–4 season in 1965. He made a number of changes in his coaching staff for 1966. He selected Fred Akers to handle the backs, Willie Zapalac to direct the offensive line, and Russ Coffee to handle the defensive backs. Jim Campbell and Charley Shira, two veteran coaches, would continue their defensive duties.

In preparing his squad for the opening game of the season against Southern California, Royal had 15 experienced veterans including Diron Talbert, John Elliot, and Barney Giles, who were voted tri-captains for the season. Two newcomers in the backfield, Bill Bradley and Chris Gilbert, were highly touted schoolboy stars. Tom Higgins and Ed Small filled the end posts, and Ron Landry and Dan Abbott were at guard. Sophomores who were to see a great deal of action included tackle Barry Stone, center Loyd Wainscott, quarterback Andy White, end Corby Robertson, tackle Mike Robuck, and Denny Aldridge, a halfback on defense.

USC, with a heavier, more experienced line and faster and shiftier backfield, took a hard-fought 10–6 win over Texas in the season's opener. But the Longhorns showed vast improvement in the next game against Texas Tech and they beat Tech 31–21. But injuries to key players in this game were to plague them throughout the season.

The Hoosiers of Indiana were no match for the steadily improving Longhorns and Texas dominated Indiana, 35–0. Still more injuries to Ken Gidney, Dan Abbott, and tackle Chris Smith left Texas hobbled as they were beaten by a strong Oklahoma 18–9, the Sooners' first win over Texas since 1957. Arkansas, taking advantage of the injuries to Texas, outlasted the Horns and took a close 12–7 game in Austin.

With three losses in the first five games of the season, the Horns came back with an aggressiveness they hadn't shown all season long. Behind the brilliant running of halfback Chris Gilbert, they racked

Texas' highly touted back, Bill Bradley (18), is helped off the field after being injured in a bruising game with Indiana in 1966.

Once again displaying some high-stepping field running, Bill Bradley (18) is on his way to score against Mississippi in the 1966 Bluebonnet Bowl.

Bluebonnet Bowl captains shake hands before the 1966 battle. Texas captains are: Diron Talbert (73), Barney Giles (80), and John Elliott (90).

up two touchdowns against Rice to edge the Owls, 14–6. Against a strong SMU team a week later, the difference was once again the superlative play of Gilbert, who was sensational with a 75-yard sprint for a score to give Texas a 12–7 lead. Then SMU recovered a Texas fumble, booted a field goal, and it was 12–10, Texas. With only three minutes left to play in the game, SMU recovered a Texas fumble. They booted a long field goal for a tense 13–12 victory as time ran out.

The following week against the Baylor Bears in Waco, it was the one-man wrecking crew, Chris Gilbert, who scored two touchdowns and established a Texas rushing record of 245 yards in 24 carries as the Horns defeated Baylor 26–14. Then David Conway booted a field goal of 52 yards and Ed Small scored a touchdown on a Bill Bradley pass to give the Horns the win over TCU, 13–3.

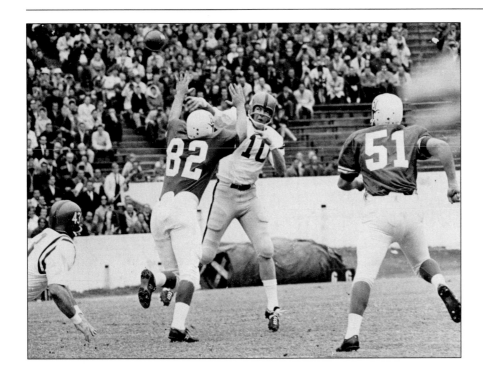

Ole Miss quarterback is rushed by Texas defenders Corby Robertson (82) and Bob Stanley (51) in the 1966 Bluebonnet Bowl.

Texas scored on the opening kickoff in the Thanksgiving Day annual against the Texas Aggies, but A&M came back to score and make it Texas 7, A&M 6. Then Bill Bradley uncorked a magnificent 61-yard pass to Tom Higgins for a touchdown. In the third period, David Conway booted 2 field goals and Texas had a 22–14 win over the Aggies. Gilbert added 137 yards to his rushing total and played another fine game.

Texas was invited to Houston's Bluebonnet Bowl against Ole Miss, who had posted an 8–2 record, and the Longhorns played their finest game of the season to defeat Ole Miss 19–0. Gilbert, Bradley, and linebacker Fred Edwards, were sensational in this final game. Gilbert added 156 yards rushing and Edwards was voted the outstanding lineman in the game. The season ended with Texas winning its last four games to wind up with a 7–4 record.

Coach Royal had his contract extended through 1977 at the start of the 1967 campaign, and Texas fans were so impressed with the

Longhorns' play against Ole Miss in the Bluebonnet Bowl that they printed up thousands of stickers proclaiming, "67, Year of the Horns."

The rosy predictions continued as the season approached. The AP selected the Longhorns as the No. 4 team in the nation as they prepared for the first game of the season against Southern California and one of the great halfbacks in college football, O. J. Simpson, who could run the 100-yard dash in full uniform in 10 seconds.

All the talk about Simpson's legendary feats were brushed aside by Longhorns fans as they pointed out the play of their two great stars, Chris Gilbert and "Super" Bill Bradley, who despite injuries had carried the Texas offense on their backs in 1966.

Bradley sparked Texas on an 80-yard drive at the very start of the USC game and Texas rolled to a 7–0 lead. Just before halftime Simpson broke into the end zone for a TD to tie the score at 7–7. Then USC drove 68 yards to take a 14–7 lead. A field goal in the final period made it 17–7, USC. Just as the game was winding down Bill Bradley led his Longhorns on a 70-yard drive for a score, and it was

17–13, USC. That was the score as the game came to a close, with the huge crowd of more than 75,000 roaring with excitement.

Texas Tech pulled into Austin with one of their greatest teams, but Bradley's fine pass to Deryl Comer for 36 yards shocked the Red Raiders and it was 7–0 before Tech knew what had hit them. Tech fought back gamely with two quick scores and a 54-yard field goal to give them a 16–7 lead. Gilbert scored on a brilliant 80-yard dash to cut it to 16–13 Tech at the half. Late in the fourth period Tech boomed a long field goal to wrap up the game by a 19–13 margin.

Oklahoma State attempted to spoil Darrell Royal's 100th game at Texas, but Gilbert, in a smashing demonstration, guided his team to three blazing scores and a 19–0 win for Texas. One week later it was Oklahoma who scored first in their game and they led 7–0 at the half. But in the second half, Bobby Layne, Jr., son of the former Texas great, kicked a field goal and in the final moments of the game, Bradley scored a TD to give Texas a hard-fought 9–7 win. Then, in rapid succession, Texas defeated Arkansas 21–12 with Bradley enjoying one of his best games with 12 complete passes; a week later Rice was beaten, 28–6; Bradley contin-

ued his brilliant passing against SMU, completing 12 of 15 for a 35–28 win; and against Baylor, Bradley connected on 10 of 21 passes as Texas defeated the Bears 24–0.

Against TCU, in the penultimate regular-season game, it was Layne again with a long field goal and then Gilbert on two magnificent dashes totaling 96 yards for a TD. Texas had a 10–0 lead. A few plays later, Gilbert broke into the clear and raced 61 yards for a touchdown late in the third period to make the score 17–6. But the Frogs came back to score a touchdown on a 78-yard sprint, and then kicked a field goal. When the Frogs got the ball back, they booted another field goal. Another last-minute touchdown by TCU gave them a come-from-behind 24–17 victory.

Just five days after the brutal TCU game, Texas faced their intra-state rivals, the Aggies. As usual, the game turned out to be a slam-bang affair. The Aggies played a tight defensive game and kicked a field goal in the first half to take a 3–0 lead. Then Bill Bradley sped through the Aggies for 35 yards, then 17 more, and finally scored from the 5-yard line to give Texas a 7–3 lead. In the final period, A&M's Long caught a pass and raced through the entire Texas defense for 80 yards and a

Glenn Halsell recovers an Oklahoma fumble to give Texas the ball. Then Bobby Layne Jr. kicked a field goal to give the Longhorns the win.

A&M star Bob Long is shown after catching an 80-yard pass to score the winning touchdown in the 1967 game. Texas defensive tackle Ronnie Ehrig (44) tries, without success, to stop the play.

touchdown that gave A&M their first win over Texas in ten years. Final score: 10–7, Texas A&M.

This was the third straight four-loss season for coach Royal and his only comment was, "No bowl game for us this year. We'll have to go back home and go to work."

Chris Gilbert, Dan Abbott, and Loyd Wainscott were named to the All-SWC Team, while linebacker Corby Robertson was selected to the all-American squad.

"It was an uneasy summer for me in 1968," said Darrell Royal. "A lot of people were beginning to question me. They were saying that after three very ordinary years where we went 6–4, 7–4, and 6–4, that football had kind of bypassed me . . . I was behind the times . . . every coach had changed his offense. Everybody had gone to two split receivers and a pro set, and here we had reverted to a full-house backfield . . . probably the only team in the country. Other teams were outsmarting us, and I had to come up with a new-type offense."

The "new-type offense" was the now famous Wishbone-T offense—a style of play that changed college football into a more high-scoring, exciting game.

Royal said, "The first time I saw this offense run was at Texas A&M under Gene Stallings, now at Alabama, and it impressed me a heck of a lot. So we started working on this idea of having the fullback a yard behind the center and the two halfbacks split. The idea of faking the handoff to the fullback had already been used and so I split the halfbacks and now we had the fullback ready to hit on quick opening plays, or pitching the handoff to either halfback to give you in fact a triple option. If we had a player with a good head and good hands, we would be able to outscore every team.

"After our coaches worked out all the kinks we were ready to use it in our first game against Houston," said Royal.

In the season's opening game, Royal started Bill Bradley at quarterback, Chris Gilbert and Ted Koy as the halfbacks, and Steve Worster at fullback. The new Texas offense sputtered and stalled, but they did produce three touchdowns and a 20–20 tie against Houston. A week later Texas Tech, aided by punt returns of 84 and 49 yards by Tech halfback Larry Alford for two touchdowns, defeated the Longhorns 31–22. It was an exciting game that saw Texas, 21 points behind in the fourth quarter, rally to score two touchdowns as James Street replaced

Bradley and guide the team in the final quarter with two accurate TD tosses.

The Oklahoma State game next on the schedule was termed by Royal as one of the most crucial in his coaching regime.

"It was a shaky time," said Royal. "So I called on the student body . . . the only time I'd ever done that. I worked at getting a student pep rally to get behind the team. And I think that helped our team in that big game."

James Street, youngest man in the backfield, was an untested but gutsy street-smart kid with great hands. He started at quarterback against Oklahoma State and threw a 60-yard touchdown pass for a 10–0 lead. Then another great Street pass and another touchdown by Mike Perrin and the Longhorns had an impressive 31–3 victory. Then into Dallas came Oklahoma with an impressive record. The Sooners flashed to a 20–19 lead over the Horns with only 2½ minutes left in the game. The game looked to be in the bag. But the savvy Street bombarded OU's defense with accurate passes of 19, 16, and then 11 yards, and then Bill Bradley smashed over the goal line to give Texas a

dramatic last-minute 26–20 win. Happy Feller kicked three field goals for the Horns, including a record 53-yard boot. Then it was Arkansas' turn and they danced into Austin with an undefeated string of wins on their way to a big bowl berth. But Street, Steve Worster, and Chris Gilbert made a shambles of the Arkansas defense, picking up 5 touchdowns and 329 yards rushing to defeat the Razorbacks 39–29 in the biggest win of the season.

Then the Rice Owls were easily beaten 38–14 as Gilbert rushed for 213 yards. It was SMU's turn next and once again it was Street handling the T like a master magician, aided by Worster and Gilbert, who ran over, around, and through the air to lead a 38–7 Longhorn romp. A week later Baylor's Bears were tamed in a devastating offensive show as Texas poured it on, 47–26. TCU was the seventh victim as Texas, operating the Wishbone with telling effect, battered TCU in a 47–21 contest.

Just five days later, in the Thanksgiving Day battle against the Texas Aggies, the Longhorns' offense under Jim Street was never better. Texas scored 35 points in the first half to completely

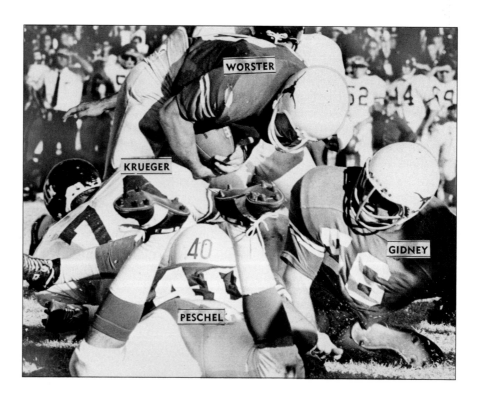

Fullback Steve Worster pounds through A&M's line with blocking from Randy Peschel and Ken Gidney as the Horns trample the Aggies, 35–14, in 1968.

Texas halfback Chris Gilbert (25) races through the A&M line for a touchdown in 1968.

demoralize the Aggies in pounding out an easy 35–14 win. Gilbert, Street, Worster, and Wainscott were outstanding as the Longhorns ran up their eighth straight victory over A&M to close out the regular season.

Darrell Royal had been greatly troubled during the early part of the 1968 season. In a year that he thought would be an outstanding season, his Longhorns had broken even in the first two games and as he studied the films he understood his problem. Bill Bradley, his quarterback, just didn't have the moves or the hands for a Wishbone quarterback, and he reluctantly replaced Bradley with James Street, a nimble, quick-thinking, five-eleven, 170-pound back with quick hands and a quicker mind. Street, a junior with stylish mod sideburns, had not even reported for spring training. He was a star pitcher on the Texas baseball team but he also had the qualities that Royal had to have in his quarterback, and Street quickly jelled with the new offense.

With Street set as the regular quarterback after the Texas Tech game, Texas began to beat everything in sight. They won eight games in a row, beat Arkansas in a great shootout by 10 points and went on a high-scoring spree that broke all school records, averaging 34.4 points per game.

In the Cotton Bowl matchup against an outstanding Tennessee team, Street, operating his options like a Las Vegas poker player, inspired the Horns to a near-perfect game as they devastated the

Vols 36–13. Street completed 7 of 13 passes for over 200 yards, and he so cleverly mixed his plays that he outguessed the Vols all day long.

The sensational manner in which Texas defeated Tennessee put to rest all the discussion about Royal being "behind the times."

Texas had scored better than 40 points per game in the final nine games of the season, and the Associated Press voted the Longhorns the No. 3 team in the nation. Royal was once again the toast of the town with a Cotton Bowl win, SWC championship, and a record of 9-1-1. Chris Gilbert closed out a stellar Longhorn season with his third straight 1000-yard rushing total and a selection to the all-American team. He and Longhorns Comer, Abbott, Worster, Wainscott, Halsell, and Brooks were All-SWC.

Like a retired undefeated heavyweight champion, James Street's legend grew. There is no equal to Street's brinkmanship in the annals of Texas football. He was the fourth-down phantom, a gutsy gambler with all the confidence of a champion.

He never lost a game. Starting at quarterback in 19 games through the 1968 and 1969 seasons, Street eventually brought Texas and Darrell Royal a second national championship.

The five-eleven, 165-pound Street faced prohibitive odds at Texas from the very day he left Longview High School. "A lot of recruiters told me that I'd spend my entire career sitting on the bench behind Bill Bradley, who was the No. 1 quarterback. But Coach Royal told me, 'Jim, if you are afraid of competition now, you'll never know if you can compete.' That did it and I went to Texas."

In 1968, after tying Houston 20–20 and then losing to Texas Tech 31–22, Royal told Bradley that he was moving him to defense and installing Street as the regular quarterback.

Texas' 31–3 win over Oklahoma State with Jim Street as the quarterback set into motion one of the greatest winning streaks in college football as the Horns won 8 straight games and finished off Tennessee in the Cotton Bowl.

In 1969, with Street at quarterback, the Longhorns defeated California, 17–0; Texas Tech, 49–7; Navy, 56–17; and Oklahoma, 27–17. The

The 1969 national champion's offensive unit. *Back row, left to right:* Billy Dale, Ted Koy, James Street, Steve Worster, and Jim Bertelsen. *Front row, left to right:* Randy Peschel, Bob McKay, Mike Dean, Forrest Wiegand, Bobby Mitchell, Bob Wuensch, and Cotton Speyrer.

Five members of the 1969 defensive unit *(left to right):* Glen Halsell, Mike Campbell, Stan Mauldin, Bill Zapalac, and Dan Lester.

Horns went on to defeat Rice, SMU, Baylor, TCU, and Texas A&M by lopsided scores and the stage was set for the game of the century between No. 1 Texas and No. 2 Arkansas. Now the two would meet on national TV for the final game of college football's centennial.

ABC-TV moved the big game to December 6. To add to the excitement, President Nixon decided to attend, announcing he would present a presidential plaque to the winner. In Texas the anticipation was at its height; every conversation ended with "going to the game?"

Arkansas had not been defeated for 15 games—since the loss to the Horns by a 39–29 score—and more than 45,000 excited fans jammed every inch of Razorback Field in Fayetteville.

On the second snap of the ball, halfback Ted Koy fumbled the ball, Arkansas recovered and in two passes, Montgomery rifled a pass to flanker John Rees and Rees got to the 2-yard line. Two plays later, Arkansas had scored.

Arkansas held their lead through the first half as both teams battled furiously, working up and down the gridiron with blocks and tackles that could be heard high up in the stands.

Early in the third period, after recovering a Texas fumble on the 47-yard line, Arkansas struck again. Montgomery's 30-yard pass to Chuck Dicus scored the TD. The kick was good and it was Arkansas 14, Texas 0.

At the start of the fourth period, it was time for the Texas' gunslinger Jim Street to join the action. On the fourth play of the period, Street faded to pass, then shot away from a couple of tacklers and drove up the middle of the Arkansas line. He straight-armed a tackler, shook loose from two more and slashed on for 42 yards and Texas' first TD. Then Street got away once more, on a counter-option play and scored the two-point conversion that Texas had to have to reach victory range. Now the score was Arkansas 14, Texas 8.

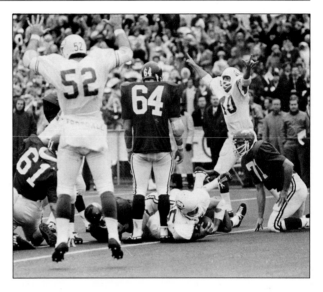

In the 1969 game against Arkansas, Jim Bertelsen (on ground with ball) scored the touchdown that gave Texas the 14–14 tie. With 70,000 fans screaming in the stands, Happy Feller kicked the extra point and Texas won one of the greatest games in their history, 15–14. Here Forrest Wiegand (52) and Randy Peschel (40) jump for joy as Texas won its tenth straight game of the season.

Fullback Steve Worster (with ball) flies through the air as he gains 20 yards against Oklahoma in 1969.

Arkansas took the kickoff and immediately began a steady drive for another score. They moved from their 20-yard line to the Texas 8-yard line. Then came the turning point.

Everybody in the stadium expected Arkansas to attempt a field goal that would clinch the game. But they did not. Instead they went into the air and tossed a pass, which Texas' great defensive back, Danny Lester, intercepted in the end zone.

Now with Texas in possession, they pounded down to their own 43-yard line with fourth down, 3 yards to go. At this moment, Street called time and went to the sidelines to confer with Royal. Royal told Street to throw the bomb to his tight end, Randy Peschel. Street shook his head in utter disbelief but started out onto the field, then stopped, and went back to Royal to ask about the play again. Royal said emphatically, "Jim, that's the play. Now call it."

Rooster Andrews also celebrates the single-point win against Arkansas in 1969 as Coach Darrell Royal trots off the field.

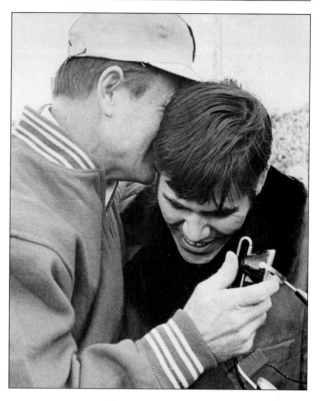

Coach Royal hugs Texas tackle Fred Steinmark during the 1970 Cotton Bowl game that was dedicated to him.

Street, back in a huddle called the play, took the pass from center, faked a handoff to Steve Worster, and then lofted a long, high-arching pass to Peschel. "When I first saw the ball coming," said Peschel, "I thought it was over-thrown, but I got a step in front of the defense, outjumped both defenders, got the ball in one hand, juggled it for a moment, and then I was down on the 12-yard line."

Two running plays later, Bertelsen had blasted through for a touchdown and Feller had kicked the extra point. It was Texas 15, Arkansas 14 as the gun sounded, ending one of the greatest games in Texas history.

After the players got to their locker room, President Nixon entered and spoke. "This was one of the greatest games of all time," he said. Coach Royal responded: "Mr. President, I know I speak for every member of our squad and the coaches when I say that when the president of the United States takes the time to come to our dressing room it is the greatest honor."

As Coach Royal and his victorious squad flew home, he was called to the phone. It was a repre-sentative of the National Football Foundation on the line who informed him that arrangements had been made for Royal and a group of Texas players to come to New York to accept the MacArthur Bowl as national champions.

It was while Royal, his tri-captains and a host of Texas dignitaries were in New York that news broke that Fred Steinmark, the popular safety and starter since his first game as a sophomore, had been injured in the Arkansas game. It was thought to be just a bad bruise, but X rays indicated it was a tumor that was malignant and Steinmark's left leg would have to be amputated. President Nixon called Freddie a few days after the operation to offer supportive words and invite him to visit the White House. Fred said that he would walk onto the grid-iron on a pair of crutches by the time the Cotton Bowl came around and that he'd finish his courses at school. He made good on all promises.

Coach Royal talks to his quarterback, James Street, about the next play against Notre Dame in the 1969 Cotton Bowl. The Irish were ahead 17–14 with two minutes to play. Then Street, on Royal's instructions, tossed a pass to Cotton Speyrer for a first down on Notre Dame's 5-yard line. After two line bucks, Billy Dale scored. Feller kicked the extra point and Texas had an exhilarating 21–17 win and its second national championship.

Irish coach Ara Parseghian congratulates Coach Royal as Texas defeated Notre Dame in the 1969 Cotton Bowl.

In the Cotton Bowl against Notre Dame, Texas came from behind with 2½ minutes left to play and defeated the Irish, 21–17. On two occasions, Jim Street converted fourth down plays on the drive—one at the Irish 20-yard line, the second time at the Irish 10-yard line.

Facing fourth and two at the Notre Dame 10, Street flipped a low pass to Cotton Speyrer, who made a sensational diving catch for a first down that laid the foundation for the winning score. After two smashes into the line, Steve Worster faked a line buck, and handed the ball to Billy Dale, who dove in for the TD. Feller kicked the extra point and Texas had a stunning, come-from-behind win, 21–17.

Texas won every wire service poll for the national championship and Bob McKay, Worster, Street, Speyrer, and Wuensch were all selected for the All-SWC Team. Darrell Royal was voted Coach of the Year.

As Darrell Royal prepared for the 1970 season, he stood at the pinnacle of success as one of college football's greatest coaches. Beginning his thirteenth year as coach of the Texas Longhorns, Royal had compiled a truly remarkable record, winning 108 games, losing 25, and tying 4. In those 13 years, Royal had built the Texas football program, making it one of the most respected in the nation. He had won the national championship in 1963—the first ever in Texas football—and again in 1969 he won his second national crown for the Longhorns.

ABC-TV network conducted a poll of the nation's sportswriters to select the leading college football coach of the 1960s. Darrell Royal was voted Coach of the Decade.

Before the season got underway, Royal spoke about the makeup of a "dream team," saying that a great team must have a number of great seniors. "I think this year's team is that kind of a team," he said.

Who were these seniors? To start with, Steve Worster, an all-American as a junior, was probably one of the greatest fullbacks Texas had ever had. When the going got tough in the Cotton Bowl against Notre Dame, Royal turned Worster loose and the big 215-pounder rushed for 155 yards and won MVP honors. Then there was split-end Charles Speyrer, who made the miraculous catch in

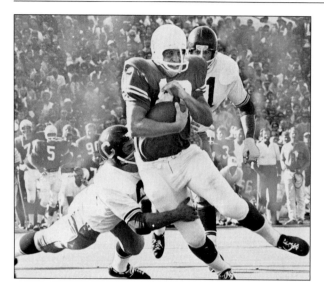

Texas end, Deryl Comer receives a pass from quarterback Ed Phillips and is off for a TD against California in a 1970 game.

the fourth quarter that enabled the Horns to beat the Irish. Next was offensive tackle Bobby Wuensch, another all-American and a tower of strength. Then there were more stars: Senior linebackers Scott Henderson and Bill Zapalac; defensive end Bill Atessis; and flashy halfback Jim Bertelsen. At quarterback, the great James Street was gone, but in his place would be Eddie Phillips.

In the opening game of the season against California, Phillips, executing the Wishbone expertly, struck for two quick touchdowns in the opening five minutes and then Texas went on to destroy California 56–15 as Worster scored three touchdowns. Texas Tech, the next opponent, was defeated 35–13 as halfback Billy Dale scored two touchdowns. Steve Worster gained 106 yards and Happy Feller starred for the Horns in a rough, slam-bang battle against UCLA. The Horns barely escaped with the win as they beat UCLA 20–17. Feller had two outstanding field goals—one of 55 yards and another of 48 yards. It was a last-minute 45-yard pass play, from Phillips to Speyrer. Then Cotton caught the ball on his fingertips and with 12 seconds remaining on the clock, crossed the goal line for the win.

Oklahoma attempted to beat Texas at their own game by utilizing the Wishbone offense, but Texas easily took the game, 41–9; with a 5-touchdown offense Steve Worster led the offense against Rice with 170 yards in 23 carries as Texas swamped the Owls 45–21. A week later, Worster was sensational as he ran for 4 touchdowns against SMU and another win for Texas by a 42–15 margin.

Texas ran its winning streak up to 27 in a row. But then they had a tough battle against Baylor, just managing to eke out a 21–14 win over the

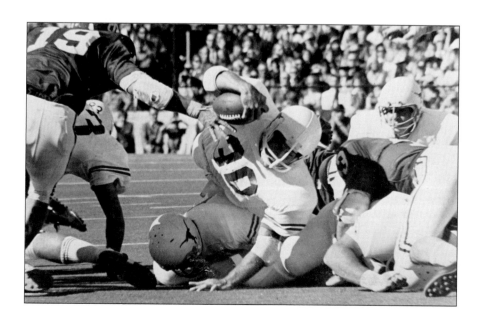

Texas fullback, Steve Worster (with ball) blasts through Oklahoma's line for a touchdown as he led the Horns to a 41–9 win over the Sooners in 1970.

The University of Texas National Champions in 1970. *Front row, left to right:* Assistant Coach Glen Swenson, Assistant Coach Leon Manley, Assistant Coach Willie Zapalac, Assistant Coach Tim Doerr, Assistant Coach Jim Helms, Head Coach Darrell Royal, Assistant Coach Emory Bellard, Assistant Coach Fred Akers, Assistant Coach R. M. Patterson, Assistant Coach Bill Ellington, Assistant Coach Mike Campbell, Assistant Coach David McWilliams. *Second row, left to right:* Donnie Wigginton, Happy Feller, Jerry Sisemore, Jim Bertlesen, Terry Collins, Mike Dean, Jim Achilles, Bobby Mitchell, Bobby Wuensch, Deryl Comer, Danny Lester, Eddie Phillips, Cotton Speyrer, Steve Worster, Billy Dale. *Third Row, left to right:* Gary Keithley, Bill Atessis, Carl White, Ray Dowdy, Scott Henderson, David Richardson, David Arledge, Rick Nabors, Alan Lowry, Stan Hicks, Stan Mauldin, Mike Bayer, Bill Zapalac, Randy Braband, Scott Palmer, Dean Campbell. *Fourth row, left to right:* Steve Fleming, Hans Helland, Bill Harrington, Jeff Zapalac, Steve Oxley, Julius Whittier, Tommy Lee, Sam McBrierty, Pat Macha, Larry Webb, John Ulrich, Steve Williams, Jim Morris, Randy Stout, Tommy Woodard, Alan Weddell, Doug Rostedt. *Fifth row, left to right:* Jimmy Dreyer, Bill Rutherford, Donny Windham, Bud Hudgins, Paul Riobichau, Keifer Marshal, Cary Kipp, Lee Lyles, Darrell Gray, Bobby Callison, Steve Adger, Mike Janda, Jack Rushing, Ronnie Tyler, Travis Roach, Bill Catlett, Tom Whiteside. *Sixth row, left to right:* Jim McIngvale, Jay Cormier, Scott Moore, R. J. Childress, Tommy Matula, Syd Keasler, Bruce Gaw, Donnie Wood, Mike Speer, Steve Valek, Mike Stephens, George McIngvale, Kevin Hutson, Rick Martin, Danny Baker, Lukin Gilliland, David Ballew, Dan Terwelp, Tony Malouf, Charles Loeffler. *Seventh row, left to right:* David Fox, Juan Conde, Bill Allison, Bubba Simpson, David Anderson, Mike Cave, Jim Lemmon, Jimmy Kay, Paul Hobbs, Barrett Gaus, Rob Schultz, Dan Steakley, Mike Rowan, Rusty Campbell, Jim Randall, Jimmy Hull, Johnnie Robinson, Jerrell Bolton, Jim Johnson, A. Y. McWright, Kim Cade, Tom Kirschner, Assistant Trainer Spanky Stephens, Trainer Frank Medina.

Bears. However, Texas' victory was a costly one as Speyrer, Palmer, Henderson, and Lowry were injured. Despite the many injuries, Texas ran roughshod over TCU the next week running up 8 touchdowns in a 58–0 win over the Frogs.

In the Thanksgiving Day game, Texas ran its consecutive winning streak to 29 in a row as they trampled Texas A&M, 52–14.

In the final game of the regular season, Texas and Arkansas were ready to resume their 1969 slugfest, which Texas won with a miraculous last-minute touchdown. This time, however, with Jim Bertelsen leading Texas with two touchdowns and 189 yards rushing, and with Steve Worster's TD and 126 yards, the Horns were too strong and simply overpowered Arkansas by a 42–7 margin.

The United Press' final poll after the Arkansas game showed Texas as the National Champions with 25 votes for first place. The National Football Foundation also selected Texas, but alongside Ohio State, as the co-champions.

Texas and Notre Dame were rematched for the New Year's Day contest at the Cotton Bowl and the Horns, despite injuries to Speyrer, Bertelsen, and Worster, were rated a 7-point favorite. As the game began, quarterback Eddie Phillips startled the huge crowd by darting 63 yards to the Irish's 10-yard line. But Notre Dame held for three downs and Feller booted a field goal for a 3–0 lead, which did not last long. With Joe Theismann passing to Gatewood again and again, the Irish scored 3 times to give them a 21–3 lead. Phillips sparked a drive that went 85 yards for a TD. Then after a 2-point conversion it was Notre Dame 24, Texas 11. All the scoring had occurred in the first half. The rest of the game was a study in futility as Texas fumbled the ball five times and the Irish played a tough defensive game to keep Texas from further damage. Final score, 24–11.

The loss to Notre Dame ended Texas' 30-game winning streak and Coach Darrell Royal was named co-winner of the Football Coaches Association's Coach of the Year award.

A couple of days before fall football practice began at Texas, Darrell Royal stood before a large gathering of Texas alumni and gave the rest of the

SWC members some bad news. "I do think this 1971 Texas team will be a very good one and it could be a great one," he said. Thus the Longhorn dynasty, featuring teams undefeated in 28 straight regular season games and SWC champions for three straight years, rolled on.

With the backbone of the great championship team of 1970 gone, the Horns still had tremendous talent: There were quarterback Ed Phillips, tackle Jerry Sisemore, halfback Jim Bertelsen, and tackle Ray Dowdy. Royal also had some promising sophomores with Bob Callison, Don Burrisk (a compact 180-pounder who could run a 4.6 40-yard split), Bill Wyman (a center), Jim Moore (a halfback), Pat Kelly, Tom Landry, and Glen Gaspard.

In the opening game of the season at California, Texas faced one of UCLA's best, coached by Pepper Rodgers. The Bruins scored first on a 42-yard TD run. But Texas tied the score with an 89-yard drive in the second period. Then a Phillips pass near the end of the half gave Texas another score. California kicked a field goal in the

Texas quarterback Donnie Wigginton (10) carries the ball against Oklahoma in 1971.

A battered Texas quarterback, Eddie Phillips, leaves the field after the game against Rice in 1971.

Attempting to come back from two straight defeats, the Horns easily defeated Rice 39–10 as Bertelsen, Wigginton, and halfback Lonnie Bennett scored touchdowns. Then in a difficult game against SMU, Texas struggled to a 22–18 win after SMU had taken an 18–15 lead, late in the third period. It was Bobby Callison who tore across the goal line in the final period for the winning touchdown. One week later, the Horns easily defeated Baylor with an impressive display of power ending in a 24–0 victory. The next week Texas demonstrated their mastery of the Wishbone offense again, taking a 31–0 win from TCU.

A Cotton Bowl match against Penn State was in the offing as Texas got ready to meet their long-time rival Texas A&M. Texas had to win to get the Cotton Bowl invitation and they did so with ease and a 34–14 score. The Texas defense held the Aggies to three first downs and scored 3 TDs in the second period to wrap up the bowl assignment.

In the Cotton Bowl championship, Texas took a 6–3 halftime lead with two field goals by Steve Valek. But in the second half, with Franco Harris and Lydell Mitchell running the ball, Penn State broke the game open and scored four touchdowns to easily defeat Texas 30–6.

Texas finished the season with a respectable 8–3 record.

third period and it was Texas 14, UCLA 10. Two more scores in the final period gave Texas a well-deserved 28–10 win. Texas Tech was beaten 28–0, and Oregon took the fall in a 35–7 Longhorn win as Texas prepared for an outstanding Oklahoma team.

"They're the best Oklahoma team we've ever faced," said Royal, "and they're a Wishbone team. And they're fast as greased lightning." Texas managed to stay close as substitute quarterback Don Wigginton, Phillips, and Bertelsen scored touchdowns. But Oklahoma had too much offensive strength; they defeated Texas 48–27. Now with another big game against Arkansas just ahead, Texas was minus two of its regular quarterbacks, Phillips and Wigginton, who were out with injuries. Texas was no match for the Razorbacks and suffered a 31–7 loss.

It seemed hardly possible that it had been fifteen years since Darrell Royal had taken over as Texas' football coach—it had all passed so quickly. So much had happened since that first season in 1957. He had won seven SWC titles, two co-SWC championships, and two national championships. Now in 1972, Darrell Royal was setting out to conquer the football world again.

In 1972 he had lost nine of the veterans who had played important parts in the 1969 and 1970 national championship years. Several members of his coaching staff had also departed to accept new assignments. Emory Bellard, who had aided in the original design of the Wishbone offense, had left for A&M. Fred Akers had replaced him and Akers and Willie Zapalac would handle the offense. Other additions to the coaching staff included Spike Dykes, Glen Swenson, and Alvin Matthews.

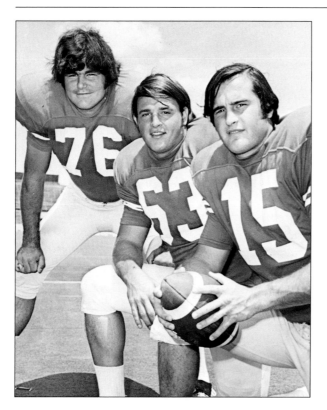

Tri-captains for the 1972 Texas team: Jerry Sisemore (76), Randy Braband (63), and Alan Lowry (15).

But without Jim Bertelsen, Eddie Phillips, and Donnie Wigginton—all big offensive stars and quarterbacks who had been able to handle the tricky Wishbone—Royal felt uneasy as he moved players in and out of the practice sessions, attempting to set a starting lineup for the first game of the season against the University of Miami.

The athletic department had completed construction of 15,000 additional seats at Memorial Stadium for the Miami game. This game was dedicated to the late Freddie Steinmark and featured three field goals by Bill Schott and touchdowns by Lonnie Bennett and Roosevelt Leaks to give Texas a 23–10 win over the Hurricanes. The second game of the season saw the Horns come from behind to defeat a hard-driving Texas Tech squad, 25–20. Texas kept Tech from a TD until the final 10 seconds of the game. Tech's kicking ace Ted Grimes booted 4 field goals.

Tony Adams, a fine quarterback for Texas in 1968 who had transferred to Utah State, starred in the next week's Utah-Texas game with 26 of 41 passes. But the Longhorns had too much experience for Utah State and, late in the game, Tommy Landry scooped up a ball and sped 55 yards for a TD. Two more Texas touchdowns late in the game gave Texas an unimpressive 27–12 win.

With a 49–0 win over Utah State, a 9-touchdown win over Oregon, and an 8-touchdown win over Clemson, Oklahoma roared into Austin with confidence. But Oklahoma stuttered until the final quarter in a defensive struggle with Texas. Then with a 3–0 lead, the Sooners surged ahead with 3 touchdowns and a field goal, defeating Texas 27–0. This was Texas' first shutout in 100 games, since a 1963 13–0 loss to LSU.

Arkansas pounded toward a 9–7 halftime lead in Texas' next game. But late in the fourth period,

Roosevelt Leaks, Texas' sensational fullback, pounds the Baylor line for a touchdown in 1972.

Leaks and Alan Lowry raced downfield for two touchdowns each and, in the best offensive performance of the year, Texas had clenched a 35–15 win over the Razorbacks who had national championship aspirations at the start of the year. In another exceptional offensive display, the Longhorns routed Rice 45–9. The following week, Texas beat SMU, 17–9, before a crowd of 72,000; Leaks, Akins, and Braband were the stars of the day.

In the next game, the great 260-pound tackle Jerry Sisemore led Texas with superb blocking and tackling as the Horns secured their seventh win of the year, defeating Baylor 17–3.

The following match, with TCU, proved to be no more taxing than the Baylor game. TCU, a 13-point underdog, fumbled 3 times in the first half. Texas' Alan Lowry accounted for 3 touchdowns and Marty Akins contributed another one as Texas claimed a 27–0 shutout.

Texas A&M kicked an early field goal in their annual contest with Texas, but the Horns jumped ahead to a 14–3 halftime lead.

In the third and fourth periods, touchdowns by Tommy Landry, Lowry, and Moore, gave Texas a smashing 38–3 win over their rivals from College Station. It was the ninth win in ten games for the

Horns and they were immediately matched for a Cotton Bowl shootout against the Crimson Tide and coach Bear Bryant.

On New Year's Day, a crowd of more than 72,000 packed the Cotton Bowl to watch the great duel unfold. Alabama quickly jumped out in front with a 50-yard field goal by Greg Gant.

Several plays later, the Tide's expert halfback Wilbur Jackson dashed 35 yards for a touchdown and Alabama had a 10–0 lead. Both teams then traded field goals and it was Alabama 13, Texas 3 as the gun signaled the end of the half.

In the third period, Texas struck back with Rosey Leaks and Alan Lowry's unstoppable play; the duo combined for 39 yards and a touchdown. Then as Alabama tried a long pass, the Horns intercepted the ball, and Lowry sprinted over the goal line, making Texas the victors, 17–13.

It was one of the seasons Darrell Royal enjoyed the most. His Longhorns had ended the year with a remarkable 10–1 season, including 7 successive wins after an Oklahoma loss—a loss that threatened the entire season's success.

After Texas' winning record the previous year, the players already had designs on another national championship in 1973. Even cavalier alumni, who

In the 1972 Cotton Bowl game against Alabama, Don Ealey (34) blocks for Texas halfback Tommy Landry, who is on his way to a big 22-yard gain.

Texas halfback Alan Lowry (15) was incredible in the Cotton Bowl against Alabama. Lowry and Rosey Leaks combined for one TD, and then Lowry scored another to win the game, 17–13, on January 1, 1973.

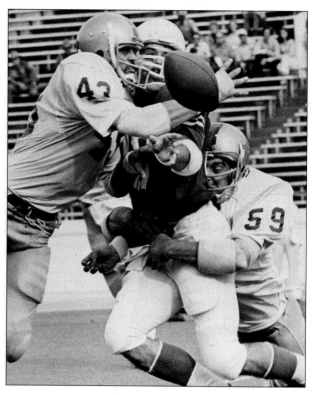

Quarterback Marty Akins attempts a pitchout as he is tackled by two Washington players in the second game of the 1975 season.

had come out to watch practice sessions in the fall, were already counting the wins. Coach Darrell Royal confidently looked forward to another outstanding season.

The big challenge was to produce a quarterback who had the ability, poise, hands, and brains to handle the complicated Wishbone offense. Royal was also troubled by his quarterback problem the season before and, now, most of the teams defeated by his specially designed offense had studied the Wishbone and would be able to handle it in 1973.

Finally settling on Marty Akins as his quarterback, Lonnie Bennett and Tom Landry as halfbacks, and the unstoppable Roosevelt Leaks at fullback, the Longhorns opened the season against University of Miami at the Orange Bowl Stadium.

The Hurricanes surprised Texas with a 20–15 defeat. Roosevelt Leaks gained 153 yards, scored two touchdowns, and was sensational. But fumbles and inept quarterback play cost the Longhorns the game. Showing some improvement in their all-around game the following week, Texas drove to a 14–0 lead over Texas Tech in the first half, then allowed Tech to score 12 points. Then Texas managed to score two more touchdowns to win by a 28–12 score. Leaks, Landry, and Lonnie Bennett all played well. Wake Forest was an easy victim as Coach Royal utilized every player on the team, winning 14–0, as a prelude to an important game against Oklahoma the following week.

Oklahoma, just off a two-year NCAA probation for recruiting violations, continued its unique football plan under a new coach, Barry Switzer. Switzer was anxious to beat Texas and hired a for-

Coach Darrell Royal talks things over with quarterback Marty Akins before the Rice game. Akins passed for two touchdowns in the 1974 game.

the worst beating from an Oklahoma team since 1908.

Texas quickly rebounded from the Sooners disaster by handing Arkansas a 34–6 defeat. And once again Rosey Leaks spearheaded the attack with two touchdowns, carrying the ball for 209 yards. The following week, against Rice, the Longhorns demonstrated their rapid improvement. Leaks scored twice again and, with Marty Akins passing for two scores, the Owls were dealt a 55–13 loss.

In their next test, SMU quickly jumped out to a 14–0 lead over Texas. But once the Horns got over the shock of SMU's striking power, Leaks, Tommy Landry, and Bill Wyman's great blocking forged the way to a 42–14 victory. Leaks rushed for a spectacular total of 342 yards, shattering the SWC record and tying him for third place in the NCAA's all-time record books.

Baylor, the Longhorn's sixth opponent of the year, was felled easily, 42–6. TCU underwent a similar battering when Texas scored 8 touchdowns, delivered by Akins, Landry, and Mike Cromeens, and won 52–7. The victory gave Texas a share of the SWC title and an invitation to face Nebraska in the Cotton Bowl. But before the Cotton Bowl matchup, Texas had just five days to prepare for the annual game against Texas A&M. This seemed to be no problem because Royal's Longhorns were on a roll after winning 5 straight games. The Longhorns methodically hammered out a convincing 42–13 win and Rosey Leaks, despite a first-quarter injury, carried the ball 16 times for 87 yards and set a new SWC rushing record of 1415 yards.

In the opening moments of the Cotton Bowl it appeared as if the Longhorns would blow away their opponent. Texas fought their way to the Nebraska 5-yard line, and then decided to kick a field goal. Bill Schott booted one from the 22-yard line and Texas had a 3–0 lead. Nebraska tied the score near the end of the half as Rich Sanger kicked a 24-yarder to tie the score at 3–3. After two Nebraska touchdowns in the second half of the game, plus a fourth period field goal, the Cornhuskers had the Cotton Bowl title with a decisive 19–3 win over Texas.

mer Texas coach, Jim Helms, who had been an assistant to Royal for several years. Helms knew every Longhorn offensive and defensive move and joined Switzer's staff just as the fall practice sessions began . . . and with a crucial Texas-Oklahoma game just three weeks away.

The Sooners had one of their strongest teams in years and had studied the game plan devised by Helms, a plan that was so effective it crippled the Texas offense. In short order, Oklahoma's long passes—one for 40 yards and two more for 47 yards—resulted in three touchdowns. Unable to stop the passing attack, Texas was no match for the Sooners and succumbed to them by a score of 52–13. It was

**Coach Darrell Royal recruited Earl Campbell, the
most sought-after prep-school halfback in Texas.
By 1975, Campbell was a threat every time he
carried the ball.**

"It was a one-sided game any way you look at
it," said Coach Royal. "We lost to a superior team.
That's all there is to it."

The defeat gave Texas an 8–3 record for the
season.

The spring after Darrell Royal introduced the
Wishbone offense with such success, Darrell got a
telephone call from Duffy Daugherty, Michigan
State's coach. Duffy was thinking about switching
to the Wishbone and he wondered if Royal would
give him some pointers. "Duffy," Royal told him,
"you don't want my offense. You want my fullback,
and he's going to be busy for two more years here at
Texas."

Steve Worster was the fullback and before he
had finished at Texas, he'd rushed for 2353 yards
and won all-American honors. Then, in 1971,
Rosey Leaks took over at fullback in the Texas

Wishbone offense and raised the power level a full
notch. Leaks rushed for 2514 yards, including an
SWC record 1415 yards in 1973 when he made the
all-American team.

By 1974, Royal had signed the most sought
after prep-school runner in Texas. Some said he was
the best ever in Texas football history. His name:
Earl Campbell. And since he grew up in rose-grow-
ing country, near Tyler, Texas, Royal dubbed him,
"My Tyler Rose."

At six-one and 225 pounds, Campbell was the
fastest Longhorn on the field. He was also bigger
than Worster or Leaks and Royal and his aides
expected the Tyler Rose to be better than either of
them.

In the opening game of the 1974 season
against Boston College, Campbell gained 85 yards
on 13 carries, and blocked and tackled with such
ferociousness that the Boston College Eagles immediately began running plays away from the Tyler
Rose. Texas piled on six touchdowns for a 42–19
win over the Eagles. Against Wyoming, Gralyn
Wyatt and Campbell carried Texas to a 34–7 win.

Texas Tech stunned Texas with one of their
best teams and three successive touchdowns. A rat-
tled Texas lost 26–3. They were simply out-played
from beginning to end. Texas returned the next
week and beat Washington 35–21 in a high-scoring
offensive battle. Campbell came into his own with
a touchdown and 125 yards in 16 carries. The following week brought disappointment when
Oklahoma won a heart-stirring 16–13 contest, scoring the game winning field goal with minutes left to
play.

On October 19, in a truly memorable clash
with Arkansas, one of the Razorback's greatest
teams was defeated by Earl Campbell's spectacular
all-around play before a national television audience. Inserted early in the game for one defensive
play, Campbell blocked an Arkansas punt that
teammate Doug English turned into a Texas touchdown. Then on Texas' first possession in the third
period, Earl set up another score with a 15-yard run
to the Arkansas 2-yard line. Earlier in the game,
Campbell hit the middle of the Arkansas line, broke
through and sped 68 yards for a spectacular TD. The

Razorbacks were paralyzed by the brilliance of Campbell's play. Texas took a 38–7 victory.

In the game against a strong Rice squad, quarterback Marty Akins set a second-half drive in motion to score 3 touchdowns and win 27–6. A week later Akins led the Horns offense in a 35–15 win against SMU as Campbell and Leaks provided both offensive and defensive strength in the victory.

Hamilton, Rosey Leaks, and Earl Campbell again were the forces that lit the scoreboard for Texas as they raced to a 24–7 lead against Baylor in the first half; it appeared to be another easy win for the Horns. But the Bears came back like a ball of fire and scored on four of the next five possessions, giving them a 34–24 upset.

Then, when it looked like Texas had lost the SWC title, the Horns destroyed TCU by running for 11 touchdowns and finishing with a shattering 81–16 rout. Akins scored 3 touchdowns, and Campbell, Jackson, and Schott delivered outstand-

ing plays. Mike Dean kicked a 56-yard field goal to set a new school record.

The Aggies needed a win over Texas in their annual game to win the SWC title and a trip to the Cotton Bowl. But Texas, playing as if it were the national championship, had a 14–0 lead with 54 seconds left in the first period. Shortly thereafter, they scored 3 more touchdowns to defeat the Aggies by an embarrassing 32–3. Campbell and Marty Akins were the Horns' stars in the big win.

Texas didn't get much contact work while preparing for their Gator Bowl contest against the sixth-ranked Auburn—a team with a fine record. Consequently, the Horns looked ragged offensley and defensley and committed several fumbles that resulted in Auburn touchdowns. Ultimately, Auburn defeated Texas 27–3 to end a disappointing season for Coach Royal. The Longhorns ended the season with an 8 and 4 record. It was an unhappy year for Royal and, in conversations with his top

Texas fullback Raymond Clayborn (24) scores against A&M, only 42 seconds after the 1974 game started.

Coach Darrell Royal, after nearly two decades at Texas, shows he's still a man on the move as he directs a workout before the 1975 Bluebonnet Bowl against Colorado. Royal watches a play that doesn't please him *(left)*, shows the players how it should be run *(center)*, and then applauds them as they run it correctly *(right)*.

assistant Mike Campbell, he intimated that "he might not coach the Horns much longer."

In 1975 Darrell Royal approached his nineteenth season as Texas' football coach and, now 51 years of age, had the pleasure of reflecting on one of the most distinguished careers in the history of college football. He had been elected president of the Football Coaches Association and had achieved an amazing record that elevated him to the level of the immortal Bear Bryant of Alabama, the late Knute Rockne of Notre Dame, Bernie Bierman of Minnesota, Fielding Yost of Michigan, and Bud Wilkinson of Oklahoma. He had won a total of 169 games—152 at Texas—and he stood fourth among active coaches in the number of wins. Royal's Longhorns finished in the nation's top ten 11 times. He won three national championships, 11 Southwest Conference crowns and played in 16 bowl games. And his teams' performances during 1960s earned him the honor of Coach of the Decade.

When Royal came to Texas, he immediately hired the nation's first football-team academic counselor. Over the years this proved wise; four out of five Texas players who lettered in football went on to get their degrees. And wherever his players were employed after they left Texas, Royal was there if they needed help. He never forgot his players.

In the intense struggle amongst coaches for victories, Royal was a champion in the battle for honesty and integrity. "He lived by the rules and never intentionally broke them," said a well-known vice president of the United States. "I'm not really a football fan," said President Lyndon Johnson a few years later. "But I am a fan of people, and I am a Darrell Royal fan because he is the rarest of human beings."

In the game against Utah State in 1975, Brad Shearer, Texas' defensive star, slams into halfback Lou Giammona.

But in 1975, Darrell confided to Mike Campbell, his best friend and chief aide, that he "was thinking of retiring for many reasons, too numerous to talk about."

But when the referee blew his whistle to signal the opening kickoff for the season, Royal's nineteenth team, with Al Jackson and John Thompson at the ends, was there. At the tackle posts, Bob Simmons and Rick Thurman; guards included Will and Charlie Wilcox; center Bill Gordon. At quarterback were Marty Akins, Jim Walker, Gray Wyatt and, at fullback, was one of the great offensive stars

of 1973 and 1974, the future Heisman winner Earl Campbell.

Against Colorado State in the opening game, Earl Campbell opened the game by rumbled 15 yards for the Horns' first touchdown of the year. By the end of the period it was 19–0, Texas. Campbell picked up 103 yards, Akins had two scores, and Landry had also scored. Colorado was smothered 46–0. Then in rapid succession, Texas beat Washington, 28–10; Texas Tech, 42–18; and Utah State, 61–7.

Then, just as the Horns were looking toward another national championship, Oklahoma, ranked No. 11 and a 7-point favorite, jolted Texas with a 24–17 defeat. Texas' poor ball handling and five fumbles in the first period led to the Sooners' first 10 points and from then on it was catch-up time for Texas. A week later, Texas was tested by one of Arkansas' top teams in a game that seesawed back and forth, until Earl Campbell took charge and raced for 2 touchdowns to take a 24–18 win.

Riddled with injuries, Texas beat Rice, 41–9, next; then SMU in a close 30–22 battle; Baylor, 37–21; and TCU, 27–11. Despite their run of success, the Horns then dropped the big game to the Aggies by a 20–10 margin.

Texas and Colorado were named to the Bluebonnet Bowl and Colorado outplayed and outfought the Longhorns to take a commanding 21–7 halftime lead. But in the second half, Texas exploded for 24 points and easily won, 38–21.

Texas back Jimmy Walker on his way to a touchdown in the 1975 Oklahoma game. Leading the interference is Texas' Gralyn Wyatt.

A blocked punt by Tim Campbell, Earl's brother, was the turning point, said Royal. Tim blocked the kick and it rolled into the end zone and Tim recovered for a Texas TD. That great block was the key to 17 additional points as Texas battered Colorado into submission for the Bluebonnet Bowl title.

Earl Campbell, tackle Bob Simmons, and Marty Akins were named to the various all-American teams. In addition, Akins was named as the SWC's most valuable player. Texas had ended another memorable campaign: They finished with a marvelous 10–2 record and the AP chose them as the sixth best team in the nation.

Darrell Royal faced his twentieth season with an increase in salary and ambivalent feelings. He had an experienced squad of veterans returning from the 1975 team. His only problem was the same one that had perplexed him nearly every other year since he had taken over in 1957. He sorely needed an experienced quarterback.

Even more important to Coach Royal were the ethical problems involving Oklahoma's and most of the other schools' recruiting, eligibility, and sportsmanship. In their fierce desire to beat Texas, other SWC coaches were quick to overlook and bypass ethical standards. It was a problem that had bothered Coach Royal before, but it seemed to be escalating. Again, he discussed retirement with his top coaching aide Mike Campbell and this time there was vehemence in his voice.

The season opened with a disappointing 14–13 loss to Boston College, wins over North Texas State and Rice, a heart-breaking 6–6 tie against Oklahoma, and a one-point win over SMU. Losses went to Texas Tech and Houston. A win over TCU came next, followed by a loss to Baylor. The next week Texas took another staggering loss dealt by the Aggies and, on December 4, Darrell Royal announced his retirement just before the season's final game against an old foe, Arkansas.

Texas won that final game 29–12 as fullback Earl Campbell, who had been on the sidelines most of the year because of an injured hamstring, rushed for two touchdowns and 130 yards to give him the school's all-time record. Russell Erxleben, Texas' trustworthy place kicker booted three field goals to put Arkansas out of victory range.

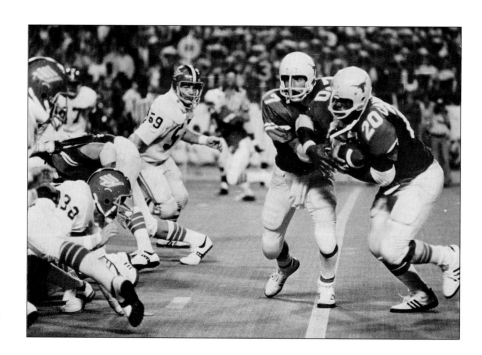

Texas quarterback Mike Cordaro (7) hands off to Earl Campbell (20) on the option play in a game with North Texas in 1976.

Johnny "Lam" Jones, at halfback, is effectively stopped by two Houston defenders in a 1976 game.

Incidentally, at the same time that Royal announced his decision to retire, Frank Broyles, his good friend and Arkansas' coach since 1958, also announced that he was quitting after the Texas game.

It was the end of a brilliant era in the Southwest Conference and the nearly 50,000 fans who witnessed this historic contest realized it. There were moist eyes in the crowd and on the field as the era-ending game concluded. Royal acknowledged as much emotion and found it necessary to brush away the tears as he put away the game ball.

"You never know how it will be and how it will end until it gets on top of you," said Royal, looking back on his final day. "The entire day seemed so confused, so hurried. For the first time in twenty-five years I didn't talk to my football team

All-American kicker Russell Erxleben kicked 3 field goals against Arkansas in the final game on the 1976 season.

In 1976, when Darrell Royal announced his resignation, his good friend, Coach Frank Broyles of Arkansas, also announced that he was leaving his post. *Left to right:* **Frank Broyles and Darrell Royal shake hands after Texas defeated Arkansas 29–12.**

after the pre-game meal. I didn't make it over there. My assistants had to do it. I blew it."

Royal said his 5-5-1 season had nothing to do with his decision to quit. "I think you are remembered for what you've done over a long period of time and not for a single season. I sure hope those years haven't been wasted." During Royal's 20 years, he had won 167 games, lost 47, and tied 5. He was the biggest winner in SWC history.

When did he decide to retire? "I can't say which straw made the camel go down on his knees. I don't think I'm too old. But I did become a head coach at twenty-eight and I'm now fifty-two. I've used up a lot of ammunition. I've always felt I wanted to quit before I was totally spent. I wanted to quit while there was still a little ham on the bone. I didn't want to overstay my leave. There will be a lot of nostalgia, a lot I'll miss," said Royal, "but I'll miss some things in a good way, I'll tell you that."

1977–1986:
THE AKERS ERA

It was peculiar that, despite the turmoil and histrionics that followed Royal's resignation, Mike Campbell, his close confidant and chief assistant for some twenty-one years, was hardly considered for the job. Royal had recommended him, but the coach's voice was unheard by the Board of Regents in the political shuffle.

Days after Royal's resignation, the board appointed Fred Akers as Texas' new coach and Royal took the post of director of athletics. Akers had been one of Royal's assistant coaches for nine years. After working for Royal, Akers had taken over a Wyoming team with a 1–9 record and within two years, had produced a team that was invited to the Fiesta Bowl.

Fred Akers was a handsome, well-manicured, and knowledgeable football man who had been a four-star letterman in high school and had played college football at Arkansas. The highlight of Akers' college career was a 28-yard field goal, kicked in the rain and mud, that gave the Razorbacks a 3–0 win over TCU. The victory gave Arkansas a share of the SWC championship— Texas was the other shareholder.

Unfortunately for Akers, he drifted away from Royal, who actually was his boss, when he assumed Texas' football fortune. It was rumored that Akers was told by someone high in the administration, "not to have much to do with Royal."

Whatever the reason, Akers hardly communicated with Royal and the relationship went sour. The stressed association worked to Akers' disadvantage, because nobody knew more about Texas football and football problems than Darrell Royal. But he did leave Akers with more than two dozen of the finest young men playing for Texas in years, including Earl Campbell, Texas' only Heisman award winner.

When Coach Akers began making plans for the forthcoming season, he said "I don't think this can be viewed as anything but a complete re-building job this year." But Akers was wrong. In Earl Campbell, Akers inherited a one-in-a-million halfback, a veritable one-man wrecking crew. A 6-foot, 235-pound senior, Campbell was one of the greatest high school backs in Texas' history. As a senior at Tyler High School, Earl led the school to the state championship, averaging 9.6 yards per carry. He scored 11 touchdowns and gained 852 yards in the five playoff games; on defense he was also a giant.

Under Coach Royal, Campbell was an immediate starter and was such a sensation that the coach said, "He's the only player I've ever seen who could have gone right to the pros from high school." In 1977, as a senior, Campbell led his Longhorns to a string of 10 consecutive wins. In every game, it was "Earl the Pearl" who distinguished himself with unrelenting line smashes, powerful drives, and bulldog determination to score every time he got the ball.

In the opening game of the season against Boston College, Texas eliminated the Eagles 44–0 in a match that featured a record-breaking 88-yard pass play from quarterback Jon Aune to Al Jackson for a touchdown and the incredible placekicking of all-American Russell Erxleben, who booted from the 45-, 57-, and 38-yard lines. In the next game the Horns routed Virginia 68–0. Campbell played less than half the game, but gained 150 yards rushing.

Earl Campbell (20) drives through a mass of Rice tacklers for a first down. Earl Campbell scored an amazing 4 touchdowns in the game.

The powerful Earl Campbell.

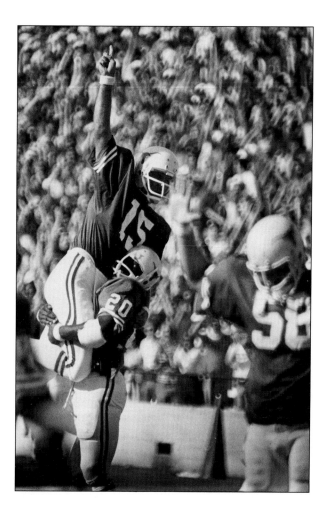

Earl Campbell, Texas' all-American back for four years, stands behind the podium after receiving the Heisman Trophy on December 9, 1977. On stage with Campbell are (left to right): Jay Berwanger, the very first Heisman recipient; Ron Cobleigh, president of the Downtown Athletic Club of New York; and the 1968 winner, O.J. Simpson.

In the opening play of the game against Texas, Rice elected to try an on-side kick. It was a play that failed as Texas recovered the ball. On the first Texas play, Mark McBath tossed a flawless 55-yard pass to Johnny Lam Jones, who scored a touchdown. The suddenness of the play shocked the Owls, and they were crushed by an onslaught of touchdowns that resulted in a 74–15 score. Campbell led the Longhorns, scoring four touchdowns and setting a school record for the number of TDs in a game.

Campbell was brilliant against Texas' arch enemy, Oklahoma, propelling the Horns to a thrilling 13–6 win that featured a brilliant 58-yard field goal by Russ Erxleben. One week after the Oklahoma win, Texas also defeated Arkansas in a close 13–9 game.

Campbell continued his rampage against SMU with 213 yards as the Horns took a 30–14 win. Texas was on a winning streak, with victories over Texas Tech, 26–0; Houston, 35–21; TCU, 44–14; and Baylor, 29–7. In the battle with A&M, Campbell wound up the regular season and the final game of his career by scoring four touchdowns and delivering a spectacular all-around performance.

Immediately after the Aggies game, Campbell was invited to New York City and to the Downtown Athletic Club to wait for the final Heisman award ballots to be counted. Campbell, Akers, Darrell Royal, Mrs. Campbell, and a number of Texas officials and friends accompanied Earl to the club for the nationally televised event. Not surprisingly, Campbell was awarded the Heisman.

In his brief acceptance speech, Earl said that when he was a small boy he would call on his mother when in trouble. Then turning to his mother, Earl said, "Well, Mom, I'm in trouble. Help me."

Texas closed out the season undefeated and was voted the No. 1 team in the nation by the Associated Press poll. The Longhorns accepted the Cotton Bowl invitation for a battle against the No. 5 team, the Fighting Irish of Notre Dame.

On New Year's Day, Dan Devine's fast-moving machine from South Bend took less than eight minutes in the second period to turn a close 3–3 game into a rout. Aided by six Texas fumbles and three pass interceptions, Notre Dame shut down Texas' offense (except Earl Campbell, who picked up 116 yards rushing) and won 38–10. Notre Dame played a tremendous all-around game, which was led by Joe Montana who tossed 25 passes with only one interception.

The loss to Notre Dame cost the Texas Longhorns another national championship, but closed out a remarkable winning season for first-year coach Fred Akers.

In the opening game of the 1978 season, the Longhorns made an auspicious showing against Rice in a 34–0 win. It was all due to Johnny "Lam" Jones, who caught four great passes and scored two touchdowns. Coach Akers' Longhorns had too much defense for the Owls; they couldn't muster more than half-a-dozen first downs during the game.

It was like homecoming for Coach Akers as Texas faced Akers' former team, the Wyoming Cowboys. Texas easily defeated the Cowboys, 17–3.

Randy McEachern's 5-yard line buck for a Texas score and Kermit Goode's 5-yard TD run, both yielding Texas scores, gave the Horns a 14–0 lead in the second period. Russ Erxleben booted a 43-yarder in the third period to nail down a 17–3 win over Wyoming.

After a week of team meetings to plan a more productive offense, the Longhorns defeated Texas Tech 24–7 as Johnny "Lam" Jones was in his best form all season and rushed for 128 yards.

With three victories in a row, the Longhorns were ready to challenge Oklahoma, the No. 1 rated team in the nation. But the Sooners, oozing confidence and trumpeting their great Heisman winner, Billy Simms, took the ball on their first possession and marched upfield 77 yards for a touchdown. And they were never stopped thereafter. Four subsequent Texas turnovers led to Sooner touchdowns and Oklahoma took a 31–10 win.

In a wild and woolly battle against North Texas, Randy McEachern came off the bench in the second period and guided Texas to three TDs and a 26–16 win over North Texas.

"I wasn't the least worried about the freshmen Ham Jones and Brad Beck in the game. They did a great job," said quarterback Randy McEachern, "and Lam was fantastic, as always."

In a thrilling come-from-behind fight against hard-nosed Arkansas, Texas defeated the Razorbacks 28–21 in a game that will long be remembered. Arkansas took a 21–20 lead in the third period, but McEachern countered with a bulletlike pass to Lam Jones for a touchdown, and then topped it off with a toss for a two-point conversion. Texas came away with their finest win of the year.

In the year's outstanding play against SMU, Johnny "Lam" Jones took an SMU kickoff in the third period, sped by five SMU tacklers, and drove the entire length of the field for 102 yards and a thrilling touchdown. The Horns claimed a 22–3 win over SMU in a game that, as Akers said, they "simply had to win."

In one of the toughest games Texas had played in many years, the Houston Cougars outlasted Texas in a difficult tussle by a 10–7 score. But the Longhorns rebounded from the Houston defeat against TCU in a game that could only mean a Cotton Bowl invitation for the winner. Next game, the Longhorns posted a significant 41–0 win over TCU with the help of quarterbacks McEachern and Donnie Little, and with the footwork of Russ Erxleben, who kicked 4 field goals for a school record. The Baylor Bears, on a prowl for a bowl game themselves and with the most talented team in years, easily defeated Texas 38–14 and eliminated any hope of a Cotton Bowl bid for Texas.

Although pride was the only thing at stake for Texas in their annual battle against A&M, it was enough for the Horns to pound out a 22–7 victory. This exhibition showcased Russ Erxleben, who booted two field goals—a 59-yarder and one for 22 yards—and kept A&M in the hole throughout the game.

In the 44th Sun Bowl, Texas demolished a strong Maryland eleven by a 42–0 score. The Jones boys, Lam and Ham, were outstanding and Erxleben's kicking was masterful throughout the game.

The win over Maryland gave Coach Akers a 9–3 season and a second place finish in the SWC. Despite the fine record posted by the 1978 eleven, the alumni were disgruntled and complained that Akers "could not win the big games," meaning the bowl games, of which he had lost two in a row. But the coaches looked forward to the fine new crop of freshman and sophomore players who had played some varsity ball in 1978 and were sure to contribute substantially in 1979. Perhaps, with any sort of break, Akers thought they might have an undefeated season. . . .

Johnny "Lam" Jones was a senior wide receiver for the Longhorns in 1979. With his six-two, 185-pound frame, great hands, and blistering speed, he could very well be the greatest wide receiver in the ranks of college football. By 1979, Jones already held six Texas receiving and touchdown records, including most TD passes in a career (12), longest touchdown kickoff return (100 yards), and best average yardage per catch (25 yards). Ask any NFL talent director about Johnny "Lam" and he'll know all about him because, among pro-level wide receivers, Johnny "Lam" leads all the rest.

"Lam may be the fastest football player in the world," said Texas Athletic Director Darrell Royal. Fred Akers agreed with his boss, "Johnny is the fastest player I've ever seen or coached. We know he's fast, we've never even bothered to time him."

In Lam's first college game, Royal used him as a halfback. He gained 45 yards on seven carries and scored a touchdown against Boston College. But by then he had already approached folk hero status on the Texas campus and in Texas sports circles.

Thousands had seen Lam at the state track championships the previous spring, when in the final event he made up almost 50 yards on the last lap of the mile relay to win the race for Lampasas High School. From there he went on to make the U.S. Olympic team, as an 18-year-old just out of high school. At Montreal he won a gold medal for his relay contribution.

But in 1979, Jones had interest only in Texas football and in the opening game against Iowa State, he scored two touchdowns. Although Iowa State was leading 9–3 in the third period on the strength of 3 field goals by Alex Giffords, they hurt themselves by fumbling three times. Texas scored and it was 10–9. Then in the fourth period, a pass interference against Iowa State gave Texas the ball on the 4-yard line and Jones cracked the line and got the TD that gave the game to the Horns, 17–9.

The Missouri Tigers never came close to scoring against Texas' awesome defense. The Horns completely stifled the Tigers and Texas took a 21–0 win over Missouri. Ham Jones scored after a 73-yard drive, while the Longhorns' ace kicker Johnny Goodson booted four field goals, one of which was a 50-yarder. Ham was the key to the Horns' attack as he raced for 142 yards in 30 carries. But the Texas defense was astonishing as they held a strong Tiger eleven to 11 first downs.

Just one week later, Texas easily beat Rice as quarterbacks Jones and Donnie Little starred in a 26–9 win. In a rough defensive battle in Dallas, Texas put down Oklahoma 16–7 in a game that was nip and tuck throughout.

After the fifth game of the season, Coach Lou Holtz explained how his Arkansas team beat Texas 17–14. "It was plain, simple football," said Lou. "We just ran the ball right at them and we came out ahead in a close one." But Texas battled until the final minute, when Goodson's 51-yard kick, which would have tied the score, fell short. SMU was the victim in the Horns' sixth game as Texas got back on track after the loss to Arkansas and scored a 30–6 win. One week later, Texas Tech went down after a fierce battle, 14–6.

The lead changed hands three times in the Houston-Texas game until linebacker Conny Hatch blocked a punt in the second period and Ham Jones recovered and burst through from the 6-yard line. In the second half, two pass interceptions by cornerback Derrick Hatchett and another by Ricky Churchman stopped the Cougars—it was Texas 21, Houston 13. Texas Christian was routed in a 35–10 battle and the following week Ham Jones caught eight passes against Baylor as the Horns shut out the Bears, 13–0.

The victory over Baylor was a costly one. Quarterback Donnie Little, who had performed admirably all season; Ham Jones; and Rodney Tate were all injured in the game and out of action for the final two games of the season.

With Little injured, the Texas offense sputtered and showed little scoring ability when Texas met the Aggies. As a result, A&M took a hard-earned 13–7 win.

As the season ended, Texas had an outstanding 9–2 record and was invited to the Sun Bowl to face the powerful Washington Huskies. In one of the most arduous defensive struggles all year, the Huskies scored a touchdown in the final period and took a 14–7 win.

Despite the loss to Washington, Texas' season ended on a high note since they had finished their second straight 9–3 season.

More than forty-five lettermen reported to Coach Akers' first 1980 practice sessions. A fine cadre of freshmen and walk-ons also made the team look promising. In the early scrimmages, Donnie Little started at quarterback, Johnny Lam Jones

Quarterback Donnie Little gets off a long pass just before he is hit by a Baylor tackler in the 1980 game.

Texas speedster, Johnny "Lam" Jones, carries the ball for a 15-yard gain against Baylor in 1980.

tested his fine runningback skills, Johnny Goodson served as an especially capable placekicker, Terry Tausch and all-American Ken Sims reconfirmed their talents as tackles. Les Koenning, Vance Bedford, Robin Sendlein, and Steve Massey were chosen as the four team captains.

In the opening game of the season, Texas had little trouble against Arkansas and beat the Razorbacks 23–17. Then in rapid succession, Texas beat Utah State, 35–17; Oregon, 35–0; and Rice, 41–28. In the toughest game to date, Oklahoma was defeated 20–13 and it looked as though the Longhorns, who had five consecutive wins, might go all the way.

But SMU upset Texas 20–6, and Texas Tech did the same by a 24–20 margin. Texas was lucky to beat Houston 15–13 and took the momentum to the next game. Texas rediscovered its strength against TCU, delivering eight touchdowns and playing the finest game of the season in a 51–26 victory. But the following weeks brought more disappointment as Baylor and the Aggies defeated the Horns. Baylor won by a 16–0 shutout and A&M, 24–14.

Despite the four losses during the season, Texas was invited to the Bluebonnet Bowl and

dropped a hard-fought 16–7 contest to North Carolina to wind up a modestly successful 7-5 season and claim fourth place in the Southwest Conference.

Fred Akers, now in his fifth season at Texas, found himself in an increasingly difficult position. He had originally been told by Allan Shivers, former Texas governor and chairman of the Board of Regents, to not "pay any attention to Darrell Royal." Shivers convinced Akers that he (Shivers) actually controlled the director of athletics' office. Therefore Akers never reported to Royal, hardly ever spoke to him, and they went their separate ways.

Because of this, Akers eventually found himself alienated by the majority of Texas fans and alumni, who practically worshipped Royal. Eventually Texas alumni, who had steered top high school football talent to Texas, gradually lost interest and by 1984 the premier Texas high school players found their way to other SWC teams—and Texas and Akers later felt the disastrous impact.

Still, in 1981, Akers had one of his finest years with only one loss—to a powerful Arkansas team, 42–11—and a 14–14 tie with Houston. With a terrific 9-1-1 season record, Texas was invited to

TONY EDWARDS   LB   TODD DODGE, QB   BRENT DUHON, WR   CHRIS DULIBAN, LB   STEVE EARGLE, OT

A few members of 1983 Longhorns squad.

play the Crimson Tide in the Cotton Bowl in a game that could decide the national championship. It would be Bear Bryant's magic against Akers' unyielding defense in what could be one of the year's most memorable matches.

At halftime, down by only 7–0, Fred Akers told his team not to worry. "You hold them in the third quarter," he said to the defense. Then turning to the offense, he said, "And you get them in the fourth period and we've got the game."

The Horns did as ordered. They had moments of confusion against Alabama's Wishbone; they had been burned by five passes for 113 yards and a touchdown. "On every play they give you a different formation, a different look," said Bill Graham, Texas safety, who led Texas interceptions with seven and was second in tackles.

Following a field goal in the fourth period, Bob Brewer, whose father Charley, currently a Dallas banker, had quarterbacked the 1955 Texas

team to a 21–6 defeat of a Texas A&M team coached by Bear Bryant, called for time. On the sidelines, Akers told Brewer to call Play 1 (the quarterback draw). The play caught Alabama by surprise as they were blitzing, and Brewer sped into the end zone to score from the 30-yard line. Texas took a 14–10 lead as Brewer again sparked an 11-play drive, including a 37-yard pass to Lawrence Sampleton at tight end. With another pass to Sampleton and a 10-yard pass to Donnie Little, Texas had the ball on the Tide's 8-yard line. Then it was up to Terry Orr, and the husky back blasted over left tackle for the 14–10 lead with 2½ minutes to play. Alabama's Walt Lewis tossed a long pass from the Texas 38-yard line. The pass was intercepted on the Texas 1-yard stripe and then after a Texas safety, the score was 14–12 and time had run out for Alabama. "I think this was the greatest win of my coaching career," Fred Akers said after the game.

Following the final game of the season, defensive tackle and two-time all-American Kenneth Simms was named winner of the Lombardi Award as the top college lineman of 1981. Simms is shown with Coach Fred Akers.

Texas linebackers Joe Monroe (38) and Ty Allert (48) make a goal line stand in the 1983 game against Oklahoma.

Texas halfback Terry Orr cracks through a strong Baylor line for a gain of 10 yards in the tense battle of two great teams. This was Texas' tenth straight win, making them No. 1 in the nation in 1983.

The 1983 season began simply in Auburn, Alabama, on September 17 as the nation watched the third-ranked Texas Longhorns defeat the fifth-ranked Auburn Tigers, 20–7. The Horns had a respectable freshman kicker, Jeff Ward; a sophomore punter, John Teltschik; three big question marks for a quarterback; end Eric Holle, an All-SWC star; Jerry Gray, an all-American safety; cornerback Mossy Cade; Jeff Leiding, a linebacker; guard Doug Dawson; Tony Degrate; and Fred Acorn. This was a team of undeniable talent and they proved it by defeating North Texas, Rice, Oklahoma, Arkansas, SMU, Texas Tech, Houston, TCU, Baylor, and Texas A&M.

But in the biggest game of the year—a game that would have meant another national championship for Texas and that was described as "nightmarish"—the Horns lost by a single point to the Georgia Bulldogs, 10–9.

Despite being inside Georgia's 34-yard line seven times, the Texas offense, led by quarterback Rich McIvor came away with only 9 points on three field goals of 22, 40, and 27 yards, all kicked by Jeff Ward. The game and the national championship hung on one play: With 4:32 to play, Craig Curry of Texas mishandled a Georgia punt and the Bulldogs wound up on Texas' 23-yard line with the ball. Three plays later, the Bulldogs scored on a 17-

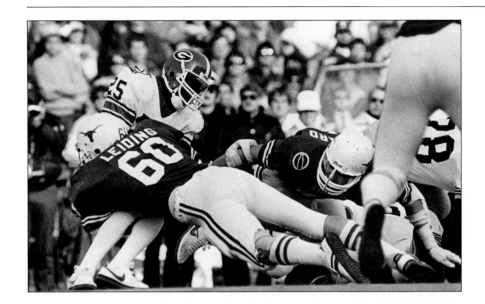

In the 1984 Cotton Bowl matchup between Texas and Georgia, Texas linebacker Jeff Leiding crushes Georgia's halfback. Texas needed a win to claim the national championship, but lost a heartbreaker that ended 10–9, Georgia.

yard pass by quarterback John Lastinger. The touchdown gave them the Cotton Bowl title by a single point, 10–9.

Texas ended the season with a notable 11–1 record and was ranked fifth in the nation. But the Cotton Bowl was the final game for thirty-one seniors' illustrious careers at Texas. "Sad part, no one will remember the eleven games we won," said Tony Degrate.

Quarterback Todd Dodge and his favorite receiver, Brent Duhon, received acclaim as one of the greatest forward passing combinations in Texas high school football when they entered Texas in 1980. But in three seasons, they had never connected on a touchdown pass. Dodge, in fact, had completed only 22 passes in three years.

But the strange drought finally ended in the nationwide TV match between Texas and the highly favored Auburn Tigers. The Tigers had the great Bo Jackson, who, everyone conceded, was on his way to winning the Heisman.

Early in the third period of the game, Dodge finally connected with a 32-yard pass to Duhon to give Texas an upset 35–27 win over the Tigers. The following week, the Longhorns displayed championship form at the Meadowlands Complex in New

Jersey as they defeated a top-ranked Penn State by a 28–3 score.

The victories over a strong Auburn team and an equally impressive Penn State team vaulted the Longhorns into the No. 1 spot in the Associated Press polls. At the same time, Akers was voted the No. 1 coach.

Texas moved on to defeat Rice but a strong Oklahoma eleven jolted the Longhorns and held them to a 15–15 tie in a tiring defensive battle. Then in successive weeks, there were wins over Arkansas, SMU, and Texas Tech. But after a 29–15 loss to Houston, Texas' hopes for another national title were lost.

Things brightened with a Texas win over TCU, but successive losses to Baylor, A&M, and Iowa in the Freedom Bowl (to the tune of 55–17) ended the season. Texas had finished a season of promise with 4 games lost and 7 won.

Now the critics began to demand Fred Akers' scalp. "He can't win the big games," they cried.

There was no doubt that the ill-fated trip to the Freedom Bowl was the beginning of the end of the trail for Fred Akers. The loss to Iowa, by a 55–17 margin, was the worst since a 49–20 loss to Oklahoma in 1952. The alumni, and even the players, were angry and distraught about the embarrassing score.

Quarterback Todd Dodge connects with a 35-yard pass to his favorite receiver, Brent Duhon. Brent scores to give Texas an upset 13–10 win over Texas Tech in 1984.

Jeff Ward, one of Texas' captains for 1986, celebrates the game-winning field goal he booted against SMU.

In 1985, the Longhorns began with wins over Missouri, Stanford, and Rice. Then Oklahoma took a one-touchdown win from Texas by 14–7. The following week things looked brighter with a 15–13 win over Arkansas, but SMU routed the Horns 44–14.

With a 4 and 2 record halfway into the season, Texas trounced Texas Tech and Houston and shut out TCU, 20–0. Next Texas beat Baylor 17–10 and with an 8–2 season, it looked as if Akers might escape the noose. But a shattering loss to the Aggies (42–10), and a loss to the Air Force in the Bluebonnet Bowl (24–15) were the last straws.

On November 29, 1986, after the Longhorns had won only 5 games and lost 6, Fred Akers was fired. This was Akers' first losing season and the first for Texas since 1956. In Akers' ten years at Texas, he'd taken the Horns to the brink of a national championship on two occasions. Six of his teams won 9 or more games. His 86-31-2 record was the fourth best percentage in the Southwest Conference. But Darrell Royal's percentage still ranked first and earned him that respect.

"It wasn't his coaching that got him fired," said DeLoss Dodds, Texas' athletic director. "It was that he divided, split the allegiance of Texas fans. People just didn't like Fred Akers."

It would be 1990 before the Texas Longhorns would once again field a team that would dominate the Southwest Conference.

1987–1992:
A NEW BEGINNING

In 1970 Darrell Royal called upon Dave McWilliams and offered him a job as an assistant freshman coach at Texas. McWilliams had completed a most successful career at Texas as a tri-captain of the 1963 national championship team. After that, he had taken a position as an assistant coach at Abilene High School, moving up to head coach from 1966 to 1969. At 24 years of age, McWilliams was the youngest head football coach in Texas.

At Texas, McWilliams put in 16 highly productive seasons as a freshman coach and then became linebacker coach. As Royal's Longhorns became one of the dominant teams in the nation, Royal named McWilliams his chief defensive co-ordinator and the Texas defense quickly became ranked among the best in the nation.

Anxious to assume the mantle of head coach, McWilliams jumped at the opportunity to take over at Texas Tech, one of the Longhorn's chief rivals. In his first season in 1986, Dave McWilliams turned around the Tech program and finished the year with an outstanding 7 and 4 record and an invitation to the Independence Bowl.

When Fred Akers was fired, Athletic Director DeLoss Dodds looked over two dozen contenders for the job at Texas. Within a few days, the list had been narrowed down to five candidates, including Alabama's Bill Curry, Dick Sheridan of North Carolina, Fisher DeBerry, and Larry Smith of Arizona. Eventually, it was McWilliams' closeness to Royal and the fact that his appointment would rejoin those fans who had divided their loyalty between Royal and Akers. Now there was goodwill among all factions.

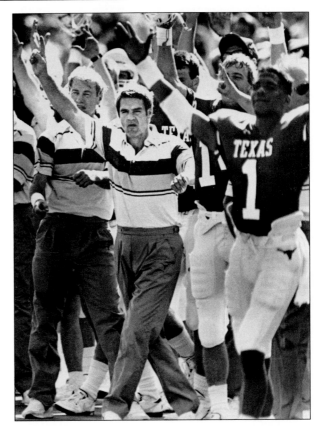

Coach Dave McWilliams leads a happy group of Longhorns off the field after their win over highly rated Arkansas 49–17 for their fifth win of the season in 1990.

On signing the Texas contract and being awarded a yearly salary of $91,000 for five years, McWilliams said, "This is a dream come true."

But the dreams of David McWilliams slowly faded as Texas was beset with injuries to key defen-

177

BEVO—the University of Texas' mascot was first brought to the campus by football manager Steve Pinckney in 1911. Pinckney was engaged in fighting Mexican rustlers along the Rio Grande River after graduating from UT and found an orange- and white-colored steer, which he brought to the campus in 1916 during Texas' 21–7 win over A&M.

UT fans give the traditional hand salute as the Longhorn squad prepares for battle against the Aggies in 1988.

sive players when they faced Auburn in the opening game of the '87 season. Three costly Texas fumbles led to scores and an eventual 31–3 Auburn win. In the Brigham Young game, the second of the season, Texas' 8 fumbles led to a 22–17 win for BYU even though the Horns outgained BYU 342 yards to their 243.

After an off week, the Texas offense began a thunderous roll of touchdowns to crush Oregon State, 61–16, and then Rice 45–26. Then Oklahoma, the 31-point favorites, took a 13–6 halftime lead in the following week. In the second half, Texas committed 7 fumbles, plus 4 interceptions, and Oklahoma destroyed them by a 44–9 margin.

At Little Rock, Arkansas, a huge crowd saw the rebirth of the 1987 Longhorns when quarterback Bret Stafford tossed an 18-bullet pass to Tony

Jones. With no time left on the clock that gave the underdog Horns a stunning 16–14 upset win.

John Hagy scored a pair of touchdowns as Texas defeated Texas Tech, 41–27. Then, in a battle against Houston, Texas fumbled 4 times and had 4 pass interceptions as the Cougars exploded for 31 points in the final period to win in a wild game, 60–40.

Then it was up to Eric Metcalf, the speedy halfback, whose father set rushing records in the NFL for St. Louis in the 1970s. Metcalf rushed for a 200-yard game and scored twice against TCU as the Horns won that battle, 24–21. Then, against Baylor, Metcalf gained 165 yards and a touchdown as the Horns won, 36–16.

In the big Turkey Day game, Texas fought A&M every minute, but the Aggies were a bit tougher and managed to nose out Texas 20–13 to win the SWC title.

Texas earned an invitation from the Bluebonnet Bowl to play a tough Pittsburgh eleven, which included 270-pound Craig Haywood, one of

Adrian Walker (#36), Texas' fleet-footed halfback, shows his heels to a horde of Oklahoma tacklers in a 1989 tussle as the Horns won an exciting 28–24 thriller.

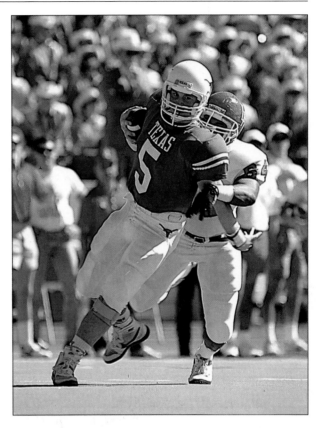

Butch Hadnot (#5), the Longhorns' outstanding running back, picks up 15 yards on this play against Houston in 1989.

the greatest fullbacks. But the brilliant star of the game was Texas quarterback Brett Stafford as he tossed passes for 3 touchdowns and a 32–27 victory over a Pitt team that was favored to win by 15 points.

It was David McWilliams' finest hour at Texas. He had taken command of a team that had posted one of the worst records in recent Texas football and turned a mediocre record into a winning 7–5 season.

In 1988, Texas was again burdened with a record number of injuries to varsity players, as well as eligibility problems. The Longhorns were only able to win games against New Mexico, North Texas, Rice, and TCU, while dropping 7 games.

Although the 1989 season looked brighter than '88's, the Horns produced a 5 and 6 record. Despite the successes, which included wins over favored Oklahoma and Arkansas, a 21–10 loss to Texas A&M cast a pall over the campus and fueled

the talk that McWilliams was too soft, too pal-like with his players and coaches.

In 1990, the fourth year of his five-year contract, Coach Dave McWilliams realized that he was living on borrowed time as head football coach at Texas. In three seasons he'd produced only one winning season, followed by two dismal years. This year McWilliams and his coaches had gone all out to produce a winner in 1990 . . . or else.

Just before the opening game of the season against Penn State at State College, on the sidelines Dave McWilliams quickly looked over a victory speech he had written the night before when he had become convinced his team would win—even though Texas had lost four straight opening games during the past four years. McWilliams wanted to show his team that he was certain they would win.

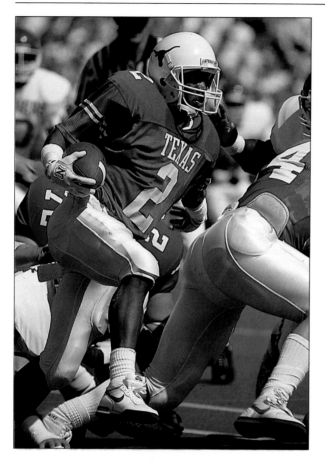

Texas' ace receiver, Mike Davis (#2), is off for a big game against Oklahoma in 1989.

The game began as Mike Pollak, Texas' kicker, booted a high kick and State's tailback, Gary Brown caught the ball on his 2-yard line and started upfield. He broke away from two Texas tacklers, then was out into the clear. It looked as if he would go all the way to the 30-, 20-, and 10-yard lines. And then suddenly, out of nowhere, Texas' linebacker, Winfred Tubbs, coming from behind like an express train, brought him down on the 5-yard line. The huge crowd of about 78,000 spectators roared their approval of Brown's sensational 93-yard return.

The Texas defense held for two downs, then tailback Thompson cracked the middle of the line and scored. The kick was good and within one minute Penn State had a 7–0 lead.

State kicked off and Texas returned the ball to the 21-yard line. Then Pete Gardere, the 6-foot, 190-pound sophomore quarterback who became a starter in his freshman year, started the Texas drive with a series of running plays by Adrian Walker for short gains. Then Gardere flipped a short pass to Chris Samuels and Texas had a first down on the 35-yard line. Then Johnny Walker made a diving one-hand stab at a bullet pass, pulling down the ball on State's 29-yard line. It was good for a 30-yard gain. The Texas drive lost steam and Pollak booted a 30-yard field goal. After four minutes of play it was 7–3 in State's favor.

In the second period, Tony Sacca, Penn's fine quarterback, was hit as he started to pass and Texas recovered the ball. The Horns' offense stalled and again Pollak kicked a field goal. The half ended Penn State 7, Texas 6.

The second half opened with State kicking to Texas and Adrian Walker fielding the ball on his 5-yard line, avoiding two tacklers, plowing through another, and suddenly breaking away into the clear as the Texas fans in the stands went wild with joy. Walker sprinted to State's 5-yard line and was tackled after a brilliant 88-yard spurt.

On the first play, Gardere handed the ball to Chris Samuels and he drove to his right and went for a touchdown. Pete Gardere faked a kick on the conversion, scrambled a bit, and then tossed a pass to Keith Cash. This set up Texas for a two-point conversion and put them in front 14–7. Late in the third period freshman Phil Brown broke loose for 42 yards to the State 20-yard line. Here the Texas attack froze, Pollak hit his third field goal, and Texas had a 17–7 lead.

As the fourth period opened, Sacca fired passes, one which went to Terry Smith and was good for 48 yards. In four plays, State scored, making it 17–13 with little time left to play.

With 1½ minutes left in the game, Sacca completed a pass. After another pass completion and a 15-yard penalty against Texas, State had the ball on Texas' 27. And now the huge crowd was in an absolute frenzy. Then there was still another pass from Sacca to Smith, and State had a first down on the 20-yard line with only 30 seconds left to play in the game.

Sacca took the pass from center, and scrambled around looking for an open man as time raced on. Sacca saw his man and hurled a bullet pass up

Chris Samuels, Texas' fine back, dives over the Aggies line for a gain as the Horns win a 28–27 battle in 1990.

the middle, but Texas defender Stan Richard had been following the play like a hawk. He batted the ball down as the gun sounded to end the struggle. Texas had pulled off the biggest opening game upset in five years with a 17–13 win.

The win over Penn State was celebrated for days, then a tough Colorado team abruptly burst Texas' bubble with a 29–22 win.

Then it was up to sophomore quarterback Pete Gardere, the young quarterback whose father played varsity football for Texas, to harness the horses and get Texas back on track. Pete did just that against Rice, tossing a touchdown pass and hitting 19 of 29 passes to defeat the Owls 26–10.

Against a highly touted Oklahoma team, it was a case of lightning striking twice. For the second straight year the Longhorns mounted a late, fourth-period drive to beat the Sooners. This time, Texas took over on its 9-yard line with about 7 minutes left to play. Twelve plays later, Texas took off with freshman Butch Hadnot's gains of 5, 7, 11, and 13 yards. Then with a pass by Gardere, Texas faced fourth down and 7 yards to go. Time was called and Peter Gardere dropped back, back, and spotted Keith Cash in the end zone. He lobbed a pass to Cash for a TD. Then Wayne Clements booted the extra point and Texas was up, 14–13. There were two minutes left.

Oklahoma then drove down to the Texas 29-yard line but, with time running out, Lasher tried a field goal for Oklahoma that barely missed and Texas had won another stunning victory.

Against Arkansas, Gardere was sensational in Texas' stunning 49–17 blitz, scoring a touchdown, tossing 15 of 24 passes and 6 for 9 in the final period as Texas erupted for 29 points in the last quarter and nailed down another great win. Now Texas was 4–1 and looking forward to one of the best seasons in years.

The Horns started slowly against SMU as Hadnot and Adrian Walker's key runs gave Texas a 17–0 halftime lead. Then Texas really took SMU

Halfback Adrian Walker (#36) flashes a dandy cross-step and picks up additional yardage to get by an Arkansas tackler in a 1990 battle.

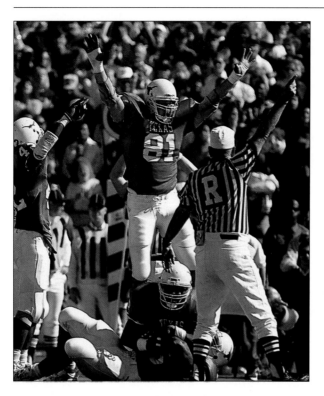

Six-foot, six-inch all-American end Shane Dronett leaps into the air and gives the Longhorn salute as Texas scores a TD against Baylor in 1990.

Peter Gardere (#10), Texas' great quarterback, races for a touchdown in a stirring battle against A&M in 1990.

Running back Pat Wilson (#39) gets a great block from a teammate and sprints 34 yards for a touchdown against A&M in a 1990 contest.

apart, ripping the Mustangs 52–3 for win number five, which the Horns celebrated through the night. Against Texas Tech, the Longhorns started slowly and were behind 7–0. But they tied the score and moved ahead as Gardere threw a pass to Kerry Cash to make it 14–7 at halftime. After two field goals by Pollak, it was 20–10, Texas. In the fourth period Texas got touchdowns from Boone Powell, Hadnot, and Lance Gunn and it became a runaway with Texas in front 41–22 as the game ended.

Undefeated third-ranked Houston rolled into Austin with its unstoppable run-and-shoot offense, led by Heisman candidate David Klinger. In the three previous years, Houston had run up an average of 57.7 points per game on Texas, defeating Texas for three straight years. This year they were top-heavy favorites to make it four in a row.

But the Longhorn defense intercepted Klinger four times and held the Cougars to 81 yards in the second and third periods, when the game was decided. Quarterback Pete Gardere had one of his greatest days, completing 20 of 28 passes for 322 yards—including a string of 10 successive comple-

Texas back Brian Howard (#19) picks up yardage against Miami in the 1990 Cotton Bowl game.

tions—while Butch Hadnot scored two touchdowns to rout Houston 45–24 and knock the Cougars clear out of any chance for the national championship. Eighty-two thousand screaming, half-crazed Longhorn fans celebrated their sixth straight win, partying all through the night.

Then TCU, with a 1 and 5 record, was easily defeated 38–10. The next week, Baylor took a 14–0 lead. But Pollak, Texas' great placekicker, made a 56-yard field goal and it was 10–3 at the half. In the second half, behind Hadnot, Pete Gardere, Adrian Walker, and Pollak, Texas drove for a 23–13 win over the Bears in an exciting down-to-the-final-gun thriller.

With a Cotton Bowl title match up for grabs, Texas was set for the biggest game of the year—the Aggies game. At game time, more than 78,000 frenetic fans were screaming in support.

The Aggies got the ball on their 20-yard line and, in 12 plays, Bucky Richardson pitched a pass to tailback Darren Lewis, who ran in from the 12-yard line, making the score 7–0, A&M. Then Pete Gardere took over after the kickoff on Texas' 32-

yard line. He attempted a pass, which was intercepted by A&M. A&M smashed ahead to the Texas 12-yard line and, on the first play, A&M scored and it was 14–0.

During the season Texas had come from behind in several games, but never 14 points against an outstanding team like the Aggies. On the first play, Gardere hid the ball, faked a handoff, and then, in a surprise move that caught A&M off-balance, burst through the left tackle and outsprinted three A&M defensive men 50 yards for a touchdown. The kick was good and the crowd roared its approval.

Then after both teams had taken turns battering each other and missing on field goal attempts, Pat Wilson, Texas' back, produced two fine runs of 15 and 18 yards and Texas had quickly moved to A&M's 10-yard line. On the first play, Gardere passed off to Cash, who drove in for the touchdown. The kick was good and now it was a 14–14 game.

Late in the third period, Texas scored from the 5-yard line. Texas was ahead 21–14 in a thrill-a-minute battle. Then Lewis of A&M drove in for a touchdown and this unpredictable contest was now tied at 21–21. Never letting up, the crowd continued to scream with excitement.

Then a magnificent Pete Gardere faked a pass, faded back, cut to his left, and sprinted 11 yards for a touchdown. Texas had the lead by 28–21, but A&M did not quit. Richardson, on an option, ran the ball and was in the clear for a touchdown, making it Texas 28, Aggies 27 with four minutes left in the game.

Texas had the ball and drove right down to the 2-yard line but before they could score, the ball game was over and Texas had won the most important, thrilling game of the year.

In the locker room, Texas accepted the invitation to the Cotton Bowl game against Miami . . . and a shot at the national championship. And the celebration across campus and all over town is one people are still talking about.

On the big day, the Cotton Bowl was jammed to capacity with some 78,000 spectators anxiously awaiting the opening kickoff as Texas faced the Miami Hurricanes.

Phil Brown cracks through the Baylor line in a 1991 game for a first down as Shay Shafie (#76) and Shane Childers (on the ground) block for him.

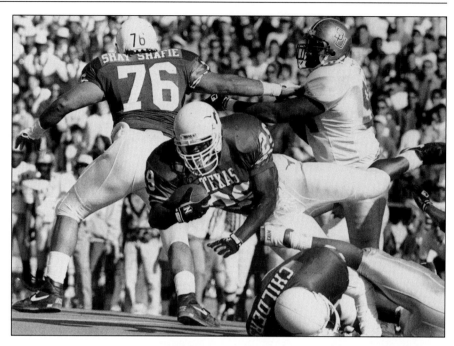

Miami kicked off and Texas failed to gain, and then kicked to the Hurricanes, who immediately began to drive upfield. On successive running plays, Miami picked up 47 yards before the Texas defense stiffened and held. But the Canes kicked a 28-yard field goal and it was 3–0.

Texas failed to gain ground and Miami took over the ball and then moved to midfield. When Texas' defense halted their offense, Miami booted another field goal—this one from the 50-yard line—and they led 6–0.

Receiving the kickoff, Texas began an aerial attack. On the second attempt, Gardere was hit hard and fumbled; Miami recovered on the 21-yard line. Then a Miami pass to Carroll was good and he took it in for another Miami score. Now the scoreboard read 12–0.

Texas finally began to move and was helped by a personal foul that gave them the ball on Miami's 33. Hadnot smashed off-tackle for 14 yards to Miami's 19, but the attack stalled. Pollak hit a 29-yard field goal and it was Miami 12, Texas 3.

Just before going into the locker room at the half, Miami scored another TD and it was 19 to 3. Texas appeared completely disoriented.

Quarterback Peter Gardere cocks his arm for a pass that was completed for a 15-yard gain against Oklahoma in 1991.

Linemen Chris Rapp (#63) and Lorenzo Lewis (#92) stop a battering drive by a TCU back in a 1991 game.

Texas' flashy runningback Phil Brown shakes off a Texas Tech tackler and picks up 15 yards in a 1991 game.

Miami took the second-half kickoff and returned the ball to the 50-yard line. But Texas halted the Miami attack, took over the ball, and began to move. Pete Gardere attempted a pass to Keith Cash, but it was a soft lob and Miami's Smith intercepted the toss and sprinted 35 yards for another touchdown, making it 26–3, Miami.

Miami scored three more times and took the Cotton Bowl title with a shattering 46–3 win over a demoralized Texas team. This was the highest score ever in a Cotton Bowl and Texas was stunned by the beating. But, overall, Texas had enjoyed the best season in 7 years and Texas fans, once they got over the Cotton Bowl massacre, believed they were getting closer and closer to the glory years of Darrell Royal.

"If we can just find some guys who can catch the ball . . . " said Coach David McWilliams as 1991's spring practice closed. "[But] I feel a lot better than I did at this point last year."

But when the season opened and Texas was without the great receivers like the Cash twins (Keith and Kerry), Johnny Walker, and a kicking game, the Horns were headed for trouble. They opened the season against Jackie Sherrill's Mississippi State team and were sandbagged by State to the tune of a 13–6 defeat. Texas was held to zero touchdowns and only scored on field goals in the first and third periods.

Auburn scored 14 points in the first period to hand Texas its second defeat, 14–10, as substitute quarterback Jim Saxton sparked the Texas offense and a touchdown after a 56-yard advance. It was Texas' first touchdown of the 1991 season.

Pete Gardere led the Longhorns to their first win of the season by scoring a touchdown and then

Newly appointed head coach, John Mackovic, just before the first game—against Mississippi State—of the 1992 season.

passing for another as the Horns easily defeated Rice, 28–7. Phil Brown and Adrian Walker led the running attack against the Owls with Walker scoring a touchdown and Brown rushing for 119 yards.

Trailing 7–3 going into the final quarter Texas' defense, led by James Patton, stripped the ball from Oklahoma back Mike McKinley. Then Bubba Jacques recovered the fumble and raced in for the winning touchdown. Quarterback Peter Gardere completed 20 of 32 passes for 220 yards. Phil Brown picked up 114 yards rushing for two touchdowns in the battle against Oklahoma, but a missed extra point conversion cost the Longhorns a 14–13 struggle in a game that became the turning point of the season.

Once again, Pete Gardere starred for Texas against SMU, as he tossed three passes for touchdowns in a second period spurt that saw Texas rip SMU for 21 points and eventually claim a 34–0 victory.

Butch Hadnot, injured most of the year, excelled in his first game as he bore the brunt of the Texas offense against Texas Tech, which the Horns defeated 23–15. Hadnot rushed for 166 yards and scored two touchdowns as Texas won its fourth game of the season.

The following week, a stirring drive by Houston, with less than 30 seconds to play, gave them a touchdown and a well-earned 23–14 victory over Texas as the clock ran out. Texas took its fifth game of the year—a 32–0 win over TCU—as Hadnot, Gardere, Walker, and Lance Gunn all contributed outstanding plays.

In the ensuing match, the Bears of Baylor, scoreless throughout three periods of play, won the game with 3 touchdowns in the final period to defeat Texas 21–11. In the final game of the season, Texas A&M took a definitive 31–14 win over the Longhorns as they scored in every period. It was Texas' sixth loss of the year after winning only 5 games. After his third losing season in five years, Coach David McWilliams resigned.

Just as Dana Bible and Darrell Royal brought freshness and great success to Texas football in the 1930s and 1950s, respectively, so did the highly respected John Mackovic, who came to Texas after four outstanding years at the University of Illinois, where his teams carved out winning records. Mackovic was twice named Big Ten Coach of the Year, and put the Illini in four bowl games in four seasons. His 1990 team tied for the Big Ten Championship.

Mackovic was an all-star quarterback and played alongside the late great Brian Piccolo to give Wake Forest the best one-two punch in their history. But the big-league polish was nurtured by Tom Landry with whom Mackovic worked for two years as the quarterback coach of the Cowboys. After working for Tom Landry, Mackovic took over as head coach of the Denver Broncos and developed

Senior defensive back Lance Gunn topped off a brilliant four-year record, in which he started every game. Gunn was an all-American selection in 1991 and 1992.

an offense that gave him a national name. When Mackovic was interviewed for the Texas post, one of the men who greeted him and gave every encouragement was Darrell Royal.

Despite an encouraging practice session with such veteran players as Lance Gunn, Adrian Walker, Bo Robinson, Jeff Boyd, Peter Gardere, and Jason Burleson, Mississippi State rolled into Austin and immediately jumped to a 16–0 lead as the Longhorns floundered in the opening game of the season.

Texas snapped out of their lethargy in the second period and hit on passes to Sam Adams and Walker. Shortly thereafter, Adrian Walker scored a touchdown. Late in the period, Scott Szeredy kicked a 37-yard field goal and at the end of the half it was 16–10, Mississippi State. In the second half, State held Texas scoreless as they ran up touchdowns in the third and fourth periods, coming away with a 28–10 win. Gardere had two apparent touchdowns called back for various infractions in the third period, but Pete completed 21 of 35 for a total of 223 yards. It was the Texas defense that gave up the game, because the defense allowed 332 yards—more than any Longhorn team had given up in the entire 1991 season.

Texas traveled to Syracuse to tackle the Orangemen and the game proved to be one of the best in college football. Texas was out for revenge as they had lost to the Orange in the 1959 Cotton Bowl by a 23–14 margin. As a 14-point underdog, Texas led the Orangemen twice and scored three touchdowns to take a 21–13 lead in the third period. The game's outcome was unpredictable until the final two minutes of play. Leading 24–21, Syracuse intercepted a Gardere pass, then with third down and five yards to go, Syracuse's quarterback, Marvin Graves, tossed a spectacular 58-yard pass to the fastest man on the field, Qadry Ismail. Ismail caught the ball and was downed on Texas' 1-yard line. On the next play, Syracuse scored the touchdown that gave them the game, 31–21, as the clock ran out on Texas. Pete Gardere had passed for three touchdowns and completed 14 of 27 passes for 246 yards.

The next week, after Texas fumbled on their first possession, the North Texas Eagles jumped to a 3–0 lead in the first period. Then Texas took over and scored touchdowns on four consecutive possessions to take an easy 33–15 win and give Coach Mackovic his first victory. Quarterback Pete Gardere continued his fine play as he threw three touchdown passes and set a new Texas career record with 26 TD passes. Gardere also completed 14 of 19 passes for 201 yards. Adrian Walker had an amazing 109 yards rushing in the first period, Scott Szeredy booted two field goals, and receiver Mike Adams

Texas quarterback Shea Morenz appears upset with his performance against North Texas State. Morenz, a brilliant prospect, should be an all-star player in 1993.

Curtis Jackson speeds upfield for 25 yards in a game against Oklahoma in 1992.

returned a punt and broke away for 59 yards and a touchdown.

Texas jumped ahead to a 16–0 lead at the half against Rice the following week, and it looked as though the Owls would be in for a drubbing. But two quick touchdowns by the Owls narrowed the score to 16–14 and the crowd, tingling with excitement, cheered as the Owls seemed to be on the verge of an upset. But late in the fourth period a pass from Gardere to Kenny Neal for 33 yards and a touchdown gave Texas the 23–14 edge that Rice couldn't match even after another scoring effort. Texas came away with a squeaker, 23–21.

Texas displayed the most impressive performance of the year in its game against the Oklahoma Sooners and took a hard-fought, knockdown battle by a 34–24 margin after both offense and defense teams played superbly. But as the game opened it looked like a "Bad Day at Black Rock" for the Horns as Oklahoma took the opening kickoff and drove 80 yards downfield for a touchdown. But Texas quickly regrouped and struck back as Gardere hit two touchdown passes, halfback Phil Brown scored twice, and Scott Szeredy kicked two field goals and the Longhorns went on to defeat Oklahoma 34–24. Jason Burleson and Justin McLemore caught passes for touchdowns as Texas' defense shut down the powerful Sooner offense.

Just before the Houston game, Coach Mackovic said in an interview with a sports editor, "In order to beat Houston you have to be able to score points." That is just what the Longhorns did on October 24 at Memorial Stadium in Austin. The Texas offense clicked as quarterback Peter Gardere led the Longhorns to a 28–0 lead in the second period and the game seemed to be over. But Houston came back like greased lightning, and scored 38 points from the second period to the fourth, while Texas only added 3 points. Then trailing 38–31, Texas took the ball on its own 20-yard line and with 7 minutes left to play, Gardere picked up two first downs. Then a pass from Gardere to Mike Adams was good for 30 yards and gave Texas a touchdown, tying the score at 38–38. Then with 3½ minutes to play, end Norm Watkins intercepted a pass and sped in for another Texas touchdown to wrap up a thrilling contest, 45–38. Adrian Walker's 88-yard touchdown gallop, Scott Szeredy's 52-yard field goal, and Gardere's three touchdown passes sparked the Texas win over the Cougars.

Texas defeated Texas Tech 44–33 for its fifth straight win of the season after dropping the first two games. In the game against Tech, it was Pete Gardere and Phil Brown, each rushing for two touchdowns, as Adrian Walker continued his sensational play and ran for 155 yards. Scott Szeredy kicked three field goals and Tony Curl added another TD to give Texas a high-scoring, but close, 44–33 win.

The following week, something happened to the Texas express that had rolled to five straight wins as TCU upset the Horns in a tough 23–14 game. This was the first win over Texas in 25 years for the Frogs in a game where nothing seemed to

Quarterback Pete Gardere breaks away from an SMU tackler for a nice 12-yard gain. Gardere was spectacular in the game as he passed for three TDs and Texas pounded out a 35–14 win.

jell for Texas. TCU scored two quick touchdowns and took a 14–0 lead, which they never surrendered. It was a mental error by Texas' defensive back Grady Cavness, who missed a punt and trailed it into the end zone, and then batted the ball out giving TCU a safety that made the score 16–7, in SMU's favor, as the half ended. Texas scored a third-period touchdown, but TCU intercepted a Gardere pass and ran it in for a TD sealing a 23–14 win.

But on a near perfect afternoon, Texas, in a complete reversal of the form they showed against TCU, defeated the SMU Mustangs 35–14. Texas completely dominated every phase of the game and Pete Gardere passed for three touchdowns to Jason Burleson, Adrian Walker, and Justin McLemore. Phil Brown's 15-yard sprint and Mike Adams' touchdown ended the Texas' scoring as the Longhorns rang up win number six.

In a day that was heavy with rain and sleet, dropped passes, controversial calls by the officials, and turnovers, Texas dropped a crucial game to

Baylor 21–20 that knocked them out of a Cotton Bowl match. Texas lost two critical fumbles, one at the Bears' 5-yard line—and the Horns were penalized 10 times for 129 yards. Baylor's three touchdowns were all controversial. One was on an interference call and on two other occasions Texas recovered Baylor fumbles only to have the officials rule otherwise. Gardere tossed a pass to Lovell Pickney for a score and rushed for another touchdown. Scott Szeredy kicked two field goals for Texas.

A crowd of 81,750 persons was on hand for the annual Texas-Texas Aggies game and it proved to be one of the most exciting of the 99 games the two rivals had played since they first met in 1898, when the Longhorns trampled A&M 48–0.

The two rivals fought each other during the first period with neither team gaining much of an edge until late in the quarter when Texas' ace kicker, Scott Szeredy booted a magnificent 52-yard field goal and Texas had a 3–0 lead.

The Aggies came back quickly as fullback Rod Thomas drove in for a touchdown, making it a 7–3 game. In the second period, Thomas ran it again in a short drive and scored his second touchdown; the Aggies had a 14–3 lead. Just before the half, the Aggies kicked a 43-yard field goal to increase their lead to 17–3.

Texas came out fast in the third period, but lost possession just as quickly and A&M took over.

After a series of short gains, Texas assumed possession and advanced to the Aggies' 40-yard line. Then Peter Gardere tossed a lateral pass to Darrick Duke. Duke then shoveled the ball back to Gardere and Pete sped 37 yards down the right sideline for a touchdown. Now it was 17–10, Texas A&M. After another field goal from Szeredy, it was 17–13 and the fans were up on their feet and screaming.

Then came a Texas A&M field goal and the score now was 20–13, A&M. Near the end of the third period, Rod Thomas drove through the Texas line for a touchdown and A&M boasted their lead to 27–13.

In the final period, Gardere came out throwing. One of his passes was intercepted by Aaron Glenn, who sped 95 yards for a touchdown to close out the game and the season for both teams. With a 34–13 win, Texas A&M finished the year in championship fashion, while the Longhorns ended their regular season with a 6 and 5 record under their new Coach John Mackovic.

And although Coach Mackovic's first season was not a howling success, it was a distinct improvement over 1991. "We've lost some fifteen top-rated players through graduation," said Mackovic, "and they will be tough to replace. But, I do think with a break here and there this year, we might have won at least two more games than we did. In 1993, I think we'll get those two or three additional wins."

APPENDIX: STATISTICS AND HIGHLIGHTS

Longhorns's Season Records Year-by Year

1893
Coach: None
Season: 4-0-0
SWC: —

18	at Dallas U	16
30	San Antonio	0
34	San Antonio	0
16	Dallas U	0

1894
Coach: R. D. Wentworth
Season: 6-1-0
SWC: —

38	Texas A&M	0
12	Tulane	0
6	Austin YMCA	0
24	Austin YMCA	0
54	Arkansas	0
57	at San Antonio	0
0	Missouri	28

1895
Coach: Frank Crawford
Season: 5-0-0
SWC: —

10	at Dallas U	0
24	Austin YMCA	0
16	Tulane	0
38	San Antonio	0
8	Galveston	0

1896
Coach: Harry Robinson
Season: 4-2-1
SWC: —

42	Galveston	0
0	at Dallas U	0
12	San Antonio	4
12	at Tulane	4
0	at LSU	14
22	Dallas U	4
0	Missouri	10

1897
Coach: W. F. Kelly
Season: 6-2-0
SWC: —

10	San Antonio	0
4	at Dallas U	22
0	at Fort Worth U	6
18	at Add Ran (TCU)	10
42	Houston Town Team	6
12	at San Antonio	0
38	Fort Worth U	0
20	Dallas U	16

1898
Coach: D. F. Edwards
Season: 5-1-0
SWC: —

16	at Add Ran (TCU)	0
48	Texas A&M	0
17	Galveston	0
29	Add Ran	0
0	Sewanee	4
26	Dallas U	0

1899
Coach: M. G. Clarke
Season: 6-2-0
SWC: —

11	at Dallas U	6
28	San Antonio	0
6	Texas A&M (S.A.)	0
0	Sewanee	12
0	at Vanderbilt	6
11	at Tulane	0
32	Tulane	0
29	LSU	0

1900
Coach: S. H. Thompson
Season: 6-0-0
SWC: —

28	Oklahoma	2
22	at Vanderbilt	0
5	Texas A&M (S.A.)	0
17	Missouri	11
30	Kansas City Medics	0
11	Texas A&M	0

1901
Coach: S. H. Thompson
Season: 8-2-1
SWC: —

32	Houston Town Team	0
5	Nashville U. (Dallas)	5
12	Oklahoma	6
17	Texas A&M (S.A.)	0
23	at Baylor	0
12	Dallas AC	0
11	at Missouri	0
0	at Kirksville	48
0	at Kansas	12
11	at Oklahoma	0
32	Texas A&M	0

1902
Coach: J. B. Hart
Season: 6-3-1
SWC: —

22	Oklahoma	6
11	Sewanee (Dallas)	0
0	LSU (S.A.)	5
0	Texas A&M (S.A.)	0
27	Trinity	0
0	Haskell	12
11	at Nashville U	5
10	at Alabama	0
6	at Tulane	0
0	Texas A&M	12

Scoring Values				
Seasons	Touchdown	Field Goal	Point After	Safety
1887-1897	4 points	5 points	2 points	2 points
1898-1903	5 points	5 points	1 point	2 points
1904-1908	5 points	4 points	1 point	2 points
1909-1911	5 points	3 points	1 point	2 points
1912-1957	6 points	3 points	1 point	2 points
1958 to date	6 points	3 points	1 point for kick, 2 points for run or pass	2 points

1903
Coach: Ralph Hutchinson
Season: 5-1-2
SWC: —

17	School for Deaf	0
0	Haskell (Dallas)	6
6	Oklahoma	6
48	Baylor	0
15	Arkansas	0
5	Vanderbilt	5
11	at Oklahoma	5
29	Texas A&M	6

1904
Coach: Ralph Hutchinson
Season: 6-2-0
SWC: —

40	TCU	0
24	Trinity	0
0	Haskell	4
23	at Wash.-St. Louis	0
0	at U. Chicago	68
40	Oklahoma	10
58	Baylor	0
34	Texas A&M	6

1905
Coach: Ralph Hutchinson
Season: 5-4-0
SWC: —

11	TCU	0
0	Haskell	17
39	Baylor	0
0	at Vanderbilt	33
4	at Arkansas (Fay.)	0
0	at Oklahoma	2
0	Transylvania	6
17	Sewanee	10
27	Texas A&M	0

1906
Coach: H. R. Schenker
Season: 9-1-0
SWC: —

21	26th Infantry	0
22	TCU	0
28	W. Texas Military	0
0	at Vanderbilt	45
11	at Arkansas (Fay.)	0
10	at Oklahoma	9
28	Haskell	0
40	Daniel Baker	0
17	Wash.-St. Louis	6
24	Texas A&M	0

1907
Coach: W. E. Metzenthin
Season: 6-1-1
SWC: —

0	Texas A&M (Dallas)	0
12	LSU	5
45	Haskell	10
26	at Arkansas (Fay.)	6
4	at Missouri	5
27	Baylor	11
29	Oklahoma	10
11	Texas A&M	6

1908
Coach: W. E. Metzenthin
Season: 5-4-0
SWC: —

11	TCU	6
27	Baylor	5
0	Colorado	15
21	Arkansas	0
9	Southwestern	11
24	Texas A&M (Houston)	8
0	at Oklahoma	50
15	Tulane	28
28	Texas A&M	12

1909
Coach: Dexter Draper
Season: 4-3-1
SWC: —

12	Southwestern	0
11	Haskell (Dallas)	12
18	Trinity	0
24	TCU	0
0	Texas A&M (Houston)	23
10	at Tulane	10
30	Oklahoma	0
0	Texas A&M	5

1910
Coach: W. S. Wasmund
Season: 6-2-0
SWC: —

11	Southwestern	6
68	Haskell	3
48	Transylvania	0
9	Auburn	0
1	at Baylor (forfeit)	0
8	Texas A&M (Houston)	14
12	LSU	0
0	Oklahoma	3

1911
Coach: Dave Allerdice
Season: 5-2-0
SWC: —

11	Southwestern	2
11	Baylor	0
12	Arkansas	0
5	Sewanee	6
6	Texas A&M (Houston)	0
18	Auburn	5
3	Oklahoma	6

1912
Coach: Dave Allerdice
Season: 7-1-0
SWC: —

30	TCU	10
3	Austin College	0
6	Oklahoma (Dallas)	21
14	Haskell	7
19	at Baylor	7
53	Mississippi (Houston)	14
28	Southwestern	3
48	Arkansas	0

1913
Coach: Dave Allerdice
Season: 7-1-0
SWC: —

14	Ft. Worth Polytechnic	7
27	Austin College	6
77	Baylor	0
13	Sewanee (Dallas)	7
52	Southwestern	0
14	Oklahoma (Houston)	6
46	Kansas State	0
7	Notre Dame	30

1914
Coach: Dave Allerdice
Season: 8-0-0
SWC: —

30	Trinity	0
57	Baylor	0
41	Rice	0
32	Oklahoma (Dallas)	7
70	Southwestern	0
23	Haskell (Houston)	7
66	Mississippi	7
39	Wabash	0

APPENDIX: STATISTICS AND HIGHLIGHTS

1915
Coach: Dave Allerdice
Season: 6-3-0
SWC: 2-2-0 (T3)

72	TCU	0
92	Daniel Baker	0
59	Rice	0
13	Oklahoma (Dallas)	14
45	Southwestern	0
27	Sewanee (Houston)	6
20	Alabama	0
0	at Texas A&M	13
7	Notre Dame	36

1916
Coach: Eugene Van Gent
Season: 7-2-0
SWC: 5-1-0 (1st)

74	SMU	0
16	Rice	2
14	Oklahoma St. (S.A.)	7
21	Oklahoma (Dallas)	7
3	Baylor	7
0	at Missouri	3
52	Arkansas	0
17	Southwestern	3
21	Texas A&M	7

1917
Coach: Bill Juneau
Season: 4-4-0
SWC: 2-3-0 (4th)

27	Trinity	0
35	Southwestern	0
0	Oklahoma (Dallas)	14
0	Rice	13
0	at Baylor	3
7	Oklahoma State	3
0	at Texas A&M	7
20	Arkansas	0

1918
Coach: Bill Juneau
Season: 9-0-0
SWC: 4-0-0 (1st)

19	TCU	0
25	Penn Radio School	0
22	Penn Radio School	7
26	Ream Flying Field	2
27	Oklahoma State	5
22	Camp Mabry Auto	0
14	at Rice	0
32	SMU	0
7	Texas A&M	0

1919
Coach: Bill Juneau
Season: 6-3-0
SWC: 3-2-0 (4th)

26	Howard Payne	0
39	Southwestern	0
0	Phillips	10
7	Oklahoma (Dallas)	12
29	Baylor	13
32	Rice	7
35	Arkansas	7
13	Haskell	7
0	at Texas A&M	7

1920
Coach: Berry Whitaker
Season: 9-0-0
SWC: 5-0-0 (1st)

63	Simmons	0
27	Southwestern	0
41	Howard Payne	7
21	Oklahoma State	0
54	Austin Col. (Dallas)	0
21	at Rice	0
27	Phillips	0
21	SMU	3
7	Texas A&M	3

1921
Coach: Berry Whitaker
Season: 6-1-1
SWC: 1-0-1 (2nd)

33	St. Edwards	0
60	Austin College	0
21	Howard Payne	0
0	Vanderbilt (Dallas)	20
56	Rice	0
44	Southwestern	0
54	Mississippi State	7
0	at Texas A&M	0

1922
Coach: Berry Whitaker
Season: 7-2-0
SWC: 2-1-0 (2nd)

19	Austin College	0
41	Phillips	10
19	Oklahoma A&M	7
10	Vanderbilt (Dallas)	20
19	Alabama	10
29	at Rice	0
26	Southwestern	0
32	at Oklahoma	7
7	Texas A&M	14

1923
Coach: E. J. Stewart
Season: 8-0-1
SWC: 2-0-1 (2nd)

31	Austin College	0
51	Phillips	0
33	Tulane (Beaumont)	0
16	Vanderbilt (Dallas)	0
44	Southwestern	0
27	Rice	0
7	at Baylor	7
26	Oklahoma	14
6	at Texas A&M	0

1924
Coach: E. J. Stewart
Season: 5-3-1
SWC: 2-3-0 (6th)

27	Southwestern	0
27	Phillips	0
6	Howard Payne	0
6	at SMU	10
7	Florida	7
6	at Rice	19
10	Baylor	28*
13	at TCU	0
7	Texas A&M	0

*1st Game in Memorial Stadium

1925
Coach: E. J. Stewart
Season: 6-2-1
SWC: 2-1-1 (2nd)

33	Southwestern	0
25	Mississippi	0
6	at Vanderbilt	14
33	Auburn (Dallas)	0
27	Rice	6
0	at SMU	0
13	Baylor	3
20	Arizona	0
0	at Texas A&M	28

1926
Coach: E. J. Stewart
Season: 5-4-0
SWC: 2-2-0 (T3)

31	S.W. Okla. Teachers	7
3	at Kansas State	13
27	Phillips	0
0	Vanderbilt (Dallas)	7
20	at Rice	0
17	SMU	21
7	at Baylor	10
27	Southwestern	6
14	Texas A&M	5

1927
Coach: Clyde Littlefield
Season: 6-2-1
SWC: 2-2-1 (4th)

43	S.W. Okla. Teachers	0
0	TCU	0
20	Trinity	6
13	Vanderbilt (Dallas)	6
27	Rice	0
0	at SMU	14
13	Baylor	12
41	Kansas State	7
7	at Texas A&M	28

1928
Coach: Clyde Littlefield
Season: 7-2-0
SWC: 5-1-0 (1st)

32	St. Edwards	0
12	Texas Tech	0
12	Vanderbilt (Dallas)	13
20	Arkansas	7
13	at Rice	6
2	SMU	6
6	at Baylor	0
6	at TCU	0
19	Texas A&M	0

1929
Coach: Clyde Littlefield
Season: 5-2-2
SWC: 2-2-2 (T4)

13	St. Edwards	0
20	Centenary	0
27	at Arkansas (Fay.)	0
21	Oklahoma (Dallas)	0
39	Rice	0
0	at SMU	0
0	Baylor	0
12	TCU	15
0	at Texas A&M	13

1930
Coach: Clyde Littlefield
Season: 8-1-1
SWC: 4-1-0 (1st)

36	Southwest Texas	0
28	College of Mines	0
0	Centenary	0
26	Howard Payne	0
17	Oklahoma (Dallas)	7
0	at Rice	6
25	SMU	7
14	at Baylor	0
7	at TCU	0
26	Texas A&M	0

1931
Coach: Clyde Littlefield
Season: 6-4-0
SWC: 2-3-0 (5th)

36	Simmons	0
31	Missouri	0
0	Rice	7
3	Oklahoma (Dallas)	0
7	at Harvard	35
7	at SMU	9
25	Baylor	0
10	TCU	0
6	at Centenary	0
6	at Texas A&M	7

1932
Coach: Clyde Littlefield
Season: 8-2-0
SWC: 5-1-0 (2nd)

26	Daniel Baker	0
6	Centenary	13
65	at Missouri	0
17	Oklahoma (Dallas)	10
18	at Rice	6
14	SMU	6
19	at Baylor	0
0	at TCU	14
34	at Arkansas (Fay.)	0
21	Texas A&M	0

1933
Coach: Clyde Littlefield
Season: 4-5-2
SWC: 2-3-1 (5th)

46	at Southwestern	0
22	College of Mines	6
0	at Nebraska	26
0	Oklahoma (Dallas)	9
0	Centenary (S.A.)	0
18	Rice	0
10	at SMU	0
0	Baylor	3
0	TCU	30
6	Arkansas	20
10	at Texas A&M	10

1934
Coach: Jack Chevigny
Season: 7-2-1
SWC: 4-1-1 (2nd)

12	at Texas Tech	6
7	at Notre Dame	6
19	Oklahoma (Dallas)	0
6	Centenary	9
9	at Rice	20
7	SMU	7
25	Baylor	6
20	at TCU	19
19	at Arkansas (Fay.)	12
13	Texas A&M	0

1935
Coach: Jack Chevigny
Season: 4-6-0
SWC: 1-5-0 (T6)

38	Texas A&I	6
6	at LSU	18
12	Oklahoma (Dallas)	7
19	Centenary	13
19	Rice	28
0	at SMU	20
25	at Baylor	6
0	TCU	28
13	Arkansas	28
6	at Texas A&M	20

1936
Coach: Jack Chevigny
Season: 2-6-1
SWC: 1-5-0 (T6)

6	LSU	6
6	Oklahoma (Dallas)	0
18	Baylor	21
0	at Rice	7
7	SMU	14
6	at TCU	27
19	at Minnesota	47
7	Texas A&M	0
0	at Arkansas (L.R.)	6

1937
Coach: Dana X. Bible
Season: 2-6-1
SWC: 1-5-0 (7th)

25	Texas Tech	12
0	at LSU	9
7	Oklahoma (Dallas)	7
10	Arkansas	21
7	Rice	14
2	at SMU	13
9	at Baylor	6
0	TCU	14
0	at Texas A&M	7

APPENDIX: STATISTICS AND HIGHLIGHTS

1938
Coach: Dana X. Bible
Season: 1-8-0
SWC: 1-5-0 (T6)

18	at Kansas	19
0	LSU	20
0	Oklahoma (Dallas)	13
6	at Arkansas (L.R.)	42
6	at Rice	13
6	SMU	7
3	Baylor	14
6	at TCU	28
7	Texas A&M	6

1939
Coach: Dana X. Bible
Season: 5-4-0
SWC: 3-3-0 (4th)

12	Florida	0
17	at Wisconsin	7
12	Oklahoma (Dallas)	24
14	Arkansas	13
26	Rice	12
0	at SMU	10
0	at Baylor	20
25	TCU	19
0	at Texas A&M	20

1940
Coach: Dana X. Bible
Season: 8-2-0
SWC: 4-2-0 (T3)

39	Colorado	7
13	at Indiana	6
19	Oklahoma (Dallas)	16
21	at Arkansas (L.R.)	0
0	at Rice	13
13	SMU	21
13	Baylor	0
21	at TCU	14
7	Texas A&M	0
26	at Florida	0

1941
Coach: Dana X. Bible
Season: 8-1-1
SWC: 4-1-1 (T2)

34	at Colorado	6
34	LSU	0
40	Oklahoma (Dallas)	7
48	Arkansas	14
40	Rice	0
34	at SMU	0
7	at Baylor	7
7	TCU	14
23	at Texas A&M	0
71	Oregon	7

1942
Coach: Dana X. Bible
Season: 9-2-0
SWC: 5-1-0 (1st)

40	Corpus Christi NAS	0
64	Kansas State	0
0	at Northwestern	3
7	Oklahoma (Dallas)	0
47	at Arkansas (L.R.)	6
12	at Rice	7
21	SMU	7
20	Baylor	0
7	at TCU	13
12	Texas A&M	6
	COTTON BOWL:	
14	Georgia Tech	7

1943
Coach: Dana X. Bible
Season: 7-1-1
SWC: 5-0-0 (1st)

65	Blackland AAF	6
7	Southwestern	14
13	Oklahoma (Dallas)	7
34	Arkansas	0
58	Rice	0
20	at SMU	0
46	TCU	7
27	at Texas A&M	13
	COTTON BOWL:	
7	Randolph Field	7

1944
Coach: Dana X. Bible
Season: 5-4-0
SWC: 3-2-0 (2nd)

20	Southwestern	0
6	Randolph Field	42
20	Oklahoma (Dallas)	0
19	at Arkansas (L.R.)	0
0	at Rice	7
34	SMU	7
8	Oklahoma State	13
6	at TCU	7
6	Texas A&M	0

1945
Coach: Dana X. Bible
Season: 10-1-0
SWC: 5-1-0 (1st)

13	Bergstrom Field	7
46	Southwestern	0
33	Texas Tech	0
12	Oklahoma (Dallas)	7
34	at Arkansas (L.R.)	7
6	Rice	7
12	at SMU	7
21	Baylor	14
20	TCU	0
20	at Texas A&M	10
	COTTON BOWL:	
40	Missouri	27

1946
Coach: Dana X. Bible
Season: 8-2-0
SWC: 4-2-0 (3rd)

42	Missouri	0
76	Colorado	0
54	Oklahoma State	6
20	Oklahoma (Dallas)	13
20	Arkansas	0
13	at Rice	18
19	SMU	3
22	at Baylor	7
0	at TCU	14
24	Texas A&M	7

1947
Coach: Blair Cherry
Season: 10-1-0
SWC: 5-1-0 (2nd)

33	Texas Tech	0
38	at Oregon	13
34	North Carolina	0
34	Oklahoma (Dallas)	14
21	Arkansas (Memphis)	6
12	Rice	0
13	at SMU	14
28	Baylor	7
20	TCU	0
32	at Texas A&M	13
	SUGAR BOWL:	
27	Alabama	7

1948
Coach: Blair Cherry
Season: 7-3-1
SWC: 4-1-1 (2nd)

33	LSU	0
7	at North Carolina	34
47	New Mexico	0
14	Oklahoma (Dallas)	20
14	Arkansas	6
20	at Rice	7
6	SMU	21
13	at Baylor	10
14	at TCU	7
14	Texas A&M	14

ORANGE BOWL:

41	Georgia	28

1949
Coach: Blair Cherry
Season: 6-4-0
SWC: 3-3-0 (T3)

43	Texas Tech	0
54	at Temple	0
56	Idaho	7
14	Oklahoma (Dallas)	20
27	at Arkansas (L.R.)	14
15	Rice	17
6	at SMU	7
20	Baylor	0
13	TCU	14
42	at Texas A&M	14

1950
Coach: Blair Cherry
Season: 9-2-0
SWC: 6-0-0 (1st)

28	at Texas Tech	14
34	Purdue	26
13	Oklahoma (Dallas)	14
19	Arkansas	14
35	at Rice	7
23	SMU	20
27	at Baylor	20
21	at TCU	7
17	Texas A&M	0
21	LSU	6

COTTON BOWL:

14	Tennessee	20

1951
Coach: Ed Price
Season: 7-3-0
SWC: 3-3-0 (T3)

7	Kentucky	6
14	at Purdue	0
45	North Carolina	20
9	Oklahoma (Dallas)	7
14	at Arkansas (Fay.)	16
14	Rice	6
20	at SMU	13
6	Baylor	18
32	TCU	21
21	at Texas A&M	22

1952
Coach: Ed Price
Season: 9-2-0
SWC: 6-0-0 (1st)

35	at LSU	14
28	at North Carolina	7
3	Notre Dame	14
20	Oklahoma (Dallas)	49
44	Arkansas	7
20	at Rice	7
31	SMU	14
35	at Baylor	33
14	at TCU	7
32	Texas A&M	12

COTTON BOWL:

16	Tennessee	0

1953
Coach: Ed Price
Season: 7-3-0
SWC: 5-1-0 (T1)

7	at LSU	20
41	Villanova	12
28	Houston	7
14	Oklahoma (Dallas)	19
16	at Arkansas (Fay.)	7
13	Rice	18
16	at SMU	7
21	Baylor	20
13	TCU	3
21	at Texas A&M	12

1954
Coach: Ed Price
Season: 4-5-1
SWC: 2-3-1 (5th)

20	LSU	6
0	at Notre Dame	21
40	Washington State	14
7	Oklahoma (Dallas)	14
7	Arkansas	20
7	at Rice	13
13	SMU	13
7	at Baylor	13
35	at TCU	34
22	Texas A&M	13

1955
Coach: Ed Price
Season: 5-5-0
SWC: 4-2-0 (3rd)

14	Texas Tech	20
35	Tulane	21
7	at USC	19
0	Oklahoma (Dallas)	20
20	at Arkansas (L.R.)	27
32	Rice	14
19	at SMU	18
21	Baylor	20
20	TCU	47
21	at Texas A&M	6

1956
Coach: Ed Price
Season: 1-9-0
SWC: 0-6-0 (7th)

20	USC	44
7	at Tulane	6
6	West Virginia	7
0	Oklahoma (Dallas)	45
14	Arkansas	32
7	at Rice	28
19	SMU	20
7	at Baylor	10
0	at TCU	46
21	Texas A&M	34

APPENDIX: STATISTICS AND HIGHLIGHTS

1957
Coach: Darrell Royal
Season: 6-4-1
SWC: 4-1-1 (2nd)

26	at Georgia	7
20	Tulane	6
21	South Carolina	27
7	Oklahoma (Dallas)	21
17	at Arkansas (Fay.)	0
19	Rice	14
12	at SMU	19
7	Baylor	7
14	TCU	2
9	at Texas A&M	7
	SUGAR BOWL:	
7	Mississippi	39

1958
Coach: Darrell Royal
Season: 7-3-0
SWC: 3-3-0 (4th)

13	Georgia	8
21	at Tulane	20
12	Texas Tech	7
15	Oklahoma (Dallas)	14
24	Arkansas	6
7	at Rice	34
10	SMU	26
20	at Baylor	15
8	at TCU	22
27	Texas A&M	0

1959
Coach: Darrell Royal
Season: 9-2-0
SWC: 5-1-0 (T1)

20	at Nebraska	0
26	Maryland	0
33	California	0
19	Oklahoma (Dallas)	12
13	at Arkansas (L.R.)	12
28	Rice	6
21	at SMU	0
13	Baylor	12
9	TCU	14
20	at Texas A&M	17
	COTTON BOWL:	
14	Syracuse	23

1960
Coach: Darrell Royal
Season: 7-3-1
SWC: 5-2-0 (T2)

13	Nebraska	14
34	at Maryland	0
17	Texas Tech	0
24	Oklahoma (Dallas)	0
23	Arkansas	24
0	at Rice	7
17	SMU	7
12	at Baylor	7
3	at TCU	2
21	Texas A&M	14
	BLUEBONNET BOWL:	
3	Alabama	3

1961
Coach: Darrell Royal
Season: 10-1-0
SWC: 6-1-0 (T1)

28	at California	3
42	Texas Tech	14
41	Washington State	8
28	Oklahoma (Dallas)	7
33	at Arkansas (Fay.)	7
34	Rice	7
27	at SMU	0
33	Baylor	7
0	TCU	6
25	at Texas A&M	0
	COTTON BOWL:	
12	Mississippi	7

1962
Coach: Darrell Royal
Season: 9-1-1
SWC: 6-0-1 (1st)

25	Oregon	13
34	at Texas Tech	0
35	Tulane	8
9	Oklahoma (Dallas)	6
7	Arkansas	3
14	at Rice	14
6	SMU	0
27	at Baylor	12
14	at TCU	0
13	Texas A&M	3
	COTTON BOWL:	
0	LSU	13

1963
NATIONAL CHAMPIONS
Coach: Darrell Royal
Season: 11-0-0
SWC: 7-0-0 (1st)

21	at Tulane	0
49	Texas Tech	7
34	Oklahoma State	7
28	Oklahoma (Dallas)	7
17	at Arkansas (L.R.)	13
10	Rice	6
17	at SMU	12
7	Baylor	0
17	TCU	0
15	at Texas A&M	13
	COTTON BOWL:	
28	Navy	6

1964
Coach: Darrell Royal
Season: 10-1-0
SWC: 6-1-0 (2nd)

31	Tulane	0
23	at Texas Tech	0
17	Army	6
28	Oklahoma (Dallas)	7
13	Arkansas	14
6	at Rice	3
7	SMU	0
20	at Baylor	14
28	at TCU	13
26	Texas A&M	7
	ORANGE BOWL:	
21	Alabama	17

1965
Coach: Darrell Royal
Season: 6-4-0
SWC: 3-4-0 (T4)

31	Tulane	0
33	Texas Tech	7
27	Indiana	12
19	Oklahoma (Dallas)	0
24	at Arkansas (Fay.)	27
17	Rice	20
14	at SMU	31
35	Baylor	14
10	TCU	25
21	at Texas A&M	17

100 YEARS OF TEXAS LONGHORN FOOTBALL

1966
Coach: Darrell Royal
Season: 7-4-0
SWC: 5-2-0

6	USC	10
31	at Texas Tech	21
35	Indiana	0
9	Oklahoma (Dallas)	18
7	Arkansas	12
14	at Rice	6
12	SMU	13
26	at Baylor	14
13	at TCU	3
22	Texas A&M	14

BLUEBONNET BOWL:

| 19 | Mississippi | 0 |

1967
Coach: Darrell Royal
Season: 6-4-0
SWC: 4-3-0 (T3)

13	at USC	17
13	Texas Tech	19
19	Oklahoma State	0
9	Oklahoma (Dallas)	7
21	at Arkansas (L.R.)	12
28	Rice	6
35	at SMU	28
24	Baylor	0
17	TCU	24
7	at Texas A&M	10

1968
Coach: Darrell Royal
Season: 9-1-1
SWC: 6-1-0 (T1)

20	Houston	20
22	at Texas Tech	31
31	Oklahoma State	3
26	Oklahoma (Dallas)	20
39	Arkansas	29
38	at Rice	14
38	SMU	7
47	at Baylor	26
47	at TCU	21
35	Texas A&M	14

COTTON BOWL:

| 36 | Tennessee | 13 |

1969
NATIONAL CHAMPIONS
Coach: Darrell Royal
Season: 11-0-0
SWC: 7-0-0 (1st)

17	at California	0
49	Texas Tech	7
56	Navy	17
27	Oklahoma (Dallas)	17
31	Rice	0
45	at SMU	14
56	Baylor	14
69	TCU	7
49	at Texas A&M	12
15	at Arkansas (Fay.)	14

COTTON BOWL:

| 21 | Notre Dame | 17 |

1970
NATIONAL CHAMPIONS
Coach: Darrell Royal
Season: 10-1-0
SWC: 7-0-0 (1st)

56	California	15
35	at Texas Tech	13
20	UCLA	17
41	Oklahoma (Dallas)	9
45	at Rice	21
42	SMU	15
21	at Baylor	14
58	at TCU	0
52	Texas A&M	14
42	Arkansas	7

COTTON BOWL:

| 11 | Notre Dame | 24 |

1971
Coach: Darrell Royal
Season: 8-3-0
SWC: 6-1-0 (1st)

28	at UCLA	10
28	Texas Tech	0
35	Oregon	7
27	Oklahoma (Dallas)	48
7	at Arkansas (L.R.)	31
39	Rice	10
22	at SMU	18
24	Baylor	0
31	TCU	0
34	at Texas A&M	14

COTTON BOWL:

| 6 | Penn State | 30 |

1972
Coach: Darrell Royal
Season: 10-1-0
SWC: 7-0-0 (1st)

23	Miami	10
25	at Texas Tech	20
27	Utah State	12
0	Oklahoma (Dallas)	27
35	Arkansas	15
45	at Rice	9
17	SMU	9
17	at Baylor	3
27	at TCU	0
38	Texas A&M	3

COTTON BOWL:

| 17 | Alabama | 13 |

1973
Coach: Darrell Royal
Season: 8-3-0
SWC: 7-0-0 (1st)

15	at Miami	20
28	Texas Tech	12
41	Wake Forest	0
13	Oklahoma (Dallas)	52
34	at Arkansas (Fay.)	6
55	Rice	13
42	at SMU	14
42	Baylor	6
52	TCU	7
42	at Texas A&M	13

COTTON BOWL:

| 3 | Nebraska | 19 |

1974
Coach: Darrell Royal
Season: 8-4-0
SWC: 5-2-0 (T2)

42	at Boston College	19
34	Wyoming	7
3	at Texas Tech	26
35	Washington	21
13	Oklahoma (Dallas)	16
38	Arkansas	7
27	at Rice	6
35	SMU	15
24	at Baylor	34
81	at TCU	16
32	Texas A&M	3

GATOR BOWL:

| 3 | Auburn | 27 |

APPENDIX: STATISTICS AND HIGHLIGHTS

1975
Coach: Darrell Royal
Season: 10-2-0
SWC: 6-1-0 (T1)

46	Colorado State	0
28	at Washington	10
42	Texas Tech	18
61	Utah State	7
17	Oklahoma (Dallas)	24
24	at Arkansas (Fay.)	18
41	Rice	9
30	at SMU	22
37	Baylor	21
27	TCU	11
10	at Texas A&M	20

BLUEBONNET BOWL:

38	Colorado	21

1976
Coach: Darrell Royal
Season: 5-5-1
SWC: 4-4-0 (5th)

13	at Boston College	14
17	North Texas	14
42	at Rice	15
6	Oklahoma (Dallas)	6
13	SMU	12
28	at Texas Tech	31
0	Houston	30
34	at TCU	7
10	at Baylor	20
3	Texas A&M	27
29	Arkansas	12

1977
Coach: Fred Akers
Season: 11-1-0
SWC: 8-0-0 (1st)

44	Boston College	0
68	Virginia	0
72	Rice	15
13	Oklahoma (Dallas)	6
13	at Arkansas (Fay.)	9
30	at SMU	14
26	Texas Tech	0
35	at Houston	21
44	TCU	14
29	Baylor	7
57	at Texas A&M	28

COTTON BOWL:

10	Notre Dame	38

1978
Coach: Fred Akers
Season: 9-3-0
SWC: 6-2-0 (T2)

34	at Rice	0
17	Wyoming	3
24	at Texas Tech	7
10	Oklahoma (Dallas)	31
26	North Texas	16
28	Arkansas	21
22	SMU	3
7	Houston	10
41	at TCU	0
14	at Baylor	38
22	Texas A&M	7

SUN BOWL:

42	Maryland	0

1979
Coach: Fred Akers
Season: 9-3-0
SWC: 6-2-0 (3rd)

17	Iowa State	9
21	at Missouri	0
26	Rice	9
16	Oklahoma (Dallas)	7
14	at Arkansas (L.R.)	17
30	at SMU	6
14	Texas Tech	6
21	at Houston	13
35	TCU	10
13	Baylor	0
7	at Texas A&M	13

SUN BOWL:

7	Washington	14

1980
Coach: Fred Akers
Season: 7-5-0
SWC: 4-4-0 (T4)

23	Arkansas	17
35	Utah State	17
35	Oregon State	0
41	at Rice	28
20	Oklahoma (Dallas)	13
6	SMU	20
20	at Texas Tech	24
15	Houston	13
51	at TCU	26
0	at Baylor	16
14	Texas A&M	24

BLUEBONNET BOWL:

7	North Carolina	16

1981
Coach: Fred Akers
Season: 10-1-1
SWC: 6-1-1 (2nd)

31	Rice	3
23	North Texas	10
14	Miami	7
34	Oklahoma (Dallas)	14
11	at Arkansas (Fay.)	42
9	at SMU	7
26	Texas Tech	9
14	at Houston	14
31	TCU	15
34	at Baylor	12
21	Texas A&M	13

COTTON BOWL:

14	Alabama	12

1982
Coach: Fred Akers
Season: 9-3-0
SWC: 7-1-0 (2nd)

21	Utah	12
21	Missouri	0
34	at Rice	7
22	Oklahoma (Dallas)	28
17	SMU	30
27	at Texas Tech	0
50	Houston	0
38	at TCU	21
31	at Baylor	23
53	Texas A&M	16
33	Arkansas	7

SUN BOWL:

10	North Carolina	26

1983
Coach: Fred Akers
Season: 11-1-0
SWC: 8-0-0 (1st)

20	at Auburn	7
26	North Texas	6
42	Rice	6
28	Oklahoma (Dallas)	16
31	at Arkansas (L.R.)	3
15	at SMU	12
20	Texas Tech	3
9	at Houston	3
20	TCU	14
24	Baylor	21
45	at Texas A&M	13

COTTON BOWL:

9	Georgia	10

1984
Coach: Fred Akers
Season: 7-4-1
SWC: 5-3-0 (T3)

35	Auburn	27
28	Penn St (New Jersey)	3
38	at Rice	13
15	Oklahoma (Dallas)	15
24	Arkansas	18
13	SMU	7
13	at Texas Tech	10
15	Houston	29
44	at TCU	23
10	at Baylor	24
12	Texas A&M	37

FREEDOM BOWL:

17	Iowa	55

1985
Coach: Fred Akers
Season: 8-4-0
SWC: 6-2-0 (T2)

21	Missouri	17
38	at Stanford	34
44	Rice	16
7	Oklahoma (Dallas)	14
15	at Arkansas (Fay.)	13
14	at SMU	44
34	Texas Tech	21
34	at Houston	24
20	TCU	0
17	Baylor	10
10	at Texas A&M	42

BLUEBONNET BOWL:

16	Air Force	24

1986
Coach: Fred Akers
Season: 5-6-0
SWC: 4-4-0 (5th)

20	Stanford	31
27	at Missouri	25
17	at Rice	14
12	Oklahoma (Dallas)	47
14	Arkansas	21
27	SMU	24
21	at Texas Tech	23
30	Houston	10
45	at TCU	16
13	at Baylor	18
3	Texas A&M	16

1987
Coach: David McWilliams
Season: 7-5-0
SWC: 5-2-0 (T2)

3	at Auburn	31
17	Brigham Young	22
61	Oregon State	16
45	Rice	26
9	Oklahoma (Dallas)	44
16	at Arkansas (L.R.)	14
41	Texas Tech	27
40	at Houston	60
24	TCU	21
34	Baylor	16
13	at Texas A&M	20

BLUEBONNET BOWL:

32	Pittsburgh	27

1988
Coach: David McWilliams
Season: 4-7-0
SWC: 2-5-0 (T4)

6	Brigham Young	47
47	New Mexico	0
27	North Texas	24
20	at Rice	13
13	Oklahoma (Dallas)	28
24	Arkansas	27
32	at Texas Tech	33
15	Houston	66
30	at TCU	21
14	at Baylor	17
24	Texas A&M	28

1989
Coach: David McWilliams
Season: 5-6-0
SWC: 4-4-0 (T4)

6	at Colorado	27
45	at SMU	13
12	Penn State	16
31	Rice	30
28	Oklahoma (Dallas)	24
24	at Arkansas (Fay.)	20
17	Texas Tech	24
9	at Houston	47
31	TCU	17
7	Baylor	50
10	at Texas A&M	21

1990
Coach: David McWilliams
Season: 10-2-0
SWC: 8-0-0 (1st)

17	at Penn State	13
22	Colorado	29
26	at Rice	10
14	Oklahoma (Dallas)	13
49	Arkansas	17
52	SMU	3
41	at Texas Tech	22
45	Houston	24
38	at TCU	10
23	at Baylor	13
28	Texas A&M	27

COTTON BOWL:

3	Miami	46

1991
Coach: David McWilliams
Season: 5-6-0
SWC: 4-4-0 (T5)

6	at Mississippi St	13
10	Auburn	14
28	Rice	7
10	Oklahoma (Dallas)	7
13	at Arkansas	14
34	at SMU	0
23	Texas Tech	14
14	at Houston	23
32	TCU	0
11	Baylor	21
14	at Texas A&M	31

1992
Coach: John Mackovic
Season: 6-5-0
SWC: 4-3-0 (T2)

10	Mississippi State	28
21	at Syracuse	31
33	North Texas	15
23	Rice	21
34	Oklahoma (Dallas)	24
45	Houston	38
44	at Texas Tech	33
14	at TCU	23
35	SMU	14
20	at Baylor	21
13	Texas A&M	34

APPENDIX: STATISTICS AND HIGHLIGHTS

Longhorn Football Overview: 1893–1992

Total Games Played: 981
Won-Lost Record: 676-263-31
Winning Percentage: .721
National Championship Teams: 1963, 1969, 1970

Undefeated and Untied Teams: 1893, 1895, 1900, 1914, 1918, 1920, 1963, 1969, 1970, 1977
Undefeated and Once-Tied Teams: 1923, 1962
Longest Undefeated String: 30 games, 1968–70

Longest Winning Streak: 30 games, 1968–70
Longest Losing Streak: 10 games, 1937–38
Top Scoring Team: 1977, 431 points

Longhorn All-Americans

1941
Malcolm Kutner, end

1943
Joe Parker, end

1944
Hub Bechtol, end

1945
Hub Bechtol, end

1946
*Hub Bechtol, end

1947
Bobby Layne, back
Dick Harris, tackle

1949
Randal Clay, guard
Bud McFadin, guard

1950
*Bud McFadin, guard
Don Menasco, end

1951
Bobby Dillon, back

1952
Harley Sewell, guard
Tom Stolhandshe, end

1953
*Carlton Massey, end

1955
Herb Gray, tackle

1959
Maurice Doak, guard

1961
*James Saxton, running back

1962
*Johnny Treadwell, guard

1963
*Scott Appleton, tackle
Tommy Ford, running back

1964
Tommy Nobis, guard/LB

1965
*Tommy Nobis, guard/LB

1967
Corby Robertson, linebacker

1968
*Chris Gilbert, running back
Loyd Wainscott, def. tackle

1969
*Bob McKay, off. tackle
Cotton Speyrer, wide
  receiver
Bobby Wuensch, off. tackle
Steve Worster, fullback
Glen Halsell, linebacker

1970
*Bobby Wuensch, off. tackle
*Steve Worster, fullback
*Bill Atessis, def. end
Scott Henderson, linebacker
Cotton Speyrer, wide
  receiver

1971
*Jerry Sisemore, off. tackle

1972
*Jerry Sisemore, off. tackle

1973
*Bill Wyman, center
*Roosevelt Leaks, running
  back

1974
*Doug English, def. tackle
Bob Simmons, off. tackle

1975
*Bob Simmons, off. tackle
Marty Akins, quarterback
Earl Campbell, running back

1976
Raymond Clayborn, def.
  back
Russell Erxleben, punter

1977
*Earl Campbell, running
  back
*Brad Shearer, def. tackle
Russell Erxleben, placekicker

1978
*Johnnie Johnson, def. back
Russell Erxleben, punter
Steve McMichael, def.
  tackle
Johnny "Lam" Jones, wide
  receiver

1979
*Johnnie Johnson, def. back
*Steve McMichael, def.
  tackle
Johnny "Lam" Jones,
  wide receiver

1980
*Kenneth Sims, def. tackle

1981
Kenneth Sims, def. tackle
Terry Tausch, off. tackle

1983
*Doug Dawson, off. guard
*Jerry Gray, def. back
Jeff Leiding, linebacker
Mossy Cade, def. back

1984
*Jerry Gray, def. back
*Tony Degrate, def. tackle

1985
Gene Chilton, center

1986
Jeff Ward, placekicker

1988
Britt Hager, linebacker

1990
Stanley Richard, def. back

1992
Lance Gunn, safety

*indicates consensus
all-American

Texas' Bowl Game Record

DATE	BOWL	RESULT
Jan. 1, 1943	Cotton	Texas 14–7 vs. Georgia Tech
Jan. 1, 1944	Cotton	Texas 7–7 vs. Randolph Field
Jan. 1, 1946	Cotton	Texas 40–27 vs. Missouri
Jan. 1, 1948	Sugar	Texas 27–7 vs. Alabama
Jan. 1, 1949	Orange	Texas 41–28 vs. Georgia
Jan. 1, 1951	Cotton	Texas 14–20 vs. Tennessee
Jan. 1, 1953	Cotton	Texas 16–0 vs. Tennessee
Jan. 1, 1958	Sugar	Texas 7–39 vs. Mississippi
Jan. 1, 1960	Cotton	Texas 14–23 vs. Syracuse
Dec. 17, 1960	Bluebonnet	Texas 3–3 vs. Alabama
Dec. 1, 1962	Cotton	Texas 12–7 vs. Mississippi
Dec. 1, 1963	Cotton	Texas 0–13 vs. LSU
Dec. 1, 1964	Cotton	Texas 28–6 vs. Navy
Dec. 1, 1965	Orange	Texas 21–17 vs. Alabama
Dec. 17, 1966	Bluebonnet	Texas 19–0 vs. Mississippi
Dec. 1, 1969	Cotton	Texas 36–13 vs. Tennessee
Dec. 1, 1970	Cotton	Texas 21–17 vs. Notre Dame
Dec. 1, 1971	Cotton	Texas 11–24 vs. Notre Dame
Dec. 1, 1972	Cotton	Texas 6–30 vs. Penn State
Dec. 1, 1973	Cotton	Texas 17–13 vs. Alabama
Dec. 1, 1974	Cotton	Texas 3–19 vs. Nebraska
Dec. 30, 1974	Gator	Texas 3–27 vs. Auburn
Dec. 27, 1975	Bluebonnet	Texas 38–21 vs. Colorado
Dec. 1, 1978	Cotton	Texas 10–38 vs. Notre Dame
Dec. 23, 1978	Sun	Texas 42–0 vs. Maryland
Dec. 22, 1979	Sun	Texas 7–14 vs. Washington
Dec. 31, 1980	Bluebonnet	Texas 7–16 vs. North Carolina
Dec. 1, 1982	Cotton	Texas 14–12 vs. Alabama
Dec. 25, 1982	Sun	Texas 10–26 vs. North Carolina
Dec. 1, 1983	Cotton	Texas 9–10 vs. Georgia
Dec. 26, 1984	Freedom	Texas 17–55 vs. Iowa
Dec. 31, 1985	Bluebonnet	Texas 16–24 vs. Air Force
Dec. 31, 1987	Bluebonnet	Texas 32–27 vs. Pittsburgh
Jan. 1, 1991	Cotton	Texas 6–43 vs. Miami

Longhorns in the National Football Foundation Hall of Fame

PLAYER	INDUCTED
Bobby Layne, quarterback (1944–47)	1968
Bud Sprague, tackle (1925–28)	1970
Malcolm Kutner, end (1939–41)	1974
Harrison Stafford, halfback (1930–32)	1975
Tommy Nobis, guard/linebacker (1963–65)	1981
Bud McFadin, guard (1948–50)	1983
Earl Campbell, running back (1974–77)	1990
Hub Bechtol, end (1944–46)	1991

Largest Victory Margin Over Conference Opponents

Arkansas	54–0	in 1894
Texas A&M	48–0	in 1898
Baylor	77–0	in 1913
Rice	59–0	in 1915
TCU	72–0	in 1915
SMU	74–0	in 1916
Texas Tech	43–0	in 1949
Houston	50–0	in 1982

Lombardi Trophy Winners

1981	Kenneth Sims
1984	Tony Degrate

Career Individual Rushing Records (Since 1939)

PLAYER	YEARS	YARDS
Earl Campbell	1974–77	4443
Chris Gilbert	1966–68	3231
Roosevelt Leaks	1972–74	2923
A. J. Jones	1978–81	2878
Eric Metcalf	1985–88	2661
Jim Bertelsen	1969–71	2510
Steve Worster	1968–70	2353
Marty Akins	1972–75	1974
Adrian Walker	1989–91	1621
Byron Townsend	1949–51	1616

Individual Rushing Plays (School Records)

Most Rushes:
Game: 38—Chris Gilbert vs. Arkansas, 1967
Season: 267—Earl Campbell, 1977
Career: 765—Earl Campbell, 1974–77
Most Net Yards Gained:
Game: 342—Roosevelt Leaks vs. SMU, 1973
Season: 1744—Earl Campbell, 1977
Career: 4443—Earl Campbell, 1974–77
Highest Average Gain per Rush:
Game: 16.0—Gib Dawson vs. North Carolina, 1951
Season: 7.9—James Saxton, 1961
Career: 6.4—James Saxton, 1959–61
Longest Run from Scrimmage:
96 yards—Chris Gilbert vs. TCU, 1967 (TD)

Longhorn Coaches in the National Hall of Fame

COACH	YEARS AT TEXAS	INDUCTED
Dana X. Bible	1937–46	1951
Darrell Royal	1957–76	1983

Single-Season All-Time Rushing Leaders

PLAYER	YEAR	ATTEMPTS	YARDS	AVERAGE
Earl Campbell	1977	267*	1744*	6.5
Roosevelt Leaks	1973	229	1415	6.2
Eric Metcalf	1987	223	1161	5.2
Chris Gilbert	1968	184	1132	6.2
Earl Campbell	1975	198	1118	5.7
Roosevelt Leaks	1972	230	1099	4.8
Chris Gilbert	1966	206	1080	5.2
Darryl Clark	1982	198	1049	5.3
Chris Gilbert	1967	205	1019	5.0
Eric Metcalf	1988	218	932	4.3

*School record

Single-Season All-Time Passing Leaders
(Since 1939)

PLAYER	YEAR	ATTEMPTS	COMPLETIONS	YARDS
Bret Stafford	1986	329*	176*	2233*
Peter Gardere	1990	282	159	2131
Todd Dodge	1984	210	100	1599
Peter Gardere	1989	186	107	1511
Robert Brewer	1982	193	91	1415
Peter Gardere	1991	228	114	1390
Paul Campbell	1949	182	91	1372
Bret Stafford	1987	245	127	1321
Mark Murdock	1988	202	98	1189
Bill Bradley	1967	153	72	1181

*School Record

Individual Passing Plays (School Records)

Most Passes Attempted:
Game: 42—Bret Stafford vs. Texas Tech, 1986
Season: 329—Bret Stafford, 1986
Career: 714—Bret Stafford, 1984–87

Most Passes Completed:
Game: 23—Shannon Kelley vs. Houston, 1987
Season: 176—Bret Stafford, 1986
Career: 380—Peter Gardere, 1989–91

Highest Percentage of Passes Completed:
Game: .909—Walt Fondren vs. Baylor, 1957 (10 of 11)
Season: .635—Shannon Kelley, 1987 (47 of 74)
Career: .562—Shannon Kelley, 1985–88 (118 of 210)

Most Yards Gained:
Game: 359—Todd Dodge vs. Rice, 1985
Season: 2233—Bret Stafford, 1986
Career: 5032—Peter Gardere, 1989–91

Most Touchdown Passes:
Game: 4—Clyde Littlefield vs. Daniel Baker, 1915
    4—Randy McEachern vs. Texas A&M, 1977
    4—Peter Gardere vs. TCU, 1990
Season: 12—Robert Brewer, 1982
    12—Bret Stafford, 1986
Career: 25—Bobby Layne, 1944–47

Highest Average Gain per Pass Completion:
Game: 29.2—Dan Page vs. TCU, 1951 (6 for 175)
Season: 20.1—Randy McEachern, 1975 (45 for 906)
Career: 18.4—Randy McEachern, 1976–78 (85 for 1564)

Longest Pass Play:
96 yards—Todd Dodge to Donovan Pitts vs. Rice, 1985 (TD)

Milestone Victories

VICTORY NO.	YEAR	GAME NO.	OPPONENT & SCORE
50	1901	eleventh	Texas A&M, 32–0
100	1910	fourth	Auburn, 9–0
150	1918	fourth	Ream Flying Field, 26–2
200	1925	fifth	Rice, 27–6
250	1933	sixth	Rice, 18–0
300	1943	fourth	Arkansas, 34–0
350	1949	tenth	Texas A&M, 42–14
400	1958	second	Tulane, 21–20
450	1963	tenth	Texas A&M, 15–13
500	1969	eleventh	Notre Dame, 21–17
550	1975	seventh	Rice, 41–9
600	1981	sixth	SMU, 9–7
650	1987	ninth	TCU, 24–21

All-Time Team Scoring Record

YEAR	OPPONENTS	SCORE
1915	Daniel Baker	92–0
1913	Baylor	77–0
1946	Colorado	76–0
1915	SMU	74–0
1915	TCU	72–0
1914	Southwestern	70–0
1977	Virginia	68–0
1910	Haskell	68–3
1932	Missouri	65–0

Single-Season All-Time Scoring Leaders

PLAYER	YEAR	TD	PAT	FG	TOTAL POINTS
Len Barrell	1914	14	34	1	121*
Earl Campbell	1977	19*	0	0	114
Michael Pollak	1990	0	39	20*	99
Jack Crain	1941	0	23	1	92
Byron Townsend	1950	14	0	0	84
Steve Worster	1970	14	0	0	84
Donnie Wigginton	1971	14	0	0	84
Roosevelt Leaks	1973	14	0	0	84
Jeff Ward	1985	0	27	19	84
Chris Gilbert	1968	13	4†	0	82
Billy Quinn	1952	13	0	0	78
Jim Bertelsen	1969	13	0	0	78
Earl Campbell	1975	13	0	0	78
Wayne Clements	1987	0	30	16	78
Raul Allegre	1982	0	41	12	77

* School Record
†PAT by two runs

TEXAS' ALL-SWC PLAYERS

1915
Clyde Littlefield, back
Pig Dittmar, center

1916
Alva Carlton, guard
Pig Dittmar, center
Maxey Hart, end
Rip Lang, back

1917
Dewey Bradford, guard

1919
Bibb Falk, tackle

1920
Hook McCullough, end
Swede Swenson, center
Tom Dennis, tackle
Grady Watson, back

1921
Hook McCullough, end
Tom Dennis, tackle
Swede Swenson, center
Bud McCallum, back

1922
Swede Swenson, center
Joe Ward, tackle
Ivan Robertson, back

1923
Oscar Eckhardt, back
Ed Bluestein, tackle
F. M. Bralley, center
Jim Marley, back

1924
Bud Sprague, tackle
K. L. Berry, guard

1925
H. C. Pfannkuche, center
Matt Newell, end
Mack Saxon, back

1926
Mack Saxon, back

APPENDIX: STATISTICS AND HIGHLIGHTS

1927
Pottie McCullough, center
Ike Sewell, guard

1928
Bill Ford, end
Gordy Brown, tackle
Dexter Shelley, back

1929
Alfred Rose, end

1930
Ox Blanton, tackle
Ox Emerson, guard
Lester Peterson, end
Harrison Stafford, back
Dexter Shelley, back
Ernie Koy, back

1931
Harrison Stafford, back
Ernie Koy, back

1932
Bohn Hilliard, back
Harrison Stafford, back
Ernie Koy, back

1933
Bill Smith, center
Bohn Hilliard, back
Charley Coates, tackle

1934
Phil Sanger, end
Bohn Hilliard, back
Charley Coates, center

1936
Hugh Wolfe, back

1937
Hugh Wolfe, back

1938
Jack Rhodes, guard

1939
Jack Crain, back

1940
Pete Layden, back

1941
Malcolm Kutner, end
Chal Daniel, guard
Jack Crain, back
Pete Layden, back

1942
Stan Mauldin, tackle
Roy Dale McKay, back
Jackie Field, back

1943
Joe Parker, end
Franklin Butler, guard
J. R. Calahan, back
Ralph Ellsworth, back
Joe Magliolo, back

1944
Hub Bechtol, end
Jack Sachse, center
Bobby Layne, back
Harold Fisher, guard

1945
Hub Bechtol, end
Dick Harris, center
Bobby Layne, back

1946
Hub Bechtol, end
Dick Harris, center
Bobby Layne, back

1947
Bobby Layne, back
Max Baumgardner, end
Dick Harris, tackle

1948
George Petrovich, tackle
Dick Harris, center
Ray Borneman, back

1949
Bud McFadin, guard
Danny Wolfe, guard

1950
Ben Procter, end
Ken Jackson, tackle
Bud McFadin, guard
Byron Townsend, back
Bobby Dillon, def. back
Don Menasco, linebacker

1951
Harley Sewell, guard
Tom Stolhandske, end
Gib Dawson, back
June Davis, linebacker
Bobby Dillon, def. back

1952
Harley Sewell, guard
Tom Stolhandske, end
Gib Dawson, back
Dick Ochoa, back
T. Jones, back
Billy Quinn, back
Phil Branch, guard
Bill Georges, def. end

1953
Phil Branch, guard
Carlton Massey, end
Gilmer Spring, end

1954
Buck Lansford, tackle

1955
Herb Gray, guard
Walter Fondren, back
Menan Schriewer, end

1959
Maurice Doke, guard
Jack Collins, halfback
Monte Lee, end
Rene Ramirez, halfback

1960
James Saxton, back
Monte Lee, guard

1961
James Saxton, back
Mike Cotten, back
Don Talbert, tackle
Bob Moses, end
David Kristynik, center

1962
Johnny Treadwell, guard
Tommy Ford, back
Scott Appleton, tackle

1963
Scott Appleton, tackle
Tommy Ford, back
Tommy Nobis, guard

1964
Tommy Nobis, guard
Clayton Lacy, tackle
Olen Ondervood, center
Knox Nunnally, end
Pete Lammons, end
Dan Mauldin, end
Harold Philipp, back
Joe Dixon, back

1965
Tommy Nobis, guard
Frank Bedrick, guard
Pete Lammons, end
Diron Talbert, tackle
Jack Howe, center

1966
Chris Gilbert, back
Corby Robertson, end
Joel Brame, linebacker

1967
Chris Gilbert, back
Loyd Wainscott, tackle
Danny Abbott, guard

1968
Chris Gilbert, back
Deryl Comer, end
Danny Abbott, guard
Steve Worster, back
Loyd Wainscott, tackle
Glen Halsell, linebacker
Leo Brooks, tackle

1969
Leo Brooks, tackle
Glen Halsell, linebacker
Bill Atessis, end
Tom Campbell, halfback
Bob McKay, tackle
Charles Speyrer, end
Steve Worster, fullback
Bobby Wuensch, tackle

1970
Steve Worster, fullback
Bobby Wuensch, tackle
Bill Atessis, end
Bobby Mitchell, guard
Scott Henderson, linebacker
Jim Bertelsen, halfback
Bill Zapalac, linebacker
Jerry Sisemore, tackle
Mike Dean, guard
Stan Mauldin, linebacker
Ray Dowdy, tackle

1971
Jerry Sisemore, tackle
Jim Bertelsen, halfback
Ray Dowdy, tackle
Greg Ploetz, tackle
Randy Braband, linebacker
Donnie Wigginton,
 quarterback
Don Crosslin, guard
Tommy Woodard,
 linebacker
Alan Lowry, def. back

1972
Alan Lowry, quarterback
Jerry Sisemore, tackle
Roosevelt Leaks, back
Travis Roach, guard
Randy Braband, linebacker
Bill Wyman, center
Glen Gaspard, linebacker
Mike Rowan, back
Malcolm Minnick, end

1973
Roosevelt Leaks, back
Bill Wyman, center
Malcolm Minnick, end
Jay Arnold, def. back
Doug English, tackle
Bob Simmons, tackle
Don Crosslin, guard
Bruce Hebert, guard
Glen Gaspard, linebacker
Bill Rutherford, end
Wade Johnston, linebacker

1974
Earl Campbell, back
Doug English, def. tackle
Bob Simmons, tackle
Bruce Hebert, guard

1975
Bob Simmons, tackle
Marty Akins, quarterback
Will Wilcox, guard
Earl Campbell, back
Brad Shearer, tackle
Bill Hamilton, linebacker
Raymond Clayborn,
 def. back

1976
Raymond Clayborn,
 def. back
Russell Erxleben, kicker

1977
Earl Campbell, back
Johnnie Johnson, def. back
Brad Shearer, def. tackle
Russell Erxleben, kicker
Rick Ingraham, off. guard
Alfred Jackson, off. end
Johnny "Lam" Jones, flanker
David Studdard, off. tackle
Lance Taylor, linebacker

1978
Johnnie Johnson, def. back
Russell Erxleben, kicker
Steve McMichael,
 def. tackle
Johnny "Lam" Jones,
 wide receiver
Jim Yarbrough, off. guard
Dwight Jefferson, def. end
Lance Taylor, linebacker

1979
Johnny "Lam" Jones,
 wide receiver
Lawrence Sampleton,
 tight end
Wes Hubert, center
Steve McMichael,
 def. tackle
Doug Shankle, linebacker
Johnnie Johnson, def. back
Ricky Churchman, def. back
Derrick Hatchett, def. back

1980
Terry Tausch, off. tackle
Kenneth Sims, def. tackle
Les Studdard, off. guard

1981
Kenneth Sims, def. tackle
Terry Tausch, off. tackle
Joe Shearin, off. guard
Mike Baab, center
Doug Shankle, linebacker
Bruce Scholtz, linebacker

1982
Herkie Walls, flanker
Kiki DeAyala, def. end
Bryan Millard, off. tackle
Darryl Clark, off. back
Raul Allegre, placekicker
Mossy Cade, def. back
Doug Dawson, off. guard

1983
Jerry Gray, def. back
Fred Acorn, def. back
Mossy Cade, def. back
Doug Dawson, off. guard
Mike Ruether, center
Eric Holle, def. end
Tony Degrate. def. tackle
Jeff Leiding, linebacker
Jeff Ward, placekicker
John Teltschik, punter

1984
Jerry Gray, def. back
Tony Degrate, def. tackle
Jeff Ward, kicker
John Teltschik, punter

1985
Gene Chilton, center
Ty Allert, linebacker
Jeff Ward, kicker
Bryan Chester, guard
James McKinney, end
Rick Houston, tackle

1986
Eric Metcalf, off. back
Steven Braggs, def. back
Brian Espinosa, def. tackle
Jeff Ward, kicker

1987
Eric Metcalf, off. back
Paul Jetton, guard
Thomas Aldridge, def. end
Britt Hager, linebacker
John Hagy, def. back

1988
Tony Jones, wide receiver
Eric Metcalf, off. back
Britt Hager, linebacker
Bobby Lilljedahl, punter

1989
Johnny Walker,
 wide receiver

1990
Johnny Walker,
 wide receiver
Stan Thomas, off. tackle
Michael Pollak, kicker
Shane Dronett, def. end
James Patton, def. tackle
Brian Jones, linebacker
Stanley Richard, def. back
Lance Gunn, def. back
Alex Waits, punter

1991
Shane Dronett, def. tackle
James Patton, def. tackle
Anthony Curl, linebacker
Mark Berry, def. back
Lance Gunn, def. back

1992
Turk McDonald, center
Scott Szerdy, placekicker
Bo Robinson, def. end
Winfred Tubbs, linebacker
Lance Gunn, safety

Single-Season Top Receivers (Since 1939)

PLAYER	YEAR	RECEPTIONS	YARDS	AVERAGE
Tony Jones	1988	42	838*	20.0
Johnny Walker	1989	55*	785	14.2
Ben Proctor	1949	43	724	16.8
Herkie Walls	1982	25	702	28.0
William Harris	1984	34	637	18.7
Alfred Jackson	1975	32	596	18.6
Johnny Walker	1990	40	565	14.1
Eric Metcalf	1986	42	556	13.2
Johnny "Lam" Jones	1977	21	543	25.9
Johnny "Lam" Jones	1979	36	535	14.9

*School record

Individual Receiving Plays (School Records)

Most Passes Caught:
Game: 12—Eric Metcalf vs. Arkansas, 1988
Season: 55—Johnny Walker, 1989
Career: 125—Eric Metcalf, 1985–88
Most Yards Gained:
Game: 198—Johnny "Lam" Jones vs. Baylor, 1979
Season: 838—Tony Jones, 1988
Career: 1842—Tony Jones, 1986–89
Most Touchdown Passes Caught:
Game: 3—Pete Lammons vs. Baylor, 1965
Season: 10—Herkie Walls, 1982
Career: 14—Johnny "Lam" Jones, 1976–79
Highest Average Gain per Reception:
Game: 36.2—Eric Metcalf vs. Houston, 1986 (5 for 181)
Season: 28.0—Herkie Walls, 1982 (25 for 702)
Career: 25.8—Herkie Walls, 1979-82 (38 for 981)

Longhorns' Academic All-Americans

1959	Maurice Doak, guard
1961	Johnny Treadwell, guard
1962	Johnny Treadwell, guard
	Pat Culpepper, linebacker
1963	Duke Carlisle, quarterback, def. back
1966	Gene Bledsoe, off. tackle
1967	Mike Perrin, def. end
	Corby Robertson, linebacker
1968	Corby Robertson, linebacker
	Scott Henderson, linebacker
1969	Scott Henderson, linebacker
	Bill Zapalac, def. end
1970	Scott Henderson, linebacker
	Bill Zapalac, def. end
1972	Mike Bayer, def. back
	Tommy Keel, def. back
	Steve Oxley, off. tackle
1973	Tommy Keel, def. back
1983	Doug Dawson, off. guard
1988	Lee Brockman, linebacker

All-Time Top Punters (Since 1939)

PLAYER	YEAR	NUMBER	YARDS	AVERAGE
Russell Erxleben	1976	61	2842	46.6*
Alex Waits	1986	48	2214	46.1
Russell Erxleben	1977	32	1470	45.9
John Teltschik	1985	59	2621	44.4
John Teltschik	1984	67	2935	43.8
Alex Waits	1987	43	1873	43.6
Russell Erxleben	1978	72*	3128*	43.4
David Conway	1965	52	2253	43.3
Bobby Lilljedahl	1988	61	2598	42.6
Alex Waits	1990	60	2557	42.6

*School record

All-Time Kicking Records (School Records)

Most Points After Touchdown:
Game: 10—Billy Schott vs. TCU, 1974 (10 attempts)
Season: 55—Happy Feller, 1970 (57 attempts)
Career: 128—Happy Feller, 1968–70 (134 attempts)
Most Consecutive Extra Points Made:
54 points—Jeff Ward, 1983–84, 1985–86

Most Field Goals Made:
Game: 5—Jeff Ward vs. Arkansas, 1985
Season: 20—Michael Pollak, 1990
Career: 58—Jeff Ward, 1983–86
Longest Field Goal Made:
67 yards—Russell Erxleben vs. Rice, 1977
Best Percentage FG Made:
.938 (15 of 16)—Jeff Ward, 1983

All-Time Kick Return Records (School Records)

Most Punt Returns:
Game: 7—Walt Fondren vs. Arkansas, 1955
Season: 44—Johnnie Johnson, 1977
Career: 114—Johnnie Johnson, 1976–79
Most Yards Punts Returned:
Game: 131—Johnnie Johnson vs. Boston College, 1977
Season: 538—Johnnie Johnson, 1977
Career: 1076—Eric Metcalf, 1985–88
Highest Average Gain per Return:
Game: 24.8—Billy Pyle vs. Texas A&M, 1947
Season: 22.3—Bobby Dillon, 1950
Career: 17.7—Bobby Dillon, 1949–51
Longest Punt Return:
95 yards—Bohn Hilliard vs. Oklahoma, 1932 (TD)
Most Kickoff Returns:
Game: 7—Eric Metcalf vs. Houston, 1987
Season: 24—Kevin Nelson, 1986
Career: 34—Walt Fondren, 1955–57
       34—Adrian Walker, 1989–91
Most Yards Kickoffs Returned:
Game: 129—Eric Metcalf vs. Houston, 1987
Season: 449—Kevin Nelson, 1986
Career: 808—Raymond Clayborn, 1973–76
Highest Average Gain per Return:
Game: 33.3—Walt Fondren vs. Tulane, 1955
Season: 32.3—Johnny "Lam" Jones, 1978
Career: 29.1—Phil Harris, 1963–65
Longest Kickoff Return:
100 yards—Johnny "Lam" Jones vs. SMU, 1978 (TD)

Longhorns' SWC Titles

YEAR	CONFERENCE			FULL SEASON		
	W	L	T	W	L	T
1920	5	0	0	9	0	0
1928	5	1	0	7	2	0
1930	4	1	0	8	1	1
1942	5	1	0	9	2	0
1943†	5	0	0	7	1	1
1945	5	1	0	10	1	0
1950	6	0	0	9	2	0
1952	6	0	0	9	2	0
1953*	5	1	0	7	3	0
1959*	5	1	0	9	2	0
1961*	6	1	0	10	1	0
1962	6	0	1	9	1	1
1963	7	0	0	11	0	0
1968*	6	1	0	9	1	1
1969	7	0	0	11	0	0
1970	7	0	0	10	1	0
1971	6	1	0	8	3	0
1972	7	0	0	10	1	0
1973	7	0	0	8	3	0
1975*	6	1	0	10	2	0
1977	8	0	0	11	1	0
1983	8	0	0	11	1	0

*Co-champion
†This marked first time in SWC history for a school to repeat as undisputed football champion.
NOTE: Texas also had best SWC record in 1916 (5-1-0) and 1918 (4-0-0), but no championships were awarded those years.

CAREER RECORDS OF TEXAS COACHES

NAME	SEASONS	YEARS	SEASON W	L	T	SWC W	L	T	SWC TITLES
No coach	—	1893	4	0	0	—	—	—	—
R. D. Wentworth	1	1894	6	1	0	—	—	—	—
Frank Crawford	1	1895	5	0	0	—	—	—	—
Harry Robinson	1	1896	4	2	1	—	—	—	—
F. W. Kelly	1	1897	6	2	0	—	—	—	—
D. F. Edwards	1	1898	5	1	0	—	—	—	—
M. G. Clark	1	1899	6	2	0	—	—	—	—
S. H. Thompson	2	1900–1901	14	2	1	—	—	—	—
J. B. Hart	1	1902	6	3	1	—	—	—	—
Ralph Hutchinson	3	1903–1905	16	7	2	—	—	—	—
H. R. Schenker	1	1906	9	1	0	—	—	—	—
W. E. Metzenthin	2	1907–1908	11	5	1	—	—	—	—
Dexter Draper	1	1909	4	3	1	—	—	—	—
W. S. Wasmund	1	1910	6	2	0	—	—	—	—
Dave Allerdice	5	1911–1915	33	7	0	2	2	0	0
Eugene Van Gent	1	1916	7	2	0	5	1	0	0
Bill Juneau	3	1917–1919	19	7	0	9	5	0	0
Berry Whitaker	3	1920–1922	22	3	1	8	1	1	1
E. J. Stewart	4	1923–1926	24	9	3	8	6	2	0
Clyde Littlefield	7	1927–1933	44	18	6	22	13	4	2
Jack Chevigny	3	1934–1936	13	14	2	6	11	1	0
Dana X. Bible	10	1937–1946	63	31	3	35	22	1	3
Blair Cherry	4	1947–1950	32	10	1	18	5	1	1
Ed Price	6	1951–1956	33	27	1	20	15	1	2 (1 co-champion)
Darrell Royal	20	1957–1976	167	47	5	109	27	2	11 (3 co-champions)
Fred Akers	10	1977–1986	86	31	2	60	19	1	2
David McWilliams	5	1987–1991	31	26	0	23	15	0	1
John Mackovic	1	1992–	6	5	0	4	3	0	—

INDEX